Related Books of Interest

Multisite Commerce
Proven Principles for Overcoming the Business, Organizational, and Technical Challenges

by Lev Mirlas
ISBN: 0-13-714887-9

In *Multisite Commerce*, Lev Mirlas—the architect who pioneered the concept of a shared multisite platform with IBM WebSphere Commerce—introduces best practices and methodologies for implementing and managing multiple e-commerce sites efficiently and cost-effectively.

Mirlas begins by reviewing why multisite commerce is necessary and yet so challenging to execute. Next, he addresses multisite commerce from three perspectives: business, implementation, and technical. You'll learn how to plan and implement a shared platform and use it to create and operate new sites that will remarkably lower incremental cost.

This book's start-to-finish methodology provides a common language that everyone involved in multiple sites—from executives to project managers and technical architects to site administrators—can share.

The New Language of Marketing 2.0
How to Use ANGELS to Energize Your Market

by Sandy Carter
ISBN: 0-13-714249-8

Use ANGELS and Web 2.0 Marketing to Drive Powerful, Quantifiable Results

Today, marketers have an array of radically new Web 2.0-based techniques at their disposal: viral marketing, social networking, virtual worlds, widgets, Web communities, blogs, podcasts, and next-generation search, to name just a few. Now, leading IBM marketing innovator Sandy Carter introduces ANGELS, a start-to-finish framework for choosing the right Web 2.0 marketing tools—and using them to maximize revenue and profitability.

Carter demonstrates winning Web 2.0 marketing at work through 54 brand-new case studies: organizations ranging from Staples to Harley Davidson, Coca-Cola to Mentos, Nortel to IBM itself. You'll discover powerful new ways to market brands and products in both B2B and B2C markets...integrate Web 2.0, experiential, and conventional marketing...maximize synergies between global and local marketing...gain more value from influencers, and more.

Listen to the author's podcast at:
ibmpressbooks.com/podcasts

Sign up for the monthly IBM Press newsletter at
ibmpressbooks/newsletters

Related Books of Interest

Search Engine Marketing
Driving Search Traffic to Your Company's Web Site

by Mike Moran and Bill Hunt
ISBN: 0-13-606868-5

The #1 Step-by-Step Guide to Search Marketing Success...Now Completely Updated with New Techniques, Tools, Best Practices, and Value-Packed Bonus DVD!

Thoroughly updated to fully reflect today's latest search engine marketing opportunities, this book guides you through profiting from social media marketing, site search, advanced keyword tools, hybrid paid search auctions, and much more. You'll walk step-by-step through every facet of creating an effective program: projecting business value, selling stakeholders and executives, building teams, choosing strategy, implementing metrics, and above all, execution.

Do It Wrong Quickly
How the Web Changes the Old Marketing Rules

by Mike Moran
ISBN: 0-13-225596-0

For decades, marketers have been taught to carefully plan ahead because "you must get it right–it's too expensive to change." But, in the age of the Web, you can know in hours whether your strategy's working. Today, winners don't get it right the first time: They start fast, change fast, and relentlessly optimize their way to success. They do it wrong quickly…then fix it, just as quickly!

In this book, Internet marketing pioneer Mike Moran shows you how to do that-step-by-step and in detail. Drawing on his experience building ibm.com into one of the world's most successful sites, Moran shows how to quickly transition from "plan then execute" to a nonstop cycle of refinement.

You'll master specific techniques for making the Web's "two-way marketing conversa-tion" work successfully, productively, and profitably. Next, Moran shows how to choose the right new marketing tools, craft them into an integrated strategy, and execute it…achieving unprecedented efficiency, accountability, speed, and results.

 Listen to the author's podcast at:
ibmpressbooks.com/podcasts

Related Books of Interest

The Greening of IT
How Companies Can Make a Difference for the Environment
by John Lamb
ISBN: 0-13-715083-0

Drawing on leading-edge experience, John Lamb helps you realistically assess the business case for green IT, set priorities, and overcome internal and external challenges to make it work. He offers proven solutions for issues ranging from organizational obstacles to executive motivation and discusses crucial issues ranging from utility rate incentives to metrics. Along the way, you'll discover energy-saving opportunities—from virtualization and consolidation to cloud and grid computing—and solutions that will improve business flexibility as they reduce environmental impact.

Lamb presents case studies, checklists, and more—all the practical guidance you need to drive maximum bottom-line value from your green IT initiative.

Can Two Rights Make a Wrong?
Reger
ISBN: 0-13-173294-3

RFID Sourcebook
Lahiri
ISBN: 0-13-185137-3

Mining the Talk
Spangler, Kreulen
ISBN: 0-13-233953-6

The New Language of Business
Carter
ISBN: 0-13-195654-X

SOA Governance
Brown, Laird, Gee, Mitra
ISBN: 0-13-714746-5

Service-Oriented Architecture (SOA) Compass
Bieberstein, Bose, Fiammante, Jones, Shah
ISBN: 0-13-187002-5

Reaching the Goal
Ricketts
ISBN: 0-13-233312-0

Eating the IT Elephant
Hopkins and Jenkins
ISBN: 0-13-713012-0

Maria Azua

THE SOCIAL FACTOR

Maria Azua

THE SOCIAL FACTOR

Innovate, Ignite, and Win through Mass Collaboration
and Social Networking

IBM Press™

Pearson Plc

Upper Saddle River, NJ • Boston • Indianapolis • San Francisco
New York • Toronto • Montreal • London • Munich • Paris • Madrid
Cape Town • Sydney • Tokyo • Singapore • Mexico City
ibmpressbooks.com

IBM® Press Program Managers: Steven M. Stansel, Ellice Uffer

Cover design concept: Ryan Mellody

Associate Publisher: Greg Wiegand
Marketing Manager: Kourtnaye Sturgeon
Acquisitions Editor: Katherine Bull
Publicist: Heather Fox
Development Editor: Ginny Bess Munroe
Managing Editor: Kristy Hart
Designer: Alan Clements
Project Editor: Jovana San Nicolas-Shirley
Copy Editor: Apostrophe Editing Services
Indexer: Lisa Stumpf
Compositors: Nonie Ratcliff and Bronkella Publishing LLC
Proofreader: Leslie Joseph
Manufacturing Buyer: Dan Uhrig

Published by Pearson plc

Publishing as IBM Press™

IBM, the IBM logo, ibm.com, IBM Press, Domino, Lotus, Lotus Discovery Server, Lotus Notes, Quickr, Sametime, ThinkPlace, Tivoli, WebSphere, World Community Grid, and z/VM are trademarks or registered trademarks of International Business Machines Corp., registered in many jurisdictions worldwide. Other product and service names might be trademarks of IBM or other companies. A current list of IBM trademarks is available on the Web at "Copy and Trademark Information" at www.ibm.com/legal/copytrade.shtml. Microsoft and Windows are trademarks of Microsoft Corporation in the United States, other countries, or both. Linux is a registered trademark of Linus Torvalds in the United States, other countries, or both. Intel and the Intel logo are trademarks or registered trademarks of Intel Corporation or its subsidiaries in the United States and other countries. Other company, product, or service names may be trademarks or service marks of others.

Library of Congress Cataloging-in-Publication Data

Himmel, Maria Azua, 1960-

The social factor : innovate, ignite, and win through mass collaboration and social networking / Himmel Maria Azua.

p. cm.

ISBN 978-0-13-701890-1 (pbk. : alk. paper)

1. Social networks. I. Title.

HM741.H56 2009

306.4'602856754--dc22

2009023428

Pearson Education, Inc.
Rights and Contracts Department
501 Boylston Street, Suite 900
Boston, MA 02116
Fax (617) 671-3447

ISBN-13: 978-0-13-701890-1

ISBN-10: 0-13-701890-8

Text printed in the United States at R.R. Donnelley in Crawfordsville, Indiana.

Fourth Printing October 2011

To my husband, Ben Himmel, who always provides inspiration, comfort, and unconditional support to me.

CONTENTS

Acknowledgments

This book represents four years of hands-on investigation and analysis of the social networking phenomenon and the perspective of 20 years in the technology industry. When I began *The Social Factor*, I never imagined that in some ways the thesis of the book would be proven in the way it came together. As the book took shape, however, I began to realize some of the limitations of social networking. Despite the generous cooperation I received from a host of friends and colleagues who shared their expertise with me, I was still faced with the daunting challenge of synthesizing all that information and creating a unified manuscript that spoke with a single voice. I quickly realized that meeting this challenge would be a solitary pursuit.

As I think of those who made this book possible, I must begin with my dear friend and IBM® vice president Gina Poole, who gathered talent and resources to produce a wealth of real-world content for the chapters on social innovation and social ideation. Gina's team of gifted collaborators included Jean Francois Arseneault, Paul Baffes, John E. Boyer, Jeanette L. Browning, Sacha Chua, Liam Cleaver, Anna Dreyzin, Jane Harper, Jean Staten Healy, Ian Hughes, Sunil Jain, Mary Keough, Aaron Kim, Wolfgang Kulhanek, Kristine Lawas, Bernie Michalik, Jeanne Murray, Jennifer A. Okimoto, Younghee Overly, Rajani Ramkaran, Delphine Remy-Boutang, Karl Roche, Joshua Scribner, Rawn Shah, Madhumalti Sharma, Ian Smith, Pete Ward, and Todd Watson.

Jon Iwata, IBM senior vice president, marketing and communications, offered his insights on the transformational power of social networking in the corporate setting, including the impact of the Jam model.

I have been lucky to be associated with a multitude of other technology leaders at IBM, many of whom I got to know during my tenure as vice president of the IBM Technology Adoption Program (TAP). Bill Bodin, Brian Goodman, and Dave Newbold are three of these leaders, and each offered the depth of his experience for the benefit of readers of *The Social Factor*.

I also want to thank my friend and trusted advisor Nick Donofrio, retired IBM executive vice president and technology industry visionary. Nick graciously provided an extensive interview regarding the strategic importance of social networking, along with thoughtful guidance as the manuscript first began taking shape. I also want to thank IBM senior vice president Steve Mills, who was also among those interviewed for current trends and experiences with social networking.

Other colleagues who provided the benefit of their experiences included Boas Betzler, Christopher Douglass, Reed Mullen, Michael Roche, and Laurisa Rodriguez.

Introduction

More than 4,000—that's the number of text messages my friend's 18-year-old daughter recently logged on her cell phone...in a single month! "Not unusual" was his casual reply when I expressed my amazement at the number.

The generation coming of age since the turn of the last millennium—including my friend's daughter—uses technology as no generation before it has done. "Millennials," also called "The Net Generation" or "Generation Y" (typically anyone born after 1977[1]), are not limited to any particular country, region, or culture. In India they're the up-and-coming generation, now more than 300 million strong, and referred to as "Zippies."[2] This new generation is found on every continent, wherever a cell phone signal or Internet connection is available. They rely on technology for information, for entertainment, and for communication. They rely on technology for shopping and socializing, and often for a combination of the two. The recommendations of friends strongly influence Millennial buying patterns and can significantly affect market penetration of both new and existing products.

In *The Social Factor* I contend that economic and social dynamics (led most notably by Millennials), along with unprecedented technological advances, have propelled us to the next great era in societal development, an era I believe will come to be known as the *Social Age*. The Social Age is fundamentally different from the preceding Information Age, which was marked by increasing efficiency in the dissemination of information via the Internet, from producer to consumer. The Social Age, on the other hand, leverages the Internet and depends on it, but the Internet is merely a conduit for the Social Age, much as the electrical infrastructure was to an Industrial Age company. *Rather than merely the next step in the Information Age, the Social Age fundamentally changes the way we communicate, socialize, and collaborate to create a better world.*

Several years ago I led an effort at IBM to tap into Social Age methods of communication and collaboration. As of the time of this writing, more than 300,000 IBMers—one of the largest worldwide workforces exploiting social tools— now contribute to internal wikis and blogs, and use a collection of new social tools. These technologies are driving a new wave of creativity and energy at IBM, as they are at other progressive organizations.

In many ways the Social Age fascinates, frustrates, and remains mysterious to those who stand to gain the most from joining it. Business people the world over often find themselves on the sidelines, like the last kid chosen for the team, unsure of what's going on around them, and not really sure how to get into the game.

So how does a business, how does *your* business effectively harness the unimaginable power of Social Age tools to stir passion and gain customer loyalty for your products and services? How do you use social tools to foster creativity and innovation *within* your company? If you suspect your business is falling behind, relying on what's "always worked," it probably is!

In *The Social Factor* we explore the thesis that a powerful new economy has emerged and profound changes in social and workplace interactions are occurring, driven by three forces: (1) information overload created during the Information Age, (2) standardization of technology that has commoditized essential conduits of communication such as cell phones, and (3) the availability of low-cost, two-way Internet communication including wikis and other social networking tools.

These three forces are irresistibly changing the way businesses compete in the twenty-first century. To effectively recruit, retain, and maximize the productivity of the Social Age workforce, and to foster collaboration with the global market, today's business must embrace and effectively integrate an array of social networking tools.

The key is to understand the dynamics of the Social Age and then accelerate the adoption of social networking tools by your organization. In *The Social Factor*, I review the events that led the world to the dawn of the Social Age. We explore the transformation of society that occurred with the advent of progressively less-costly methods of communication—from the phone, to the personal computer, to the Internet, and finally to social networking tools and services that connect the world in amazing ways.

We look at wikis, blogs, instant message, and other social networking services and discover that all these tools are increasingly available on any device—mobile or fixed, allowing you to connect with collaborative communities—any time, anyplace. Social networking has extended to the world of software development as well, and we spend a chapter discovering the powerful benefits available to your organization through open software development. We also devote two chapters to the emergence of "clouds." These clouds can either be "clouds of knowledge"—developed through the process of "tagging," or computer clouds, in which the power of massively scalable computers is available on-demand, for development, storage, or for launching a new application. We also spend two chapters discussing ideation and innovation processes in the enterprise—two areas that use social networking tools in a particularly powerful way. In the ideation chapter we also explore the fascinating organic foundation for all the social interactions—the remarkable human brain.

Throughout *The Social Factor*, we provide you with proven methods to tap into the incredible power of social networking—to ignite innovation, empower your employees, win new customers, and make existing customers even happier with your products or services.

The Social Age is here. Is your business ready? Are *you* ready?

Dawn of the Social Age

Historic eras by definition can be fully understood only with the passage of time. Perhaps you witnessed the World Trade Center attack on September 11, 2001. It was a singular event, but we now recognize that it foreshadowed the long, expensive, and painful "war on terror" in Iraq and elsewhere, and it led to a soul-searching re-evaluation of U.S. foreign policy. Perhaps in August 1981 you heard that IBM® had introduced the personal computer, which made computing available to everyone for the first time—a singular event, but one that marked the beginning of one of the most remarkable eras in the history of humankind.

To better understand how we arrived at the Social Age, a brief overview of the shape and impact of earlier eras is vital. Perhaps most notably, these eras were marked by an ever-*decreasing* cost of both communication and transportation. Together these decreasing costs were fundamental to the eventual dawn of the Social Age.

We need to return only to the mid-nineteenth century to see the first seeds of the Social Age being sown. At an early stage of the Industrial Revolution, there was a massive transformation of the labor force. A shifting skill set naturally followed the financial rewards, which were no longer found in farming, but in manufacturing. Because manufacturing was concentrated in large population centers with deep labor pools, the bucolic, community-oriented farming lifestyle vanished for many. In its place were congested cities and noisy, overcrowded, and dangerous factories. Apart from conversations with neighbors or coworkers or the occasional letter, communication for these people was rare and expensive. Long work hours, low wages, poor working conditions, and poor transportation all made extensive communication an unaffordable luxury.

America, Connected

The events that followed transformed America forever and represented the first quantum leap toward the Social Age. The steam engine, an ever-growing rail system, and perhaps most profoundly, the advent of inexpensive long-distance communication by telegraph, all served to dramatically catapult both social and economic growth.

In 1849, Samuel F. B. Morse simplified bulky and unwieldy telegraph designs into a practical and easily deployable device.[1] Not content with merely increasing communication efficiency, Morse quickly leveraged his telegraph technology into a revolutionary system that automatically signaled the location of trains, dramatically increasing safety on the growing rail system. Telegraph lines deployed at the same time as new railroad track ensured that telegraph would become the de facto communication standard of the early Industrial Age.

Coupled with Morse code, these extended telegraph lines served to provide a quick and low-cost communications channel. Although there was nothing intuitive about Morse code (short and long signals could be sent and deciphered only by highly trained telegraphers), it was nevertheless by far the fastest communication method of its time. As we explore in detail later in this chapter, the railroad safety features offered by telegraph and the broad deployment of the vastly improved telegraph technology are excellent examples of the way standardization plays a key role in lowering barriers to adoption.

Communication expanded still further with President Lincoln's signing of the Pacific Railway Act, which was created as part of Lincoln's ongoing vision of national unity. Subtitled "An aid in the construction of a railroad and telegraph line from the Missouri river to the Pacific Ocean, and to secure to the government the use of the same for postal, military, and other purposes,"[2] the act was signed in 1862, and the project was completed in 1869, four years after Lincoln's death.

For the first time, the East and West coasts were knitted together by rail and telegraph lines. Some of the first telegraph lines in the project were used by Lincoln to receive Civil War battle reports, and the general public used them to communicate across the country with loved ones. For the first time, people could stay connected quickly and at relatively low cost with people who moved West during one of America's greatest periods of migration.

The monumental scope of the Pacific Railway Act is difficult to fully appreciate today. To ensure the success of the project, the government provided more than 175 million acres of land to build it on, 3 million acres more than the size of the state of Texas[3] (Figure 1.1). Although government assistance was important, further efficiencies in the Pacific Railway construction were possible through standardization of railroad track and significant advances in the development of steel. The railroad was one of the largest and most important government projects of the Industrial Revolution, and it stands as an engineering marvel of its time.

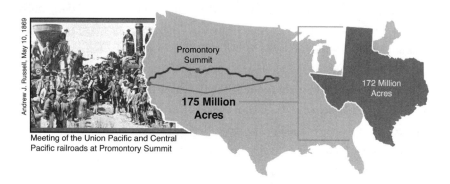

Figure 1.1   The 175 million acres donated by the U.S. government to build the Pacific Railroad is greater than than the size of Texas. A celebration on May 10, 1869, at Promontory Summit, Utah, marked the completion of the heroic effort to join America from coast to coast by rail for the first time.

The competitive advantages gained by the completion of the railroad are immeasurable and quickly propelled the United States to a position of global economic power, which it retained for many years. Telegraph cables were soon ubiquitous across the United States, and in due course were laid across the bottom of the Atlantic Ocean, creating a connected world—via Morse code—for the first time. The Associated Press was a creature of the telegraph, formed by newspaper publishers who recognized the tremendous profit potential of instantaneous worldwide news bulletins.

The Pacific Railway Act transformed an expensive and often life-threatening westward journey of more than three months to just over one week of relative comfort and low cost. The act not only lowered transportation costs but also enabled vastly improved communication across the nation.

This lower cost of transportation and communication, enabled by the railroad and telegraph lines, transformed the nation and supported the collaboration required by the rapidly expanding country.

The Telephone: Talking on the Wires

The next phase of the Industrial Revolution, which some historians call the "Second Industrial Revolution," occurred from 1875 to the 1920s, and represents another leap in economic and social development. Electricity, petroleum, automobiles, telephones, and new steel industrial applications generated a host of innovations. Together these advances enabled increased economies of scale through lower cost of communication and manufacturing; and more importantly, for the first time they provided workers with affordable transportation that made longer-distance commuting possible.

The combination of the automobile, electricity, and telephone created the momentum that generated explosive urban development. The automobile increased the distance and speed that food and other goods could be transported. Electricity powered a host of innovations, including electric-powered refrigeration, which also increased the distance goods could travel and their shelf life after they were delivered to a customer. Finally, the telephone was instrumental in maintaining connections over long distance in the new urban and dispersed society. These inventions changed society by empowering and freeing individuals to communicate better and travel farther and faster, at a lower cost.

Alexander Graham Bell's telephone, invented in 1876, leveraged the established telegraph infrastructure to vault communications to the next level. The telephone established a new, low cost communication, which consequently supported further dispersal of communities into the suburbs and encouraged better long distance communication.

Now a community included not just those we talked with face to face; now it included anyone we could talk with on the telephone, no matter the distance. As communication cost decreased still further, it supported a rapidly expanding and more complex society, which in turn fostered even more societal dispersion. It was increasingly apparent that communities dispersed as the cost of communication decreased. Here was early evidence, now fully proven in the Social Age, that productivity doesn't always require face-to-face interaction.

Rather than revolutions, the first and second Industrial Revolutions can perhaps better be thought of as the evolution of technologies from earlier, less-efficient—and less-effective—predecessors. Much like Darwinian organic evolution, technology progresses through a natural selection process in which those traits most useful to society are propagated and further enhanced with more innovations. Incremental advances occur as less-efficient systems are abandoned or improved—the telegraph becomes the telephone, and the stage coach becomes the railroad.

Technologies that evolve and constantly provide increased value will survive. Each technical advance is driven by an increased need for efficiency and effectiveness, which in turn is driven by the understanding that the delivery of increased value results in increased value received—revenue and profits. Henry Ford recognized the incredible power of innovation to drive profit:

> We regard a profit as the inevitable conclusion of work well done. Money is simply a commodity which we need just as we need coal and iron. If money be otherwise regarded, great difficulties are inevitable, for then money gets itself ahead of service. And a business that does not serve has no place in our commonwealth.[4]

Incremental Change, Big Consequences

In some cases, the evolution of technology is so dramatic that little remains of the foundational idea on which the technology is based. But there are times when even a small incremental change can lead to an innovation with tremendous social and economic impact. Modern electricity represents such an incremental change.

Three main players are on stage for this historic moment in 1887. The first is Thomas Edison, the visionary "Wizard of Menlo Park," with his 1,000+ patents. Next is the insightful businessman George Westinghouse, the chief rival of Edison, best known to that moment for his invention of a revolutionary air brake system still in use on trains today.[5] And last is Nikola Tesla, the brilliant young inventor with the photographic memory and a reputation for efficiency in the inventive process.

Edison made great progress leveraging direct electrical current (DC). With DC, he created a collection of electric appliances and the first light bulb, all of which had lasting impact on the world. But DC was inefficient and difficult to transport over long distances. It was Tesla's ingenuity that transformed DC to alternating electrical current (AC) and enabled electricity to be transported over long distances at low cost, establishing our current modern electrical grid.

It was a small change, but AC vastly improved electrical power. George Westinghouse bought Tesla's AC patent, and together they created the technology that transformed modern life, which even today is used to power the world. Businesses became more efficient and mass production costs were reduced dramatically with a new electric utility enabled by the AC technology. Powerful mass communication devices such as the radio would soon become a reality.

Ahead of His Time

Benjamin Abrams' Emerson Radio and Phonograph Corp. produced more than one million low-cost, high-quality radios in each of the years leading up to World War II. Abrams' business philosophy was simple: "I have never regarded low price as being the paramount issue," he said. "Value, utility, [and] service have been and always will be, greater considerations."

Although these three factors were most important to Abrams, it is evident that low price was the deciding factor that drove so many Depression-era consumers to his product. In only nine years, from 1932 to 1941, the number of radio listeners more than quadrupled, from 12 million to 55 million, due in large part to Abrams' low-cost radio.[6]

Radio Comes of Age

Like electricity, radio also evolved incrementally through many small but significant steps. Through the groundbreaking 1897 work of Guglielmo Marconi—known as the "father of wireless telegraph"[7]—telegraph was no longer bound by copper wire. Leveraging the electromagnetic waves theory first postulated by James Clerk Maxwell in the middle 1800s, Marconi transmitted telegraph through the air and paved the way for the next revolution in mass communication—the radio. In 1907 Lee de Forest created audion, a feedback amplifier and oscillator that used Marconi's wireless telegraph principles to send the human voice across the airwaves for the first time.[8]

Ten years after Lee de Forest's audion, the radio became a household fixture. The radio helped keep the nation together through the Great Depression and two world wars. Such a means of mass communication was without precedent in human history. Radio was affordable to most Americans, and listening soon became a national pastime.

Perhaps the greatest validation of the radio as the primary means of mass communication came immediately after the December 7, 1941, attack on Pearl Harbor.

Within 24 hours of the attack, President Franklin D. Roosevelt (Figure 1.2) was heard on the radio delivering his most memorable speech to Congress about "[the] date which will live in infamy."[9] This was a historic moment because a U.S. president used radio to gain immediate access to an entire country and inspire them to work together to win the war. The low cost of the communications medium made Roosevelt's appeal available to the broadest possible audience in real time.

Figure 1.2 Roosevelt speaking to the nation in 1934.[10]

Social Networking and the Social Age

In our consideration of the Social Age, Roosevelt's example is also instructive. Roosevelt found that the best method of effective organization was to speak to the *largest number of people possible over the least expensive medium.* He was leveraging the social aspect of radio to create an unprecedented sense of unity in the country and support for the war. As Roosevelt demonstrated, and as we've seen repeatedly in the Social Age, the greatest value of low-cost communication is its capability to enhance the effectiveness of crowds and organizational efforts across a wider range of communities.

The radio also dramatically compressed the time required for news to be distributed, and at a much lower cost than newspapers or other traditional methods. The invention of the television followed with even greater communication power. In fewer than 30 years— from 1950 to 1978—households owning televisions in the United States rose from 9 percent to 98 percent.[11] Television is a prime example of the way communication cost has steadily decreased in the modern era, as illustrated in Figure 1.3.

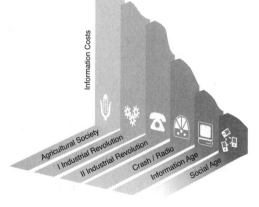

Figure 1.3 Decreasing cost of communication in each modern historical era.

Although television was an early step in the Information Age, the advent of computers—particularly personal computers—marked the high point of the Information Age and laid the foundation for the Social Age. Beginning in 2000, we entered the transition from the Information Age to the Social Age as fully enabled and "smart" electronic networks were rapidly becoming populated with social services and tools such as Classmates and YouTube. Mass communication up to that time was essentially a unidirectional medium. But now, for the first time, meaningful two-way communication was possible on the Web, using Web 2.0-enabling technology that arrived on the scene around that time.

The Semantic Web

Social networking tools such as wikis and blogs are possible only because of a bidirectional communications technology known as the Semantic Web. The Semantic Web created the concept of a smart document that is aware of its own content via Extensible Markup Language (XML) tags. A host of technologies support this trend including Resource Description Framework (RDF), Web Ontology Language (OWL), and other XML extensions. For example, if you update a page that is content-aware, the update will be reflected in other related sites. Simply put, when someone changes something on a content-aware Web site "A," Web sites "B," "C," and "D" have their content dynamically updated as well.

The Semantic Web innovations, combined with two-way communication-capable web pages, such as wikis, blogs, and other social networking tools, created a completely new way to get organized, provide information, and collaborate. In turn these changes created even greater efficiencies and propelled social tools to broad acceptance by the general public.

These changes are also happening inside the protected environment of the corporate firewall. For the first time, lower-cost Internet communication and two-way web technologies have enabled businesses to collaborate and leverage large and diverse internal and external communities through social networking services.

Social networking is a critical long-term shift of the Internet revolution and is the primary catalyst of the Social Age. Suddenly, smart content and two-way communication empowers the individual to be heard in a meaningful way. Each person's opinion carries the same weight as fellow collaborators. Everyone's credibility is enhanced and his or her opinion is important. Particularly in decision making, the opinion of the crowd is now vital to final outcomes.

As social networking tools gained popularity, the world became increasingly instrumented. Through radio frequency identification (RFID) tags, and other technologies, the previously insensate world suddenly got "smart." New two-way communication devices can sense human activity, monitor supply chain workflow for bottlenecks, and even analyze weather patterns, making our world smarter and more efficient.

> *Social networking is a critical long-term shift of the Internet revolution and is the primary catalyst of the Social Age.*

In comments to the Council on Foreign Relations in November 2008, IBM's CEO Sam Palmisano picked up on this theme. "The world will continue to become smaller, flatter…and smarter," he said. "We are moving into the age of the globally integrated and intelligent economy, society and planet." He concluded with a challenge: "The question is what we are going to do with that?"[12]

This is certainly a question we do well to ask ourselves, and one we address in more detail in Chapter 2, "Social Age Organizations."

Standardization + Low Cost = Increased Adoption

As we've seen with earlier innovation, the adoption of Social Age technology is accelerating proportional to the decreasing cost of communications. In many ways social networking is following a short, steep pattern of growth reminiscent of other recent transformational technologies such as the personal computer (PC).

Another example of such growth is the cell phone, which achieved 70 percent market penetration in only seven years. Even with a recession in 2008, the worldwide penetration of cell phones continues to grow at an unprecedented rate. Emerging regions such as Africa and Asia drive much of this increased demand with approximately 250,000 cell phones shipped to those regions in the first quarter of 2008. By comparison, television took nearly 20 years to reach 70 percent penetration. Industrial-Age automobiles took even longer to reach comparable acceptance—more than 100 years.

As each new technical innovation reaches the marketplace, the speed with which it is adopted becomes shorter and shorter. The acceleration of technology adoption has been caused by better communication and increased standardization, which ultimately leads to a lower cost of technology. In this way innovation creates a virtuous cycle—incremental improvements generate lower cost of production, which in turn leads to increased adoption and greater value to society.

Technology Standardization

By using the assembly line, Henry Ford was among the first to leverage the cost efficiency available through standardization. Perhaps the best illustration of Ford's philosophy of standardization was his decision to offer his Model T in "any color, as long as it's black."[13] More importantly, Ford understood the critical necessity of establishing his technology with early adopters before any of his competitors. Ford leveraged the assembly line to lower cost of production that, in turn, lowered the cost of the Model T, making it among the most affordable cars of its time. Early adopters of the Model T drove strong growth and exceptional profitability for Ford, which encouraged competitors to enter the market using similar standardization and assembly line practices.

The Model T is an excellent example of the way early adopters drive a steep demand curve for new technology, which is the part of the adoption cycle with the highest profit margin. Although the initial penetration of the automobile market by early adopters was fast, overall market penetration didn't achieve the 75 percent mark for 125 years. Today, 75 percent market penetration can be reached with new technology in only a few years, as illustrated in Figure 1.4.

As Ford demonstrated with the Model T, timing is everything to win in any new market. Ford not only reaped the profitable benefits of being first to market with his automobile, he was also the first to transform manufacturing processes with his new assembly line production approach. The result was a standardized product that many could afford, which ultimately led to the commoditization and mass adoption of the automobile. Ford and other entrepreneurs from earlier eras had at their disposal only unidirectional communication such as radio and television to advertise their products. In the Social Age, however, rapid market penetration and adoption of new technology happens much more quickly, and success increasingly depends on effectively marketing to social networking communities.

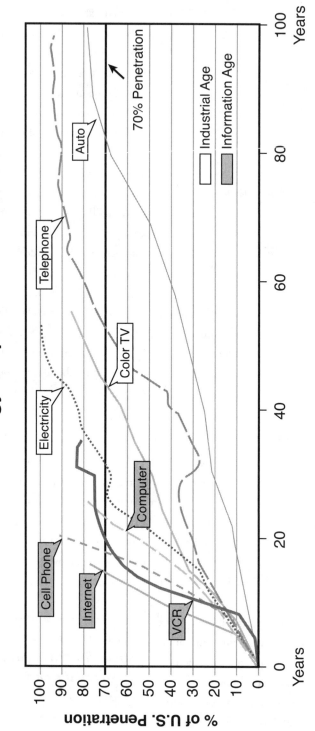

Figure 1.4 Number of years for each technology to penetrate 70 percent of market.[14]

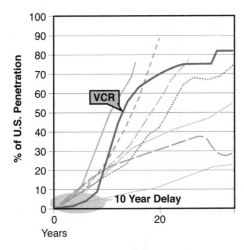

Figure 1.5 Adoption of VCR was delayed for ten years during format battle between Betamax and VHS.

For an example of the dangers of *failing* to standardize, we need look no further than the competitive battle that raged in the mid-1970s between Sony Betamax and the VHS format of video recorders. Broad acceptance of the VCR was hindered primarily through a lack of standardization. Betamax and VHS were offered simultaneously, dividing the market for ten years (see Figure 1.5), and causing many consumers to delay their buying decisions—no one wanted to get stuck with obsolete technology! As we witnessed recently in the brief, two-year battle between Toshiba HD DVD and Sony's Blu-ray format,[15] such conflicts are quickly resolved in the Social Age. Social networking tools promote conversations about new technologies across a wide community. These conversations quickly result in a consensus about the superior technology, leading to standardization and broad acceptance.

Technology Commoditization

Importantly, history demonstrates that standardization also quickly leads to commoditization. As standardization is achieved, economies of scale drive costs lower, which in turn further propels adoption of the technology. Commoditization then leads to rapid global acceptance. Faster and lower-cost communication further accelerates the adoption of standardized technology. Two technologies that have commoditized recently—both within the context of fast, low-cost communication—are the personal computer and the cell phone, as demonstrated by their parabolic growth curves in Figure 1.4.

The cell phone is perhaps the most current example of the way low-cost communication has created a massive adoption of technology, which has benefited the Social Age, offering an additional medium of communication. In addition to low cost, the enthusiasm for cell phones

Social networks accelerate standardization of products through their massive influence and buying power.

is driven by several factors, including its highly customizable design, or its plasticity. From personalized games to ring tones, cell phones can be tuned to communicate any way their owners want. This plasticity will soon lead to cell phones becoming the primary means for collaboration and communication in the Social Age.

With new sensors embedded in cell phones, even credit cards as we know them might become obsolete, using applications such as e-wallet, an IBM-patented technology. E-wallet enables instantaneous connection with credit card companies, banks, and other payers from a cell phone, simplifying the point of sale process.[16] Further transparency for mobile device users becomes available as they enable sensors that are context-aware. By always knowing where their users are, and communicating that information to others, mobile devices will essentially become social coordinators and electronic proxies for their owners.[17]

Social Networking: Transforming Our World

In many ways, the Internet revolution was just the beginning; the real revolution, taking place now, is social networking. As we discuss in the following chapters, social tools such as wikis, blogs, tags, interactive games, and ratings that enable folksonomies[18] (among others) are at the heart of the Social Age and represent a key value proposition for your business.

The speed with which social networking tools have been embraced is stunning. Every month millions of people and businesses are jumping to get connected, whether to satisfy a basic social need or to sell their products through this powerful new "electronic word of mouth."

As recently as 2002, blogs were considered arcane technology used mostly by geeks to share their thoughts and witticisms. But the plummeting cost of communication and pervasive social technology has in many ways encouraged the soaring adoption of blogs and other social networking tools in just a few years.

> *The real revolution, taking place now, is social networking.*

Today, a tsunami of blogs comes from all levels of expertise, from professional writers to rank amateurs. People can't get enough of social tools. Seemingly overnight there are a host of social tools available online, including MySpace, Facebook, Friendster, Orkut Windows Live, Classmates, Cyworld, Bebo, Hi5, and others.[19] Like-minded enthusiasts can connect on 24hTennis, Taltopia, Travellerspoint, Librarything, GoodReads, MyArtSpace, CakeFinancial, and others.[20] You can celebrate your heritage on BlackPlanet, MiGente, Geni, and many others.[21] While you're at it, why not expand your business network with LinkedIn and Plaxo?[22] All these relatively new sites, attracting tens of millions of visitors each day, are the direct result of the revolutionary changes of the Social Age.

Social Age, Exabyte Age

An exabyte is one quintillion bytes—a *billion* gigabytes. It seems like only yesterday, just when we had learned how many bits were in a byte, that we were suddenly asked to learn about megabytes and gigabytes. Now we need to keep track of exabytes!

IDC said that as of 2007, the digital universe was 281 exabytes in size.[23] IDC predicts that the digital universe will reach nearly *3,000* exabytes by 2010 (3,000,000,000,000 gigabytes). This is actually a conservative estimate, which excludes specialized data from scientific experiments such as the Large Hadron Collider and digital telescopes that generate several exabytes *per week.*[24]

A computer-age pioneer, Frederick Brooks, Jr., looked back with nostalgia on his early, slower-paced years in the industry and forward with anticipation of the bright future ahead:

> When I was a graduate student in the mid-1950s, I could read *all* the journals and conference proceedings; I could stay current in *all* the disciplines. Today my intellectual life has seen me regretfully kissing subdiscipline interests goodbye one by one, as my portfolio has continuously overflowed beyond mastery. Too many interests, too many exciting opportunities for learning, research, and thought. What a marvelous predicament! Not only is the end not in sight, the pace is not slackening. We have many future joys.[25]

Brooks penned those words in 1994. Much has happened since then. Not only has the pace "not slackened," but an exponential acceleration in knowledge has forced us to rethink almost everything about the ways we learn, interact with each other, and get our jobs done.

Shift Happens

The video sharing Web site YouTube.com has a number of provocative five- to six-minute videos about the pace of change in our technological world, all of which were apparently inspired by 2007's *Shift Happens* (also known as *Did You Know?*).[26] Originally produced for a teacher's conference to spark discussion about trends in education, *Shift* asks a series of questions about the state of world culture and demographic trends.

Shift points out, for example, that the first commercial text message was sent in 1992, and in 2006, the number of text messages sent *each day* exceeded the total population of the planet. In 2006, there were 3,000 books being published *daily*. The amount of technical information was doubling in 2006 every two years, and by 2010, technical information is expected to double every *72 hours*. In 20 years or so, this means a college freshman studying technical disciplines will learn things that will likely be obsolete by the time he or she graduates.[27]

Social networking certainly contributes to this mind-numbing growth of information, but ironically, social tools are also the best way to deal with this explosion.

So what does all this mean as you consider the impact of the Social Age on your life and business? History has shown that major revolutions—in technology and in politics—create disruption and uncertainty as the old order is threatened and at last replaced by the new. Smart businesses see this disruption and uncertainty as an opportunity. They rush to bring innovations and value propositions to corporations, to the government, and to society at large. Disruptive innovations and solutions confront lower barriers to entry during times of uncertainty and often serve to facilitate the establishment of a new social order.

> *"The entrepreneur always searches for change, responds to it, and exploits it as an opportunity."*[28]
>
> Peter F. Drucker

In the present context, the Social Age, with its communication and collaboration-centric approach, will unleash powerful synergies that can create value for your business and personal life. The following chapters provide additional groundwork for ways to transform your business and leverage social tools to create collaboration among employees and across organizations to tap into the incredible power of the Social Age revolution.

Summary

- The main thesis of *The Social Factor* is that three forces led to the revolution we call the Social Age: information overload created during the Information Age, standardization of technology that has commoditized key conduits of communication such as pervasive devices like cell phones, and low-cost two-way Internet communication including wikis and other social networking tools.

- Technology revolutions are more appropriately thought of as iterative evolutions from less-effective and less-efficient predecessors to solutions that provide more value to society. An example is the telegraph evolving into the wireless telegraph and eventually into the radio.

- Faster and lower cost of communication combined with standardization leads to more rapid market penetration of technologies.

- The enormous social networking capabilities of the cell phone are transforming it into a genuine social extension for the user.

- Social networking tools are an excellent way to manage the overwhelming flood of information generated by the fast pace of our society.

2
Social Age
Organizations

The compounded technological advances of the past 200 years have reduced the cost of communication to a point that many take it for granted. Low-cost communication has created dramatically increased efficiency, which has become a catalyst for entirely new social and business organizations. More complex social structures and intricate business collaboration networks are now possible and generate incredible organizational efficiencies in businesses of all sizes.

Traditional hierarchical structures have great value to organizations where information is controlled or consolidated at the top. Military services depend on a rigid and well-defined hierarchical structure, but dynamic market forces have forced businesses to rethink this traditional, top-down approach. Business strategists realize that hierarchical structures just don't work as effectively in the Social Age. In an earlier stage of development, businesses focused on economies of scale, growing as fast as possible, and relying on highly centralized company structures. Strategists and executives had the information required to lead the organization, and they pushed the information down to the workforce through organizational layers.

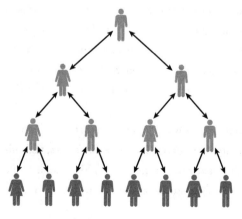

The Globally Integrated Enterprise

In the Social Age, information resides in the network, *within* organizational layers. This creates a new world order of communication, requiring different ways of working and thinking. Add market pressures, and increasing globalization, and any business that hopes to survive must respond aggressively. As businesses "globalized," organizational evolution quickly moved from highly centralized hierarchies to multinational structures with independent businesses empowered to optimize for local markets.

But the multinational structure has proven to have some drawbacks. The primary deficiency of this model has been the duplication of services driven by local business units optimizing for their markets, but failing to take into consideration the overall corporate financial perspective. For example, businesses structured around the multinational model tend to create duplication of IT solution procurement and fulfillment as they satisfy specific requests from each regional team. This can create a plethora of solutions that drive IT costs higher and introduce operational inefficiencies. These same needs can be addressed more cost-effectively with a well-defined supply chain IT solution to optimize the business. A more effective way to handle this problem is through the establishment of a shared service that can be customized but not duplicated by the regions.

The Globally Integrated Enterprise addresses the deficiency of the multinational model. The Globally Integrated Enterprise is a more efficient organizational model in which common business processes are standardized to lower the cost of IT and simplify overall end-to-end delivery. Increasingly, companies are moving toward the Globally Integrated Enterprise model—radically challenging their existing business model, embracing disruptive technologies such as cloud computing, and most importantly, providing the tools and encouragement for employees to work in communities. In the Social Age, companies will continue to transform their organizational structures to become more agile and community-centric. They will have loosely connected structures arranged around business communities that are fluidly formed and disbanded based on new projects, innovation efforts, and market demands. Employees will come together for a project, based on their relevant expertise, and then disband when the project concludes.

New collaboration and social networking tools also help create better global perspectives. Teams collaborate across country boundaries, language differences, and cultural barriers to ensure everyone has an equal voice in the process. These tools create a flatter, smarter, and more nimble business structure—a business structure that truly leverages the benefits of a global marketplace by integrating the power and energy of a worldwide "business crowd."[1] These expanded business communities offer a clear competitive advantage to organizations that embrace them. Social networking tools enable the entrepreneurial team of a company to more easily come together around difficult challenges and efficiently create innovative solutions.

Communities supported by social networking tools typically encompass a variety of skills, cultures, and locations, but common goals and passions motivate them and bind them together. The low cost of participation—in both effort and expense—often leads to these communities being noncollocated. By expanding the community geographically, those who participate are often among the recognized experts in their fields. Ease of participation and higher levels of expert participation create more valuable outcomes, and participants tend to work together better and share information more readily than traditional collocated groups.

Just as happens in society at large, these ad hoc communities also develop their own sense of identity and culture that might only be loosely associated with the corporate "vibe." Although everyone might not wear a company-logoed shirt, these communities are typically marked by a drive to excel and to contribute to the business in a meaningful way. Participants are respected for the value they provide to the community, rather than for their hierarchical corporate position or social status. In many ways these communities create their own work ethic that encourages members to contribute and generate value through healthy peer pressure.

Objections might be raised by those who are new to this model. "How can someone halfway around the world relate to and work with someone here in the states? After all, aren't the nonverbal cues we receive from our colleagues, along with our powers of observation about their workspace, important in our working relationship?" Both of these are excellent questions and both get at the heart of what makes socially networked communities so powerful.

In today's global marketplace, teaming with people you've never met face-to-face is increasingly common. These colleagues might be from completely different cultures, have completely different business practices, and even be working while you're sound asleep, ten time zones away. But to get the job done, you have to effectively collaborate with these distant colleagues, just as you do with the team in the offices and cubicles all around you.

In a face-to-face work environment, verbal and nonverbal cues help you work with colleagues. Through casual conversations, or by observing coworkers interact with each other, you gain valuable insight into personality and work style. Even the way people decorate their offices can help you connect with them. Knowing the whole person can be vital for team success. We all tend to gravitate toward people we like, and knowing someone socially can build a better working environment. The challenge is to foster this same interpersonal connection and team spirit among people who sometimes work in locations separated by 10,000 miles or more.

Social networking, in this case, becomes something of a virtual representation of your workplace. What do people in your office know about you just by observing your work space? Malcolm Gladwell says that the best way to find out about a job candidate is not by any of the usual methods. "Forget the endless 'getting to know' lunches. If you want to get a good idea of whether I would make a good employee, drop by my house one day and take a look around."[2]

With social networking we can hang our family pictures on the virtual walls of our blog. We can share the latest news about our local sports team, or highlight a competitive sales win. Did you just finish your first marathon? Perhaps you'll find that five people in the Mumbai office are marathon runners as well. In addition to chatting around the water cooler about a recent customer experience, many employees are now blogging about it as well.

Share bookmarks with your teammates by using a social bookmarking site where your collective knowledge is always available. Show your preference for a sports team by joining a fan club on a social networking site. You can also share your membership in professional organizations. With social networking tools there are countless ways to let your colleagues know you better, which ultimately improves teamwork and camaraderie.

Socially networked business communities work together continuously, leverage external channels, and remain loosely connected to other teams and business units. This structure is successful because of constant information sharing and the transparency created by technologies such as wikis, blogs, and other services that socialize the enterprise in a way that information becomes equally accessible to everyone in the business.

The Social Age Corporation: Hungry for Change

The openness and transparency of collaborative communities—both outside and inside the confines of corporate firewalls—represent a significant shift that overturns traditional delivery and management approaches.

The loose structure of these communities provides profound benefits to the organization. Rather than being constrained by traditional department boundaries and hierarchies, Social Age organizations can quickly redeploy resources or restructure within the social networking model as opportunities or challenges arise. For the Globally Integrated Enterprise, such nimbleness is a powerful competitive advantage.

Unlike monolithic corporations of an earlier age, the Social Age organization is not threatened by change but is hungry for it. The Social Age organization is interested in innovation as a way to continually generate value for customers and society. It is truly integrated globally and driven by the energy of its communities. It is disruptive by nature, always questioning the status quo and responding quickly to opportunities. Perhaps above all, the global corporation of the Social Age is *genuine* with its employees, not just generous. This is significant because Social Age employees often seem to value transparency, honesty, and camaraderie in the workplace more highly than they do additional compensation. The unprecedented wealth experienced by the Net generation has created profound social needs and expectations of higher ethical behavior in the work place.

As we explore later, there is an abundance of retail social tools available on the Internet from which your business can choose. These tools enable anyone to create a Web site to exchange ideas, brainstorm, or collaborate with others. These services are typically free if you're willing to give up some privacy, receive advertising, or tolerate occasional service outages. Similar tools have been adopted internally at many corporations, but with key adaptations to provide more reliability, privacy, and business efficiencies. Advertising has similarly been stripped out of these tools, which is seen as an unnecessary distraction in most corporate settings.

Along with easy-to-access and user-friendly tools, the Social Age will be marked by communication that continually becomes more effective and affordable. Any business can use—and take for granted—wikis, blogs, micro blogs, instant messages, collaboration tools, tag services, smart phones, cloud data storage, 3D virtual office spaces, customized business search engines, standardized transaction services, and many other services that enable formation of business communities.

CEOs and CIOs are increasingly acknowledging and validating social models of interaction and communication. We have seen investments of up to 20 percent of IT budgets in collaboration and innovation initiatives with customers and employees. European conglomerate Rheinmetall is a good example of a company with a substantial commitment to social networking and collaboration tools.

Social Networking at Rheinmetall

With multibillion Euro annual revenues, Germany's Rheinmetall is a leading auto-motive and defense technology company with locations in Europe, North and South America, and Asia. Rheinmetall has offices in 17 countries and 60 locations, and uses a variety of social tools to support its worldwide workforce of 19,000 employees.

CIO Markus Bentele talked about the challenges of implementing social software at Rheinmetall. "We have a legal structure for the organization we must maintain," Bentele said, "but we wanted to build a virtual structure spanning these different entities, and [social tools] are enabling us to do this." The automotive business of Rheinmetall has five product divisions with a total of nearly 12,000 employees. "We wanted them to be able to network and tap into the entire organization for expertise, help, and ideas,"[3] said Bentele. Rheinmetall needed to connect people from various parts of the organization into virtual teams and communities to effectively drive the business.

"Along with subsidiaries in Europe, North America, and Asia," Bentele said, "we maintain a tightly woven network of branches and company representatives. Proxim-ity to the customer is one of our most important principles. Rheinmetall needed a single point of entry for all employees worldwide that would give them access to the collaboration tools and all their intranet and business intelligence systems."

Social networking was strategic to Rheinmetall for growing its business. "We experimented with a few social tools like wikis and blogs," Bentele said, "to see how they could be used in business environments, and users asked for more. We also iden-tified that we needed to implement a social computing system for several important reasons."

Bentele went on to list three primary drivers of social networking at Rheinmetall:

- **A tool in the recruiting war for talented employees**—Social networking pro-vided Rheinmetall with credibility as a Social Age company in the eyes of job candidates.

- **A paradigm shift in communications**—New employees and trainees commu-nicate in different ways—they don't use e-mail, or write things down; they are expert at communicating via instant messaging and social tools such as blogs. Without social networking, communication at Rheinmetall would suffer and collective knowledge would be limited.

- **Evolutionary changes in information location**—No longer do Rheinmetall employees "go it alone" when it comes to research. Millennials, including those at Rheinmetall, grew up with Wikipedia. They get information from established networks and rely on those networks to get things done.

It is fascinating to hear Bentele explain the role of demographics in the use of social tools at Rheinmetall: "We have four generations working at our company," Bentele said. "The first are the older executives who still like to work with paper. The second generation work mostly with e-mail and groupware; the third use instant messaging, and the fourth—the newest recruits—work in wikis and blogs."

Bentele said that these different approaches aren't so much a function of age as they are a function of cultural influence and mind-set. As a result, Rheinmetall offers flexibility in the use of social and communication tools, which Bentele believes fosters a more productive environment. "It is [simply] not possible to mandate that everybody use the same tools," says Bentele.

> *"This technology is not just an opportunity; it is a necessity."*
> Markus Bentele, Rheinmetall CIO

For other CIOs considering social tools, Bentele offers an enthusiastic endorsement: "This technology is not just an opportunity; it is a necessity."

The Social Age: Great Expectations

Social networking was embraced by the general public before it was embraced by most businesses, and its influence continues to grow in all areas. The Social Age generation is being conditioned—as no previous generation has been—to feel comfortable sharing information, collaborating with distant colleagues and acquaintances, having a global mind-set, and valuing (not just *tolerating*) transparency.

Our expectations during the Social Age have risen as well. In the dot-com era we were pleased with a web page that was fairly current that could execute a commercial transaction. The Internet was originally thought of as only a static content delivery model. As such it was just a better, faster print medium; it was primarily unidirectional—content producers to readers. There was little if any bidirectional capability in the early days. If someone had valuable information to share with others, there was no easy way to get the word out. Although everyone could set up their own Web sites, this just exacerbated the problem—now there were just that many more isolated islands of information.

During the dot-com era, a plethora of Web sites were created with no collaboration interfaces between them. New web crawlers and search engines tried to bridge the gap between these isolated data sources but didn't provide the interactive experience that most people instinctively desire as a natural social behavior. After all, we are social animals!

The transformation to dynamic bidirectional interaction—a social-centric Internet—was driven by Web 2.0 technologies, higher bandwidth capacity, and easily accessible new media. Users today expect web applications to be interactive—capable of receiving input from readers and benefiting from the input of others using the application. Customers now demand a way to rate products and have an easy way to complain about or praise a product. The pressure is building for all businesses to provide a channel for customer feedback and social collaboration.

For your business, however, the Social Age means much more than just creating an electronic suggestion box or customer feedback form. True social networking transformation creates self-sufficient communities that can actually help run part of your business. For example, a business can foster a socially networked customer community to work jointly with its own support team to provide better customer service. These business communities can help fix bugs, build an effective communication campaign, select the next product enhancement, or even share ideas for new business directions. No business has a monopoly on good ideas. Why not tap into what might be your best source of new ideas for your product—those who already use it!

More powerful social networking solutions are now being created for businesses through Services Oriented Architecture (SOA)[4] and *web services*, which standardize social networking tools and allow them to be connected with other business services. The current barrier between retail social networking applications and enterprise social networking tools behind the firewall will continue to diminish as these open interfaces are embraced. This standardization of web services has enabled corporations to exploit external services through a set of modular encapsulations of services or *composite applications* that can be used with enterprise web applications.

New social networking services, based on web services, will accelerate business transformation and fundamentally restructure the enterprise around communities. Loosely coupled social connections—those connections that you create through social networking, with people you barely know, but with whom you associate by profession, interest, or project—will play an important role in this transformation. These communities, empowered by SOA and web services, will realize the full value of social connections to collaborate with knowledgeable external and internal participants, and facilitate globalization of the enterprise.

Social networking tools in the business world are about transformation. They are about supporting a new world order that democratizes and socializes business processes. They create more productive and efficient environments for communities to collaborate on projects—with local flavor and worldwide scope.

Social Networking in Your Organization

Organizations of all sizes are exploiting Social Age tools to encourage more effective collaboration by their employees, clients, and business partners. Employment agencies make extensive use of professional networking sites such as LinkedIn.com to identify potential candidates. Likewise, employers use LinkedIn.com to advertise jobs. Retail companies use social networking tools to drive sales and marketing. Everyone, it seems, from giant corporations to grade-school students, are selecting products and suppliers with reference to satisfaction ratings and reviews. But for most organizations, the greatest value in social networking is found in these six areas:

- Teaming and collaboration
- Content and expertise capture
- Succession planning
- Skills development
- Recruitment and on-boarding
- Innovation

Teaming and collaboration are the primary drivers of social networking at most organizations. These tools provide valuable support to employees, business partners, and clients. The agility and reach of the organization is improved when tools are available that help people get to know each other better, ultimately leading to more effective team building and productivity. Particularly in the area of research and development, effective collaboration around key initiatives is vital to the future of your organization. In a 2008 paper, the journal of the International Association for Human Resources said that people with better social capital:

- Close deals faster

- Enhance the performance of their teams

- Help their teams reach their goals more rapidly

- Help their teams generate more creative solutions[5]

Recruitment and on-boarding of new employees is improved with access to social tools. Services external to the firewall (such as LinkedIn.com) can be used to advertise for and find potential hires. A new hire can then access internal social tools to quickly become productive. For example, wikis offer extensive how-tos. Profiles and blogs provide access to mentors, along with the capability to "follow" someone by subscribing to a feed of their activity, as we discuss in Chapter 7, "Social Media and Culture." In addition, the new hire can find corporate information and navigation assistance in wikis and FAQs. In 2008, the International Association for Human Resources also noted, "Social capital is a key driver in employee retention."[6] Social tools are useful in recruiting talented employees, but the sense of camaraderie these tools build within the organization is vital for retaining talent.

Skills development is accelerated by being socially networked to existing communities of expertise or interest, and exploring e-learning content adds depth to those skills. Weaving social tools into e-learning has reinvigorated this technology over the past five years, making it more relevant. Everybody can contribute content to e-learning, and social tools allow tagging, ratings, and recommendations. Also, while consuming e-learning, users can now have access to other learners, experts, and communities—in context—through social networking.

Succession planning is more easily accomplished when expertise profiles and skills assessments are current and complete. Social networking tools provide the information vital to succession planning at all levels of the organization. For western companies, which are planning for large numbers of retirees in the next decade, this issue is particularly important.

Content and expertise capture, or the accumulation of *tacit knowledge,* is significantly enhanced with social tools. The longer someone participates in a social networking community, the more they contribute. This low barrier to entry leads naturally to the next stages of social networking involvement—contributing media, new or updated content on wikis, and developing personal profiles. Media contributions can include anything from spreadsheets and documents to more social forms such as video and podcasts with presentations or screenshot content. Users might ultimately publish blogs or create and lead new communities.

Finally, *innovation* is arguably the area where social networking is having its most powerful impact in business. In Chapter 10, "Social Innovation," we explore this topic in detail, using an extensive real-world example at IBM where more than 125,000 contributors collaborated on literally hundreds of exciting new technologies.

Accelerating Particles
and **Collaboration**

In 2008, the Oxford Internet Institute (O.I.I.) conducted case studies with two physics experiments developed at the CERN Large Hadron Collider (LHC) in Switzerland. One experiment was developed using a traditional hierarchical project management, and the second (Atlas) was developed using new Social Age project management techniques. The latter was found to take longer to establish priorities and agreement, but, when started, was executed more effectively. Importantly, the Atlas experiment was shown to deal better with setbacks and problems encountered during development. The Atlas project comprised over 2,000 scientists and 165 working groups across the globe.[7]

Degrees of Separation: An IBM Experience

For a more empirical understanding of the effectiveness of social networking in the business environment, my team created a project in which IBMers could join a study about the degrees of separation between IBMers and their patterns of communication.

The study was performed under a rigorous scientific process and strict privacy rules were enforced on communications related to e-mail, instant messages, blogs, and wikis. This strictly volunteer project was by invitation only, and anyone who wanted to participate had the opportunity to sign in. Anonymity was ensured through replacement of personal information with numbers. Company confidential and personal sensitive data were also removed.

One of the studies included approximately 30,000 employees using e-mail and instant message, while the second study included approximately 157,000 employees using wikis. These studies provided powerful examples of the ways socially networked business communities exchange information and work together.

The study revealed that communities had a few participants who performed the majority of the communication that held the team together. Also, more frequently than expected, the true community leader was neither the formal leader nor the primary keeper of the information (*institutional memory*).

Instead, as illustrated in Figure 2.1, the communities behaved as organic entities that organized around people whom Malcolm Gladwell described as *connectors*.[8] These connectors kept the team moving and were instrumental in conflict resolution. In essence, these communities formed an effective informal organization. All these organic entities were free to collaborate and solve problems as the situation and business changed. Natural leaders emerged depending on the expertise required and the problem confronted. This community behavior is characteristic of the Social Age, when the organization is given freedom to interact organically and is coupled only loosely with a formal business structure.

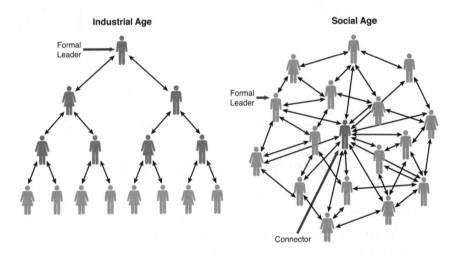

Figure 2.1 The true community leader in the center of the Social Age organization (right diagram) is not the formal leader, but is providing most of the communication and is linking the team members together. The formal leader is often a peripheral contributor rather than at the top of the organization as in the Industrial Age.

Knowledge Is Still Power

The old adage "knowledge is power" remains true, but in the Social Age there's a shift underway. Individuals previously held information as a way to hold onto power. Now information is everywhere, and those who are most adept at *sharing* that information are the ones who suddenly have the power.

With all social networking, the value of information increases with the number of people contributing to or distributing it. This is one of the tenets of all Web 2.0 systems, as exemplified perhaps most dramatically by Wikipedia. Another factor encouraging the sharing of information is the incredible speed with which some information becomes "old news." There's a drive to gain recognition for sharing the information but also for being "first." A healthy competition to share information quickly is unique to social networking.

Likewise, employees make valuable connections using social tools, both inside and outside the organization. Mark Granovetter, in a 1973 paper, talked about Weak and Strong ties in traditional (nonelectronic) social networks. (A theme also explored by Malcolm Gladwell in *The Tipping Point.*[9])

Granovetter suggested—perhaps counterintuitively—that weak ties are more valuable. In other words, when people are less strongly connected, there is often more value in a relationship.[10]

The example often cited to support Granovetter's thesis is a job search. You are more likely to find useful job leads through weaker ties in your network (a friend of a friend) than you are from your strong ties, such as immediate family and work colleagues.

Granovetter took up the topic of social ties again in 1983, when he acknowledged the importance also of strong ties. "Weak ties provide people with access to information and resources beyond those available in their own social circle," he said, "but strong ties have greater motivation to be of assistance and are typically more easily available."[11]

Social networking in an organization can help to form and cultivate new weak ties while strengthening and maintaining strong ties.

The following chapters reveal the way employees can leverage the power of social tools to improve internal enterprise processes, create new business opportunities, satisfy internal social needs, and enhance their world. We also explore more closely the social instincts that are behind the strong human tendency to collaborate around communities.

Summary

- The Social Age is leading to the rapid reappraisal of traditional "top-down" management hierarchies and tapping into the information that resides *within* the organizational layers. Loosely structured and highly efficient communities, focused on specific tasks, are replacing less efficient traditional organizational models.

- The successful Globally Integrated Enterprise uses social networking to radically challenge its business model, embrace disruptive technologies, and facilitate and encourage employee communities.

- Social networking tools are widely available, and the increasing uses of SOA technologies allow enterprises to leverage external services and interact with a variety of social networking tools.

- Company blogs are a great way to record institutional memory and provide a channel for expression to the most innovative employees.

3
Wikis: Bringing the Crowds to You

After reviewing how we got here and seeing the restructuring necessary for your company to thrive in the Social Age, we can turn our focus to some of the tools that increase organizational transparency and efficiency.

Regardless of size, companies know that excellent communication is a competitive advantage. Conversely, poor communication can be painfully costly—in lost customers, high employee turnover, and decreased productivity. Much like Guttenberg's printing press, the Social Age has created a worldwide communications revolution of historic proportions. Fueled by Web 2.0 technologies, social networking sites, wikis, and blogs, the Social Age is emerging everywhere, seemingly overnight.

The Social Age dawns just as profound changes are dramatically sweeping through the global economy, through society, and through technology. An increasingly complex and connected world calls for creative multidisciplinary approaches to solving novel challenges—traditional or conventional collaboration methods just won't cut it anymore. Savvy enterprises must embrace the Social Age or be left in the dust by those who do.

These three factors—economic pressures, societal changes, and advances in technology—although seemingly unrelated to the current frenzy for wikis and blogs, have accelerated their acceptance and massive adoption, both inside and outside corporations. Companies are increasingly leveraging Social Age collaboration among their employees and with customers to accelerate innovation and enhance productivity.

Perhaps the most well-known example of Social Age wiki collaboration is Wikipedia, the ninth most-visited site on the Internet.[1] Wikipedia contributors from around the world collaborate continuously to create an extraordinary online encyclopedia. If you haven't visited Wikipedia, perhaps you have friends or children who collaborate on a personal or business wiki.

Wikis—led most obviously by Wikipedia—have changed forever the way we communicate and gather information; and they are certainly not just another chat room or forum. The same technology that enabled two-way communication and collaboration in Wikipedia, using a free-form editing style, has enabled the creation of many other types of wikis. New wiki applications empower users to collaborate and build solutions together. With wikis, we can track action items, distribute work loads, and create an entirely new work experience. In many cases, wikis make face-to-face meetings obsolete. Regardless of location, employees can now use wikis to be part of a productive, enthusiastic, and supportive team.

Certainly some people continue to look with suspicion on wikis and other Social Age communication tools, but social changes and economic factors will drive increased adoption. Although some users might accept wikis and blogs more slowly, Millennials and mid-career professionals are responding enthusiastically and embracing them with a passion. They see wikis and blogs as career accelerators. They provide an easy way to make highly visible contributions through effective collaboration and communication.

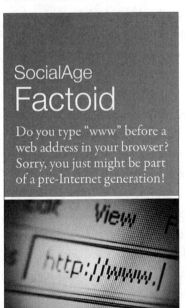

SocialAge

Factoid

Do you type "www" before a web address in your browser? Sorry, you just might be part of a pre-Internet generation!

Wikis and blogs are not just a new expression of the traditional "vanity press." In many ways, wikis and blogs have instead become the ultimate expression of free speech. Wikis and blogs can also ensure that only the best ideas and writing emerges from the collaboration of experts in a particular discipline. Passionate, expert minds converging in a single space can produce amazing results. Finance, education, government, and technology are among the fields benefiting greatly from wikis and blogs. In fact, blogging has now hit the business mainstream and is quickly becoming a preferred method of corporate communication. We look at blogs in more detail in Chapter 4, "Blogs: Your Personal News Outlet."

What About Intellectual Property?

One of the long-term barriers that kept both corporations and academia from using social networking tools such as wikis and blogs was the earlier inadequate protection of intellectual property. Without safeguards, what would become of the competitive advantage provided by intellectual property? What would keep somebody from claiming credit for something he'd seen on a corporate or university blog?

This challenge has largely been overcome by instrumentation of social networking tools with security identification, metadata, and tags. Wiki tools are now capable of establishing audit trails for updates, postings of information, and maintaining a record of publication dates.

Even in academia, in which "publish or perish" (papers, books, and articles) is a mantra, and in corporate research labs, in which intellectual property concerns have always been paramount, many serious scientists and researchers are now active bloggers. Corporate and academic bloggers are free to share ideas without fear of readers taking ownership of ideas illegitimately.

Wikis

So what is a wiki? Is it an over-hyped fad that will fade just as quickly as it arrived? Well, perhaps like me you're overloaded with e-mail and have a to-do list that never seems to get shorter. You know you need help, but you don't know how to get help or how to ask for it. Until now you might not have realized it, but you need a wiki!

At IBM, we were pleasantly surprised a couple of years ago when we launched a wiki initiative, and within a year, more than 150,000 IBMers were contributing to internal wikis. That's a powerful success story that we explore in detail later in this chapter. Let's first consider a brief explanation of wikis and their place in the enterprise.

Wikis serve at least three functions inside the enterprise. First, some employees use wikis simply to create static Web sites to communicate with large communities. Using a wiki simplifies the content management and publishing processes. Wikis can also be configured to create private team spaces where a limited audience shares collateral, plans, and documents. Finally, as in the case of the well-known Wikipedia, wikis are used inside the enterprise for dynamically cataloging and defining historical facts and processes. A company wiki is surprisingly attractive to employees and a powerful way for employees to catalog their experiences.

In each case, a wiki is a powerful collaboration tool that brings teams together and simplifies communication, especially among geographically dispersed team members. Wikis also create tighter relationships within matrix organizations, lowering the degree of separation between individuals. Wikis create a level playing field in which team members have equal access to information and tools to contribute to the success of the business. In this way, wikis encourage transparency by democratizing business processes. Clear business strategy, intent, and direction are all important to employees. In this environment, the transparency provided by wikis becomes an obvious organizational strength.

And perhaps most importantly, wikis align nicely with the organizational trends in the enterprise we discussed in Chapter 2, "Social Age Organizations." Rather than a hierarchical structure, the enterprise increasingly embraces a looser, more project-specific organizational structure. As we said, these new groups might still have a formal leader, but true leadership often rests with someone else within the group. The strength of these groups is seen in their capability to quickly form and disband based on business need and their ability to attract the best talent to accomplish a given task.

Success Through Tacit Knowledge

In addition to the benefits of wikis previously listed, they are also an excellent way to distribute skills and experiences within the wiki community. "Hard" technical skills—often learned in a classroom setting—and real-life experiences are fundamentally different competencies. Companies struggle with the best way to disseminate institutional, experiential knowledge—also known as "tacit knowledge"—to employees. Tacit knowledge is the insight gained by personal experience in the day-to-day difficulties and successes of the job. Such knowledge is often difficult to communicate in books or methodologies. Wikis help increase basic technical skills, but more importantly they increase the level of collaboration that serves to build and strengthen core competencies, including the crucial aspect of tacit knowledge. Although wiki collaboration is a nontraditional face-to-face activity, it still generates experiences that are the

Tacit knowledge is the insight gained by personal experience in the day-to-day difficulties and successes of the job.

essence of tacit knowledge. The result is dramatic advances within the wiki community in knowledge sharing, collaboration, team-building, and trust. Essentially, wiki
collaboration taps into the incredible power of shared experiences.

Active wikis can also improve technical skills in a team faster than traditional learning activities such as reading books or corporate training. This is especially true on
development teams that follow Agile Methodology. In the knowledge-sharing context of a wiki, the skills of the team quickly accelerate to a point of parity. As a result,
everyone contributes to the project at similar levels.

Efficiencies are obtained from factors already mentioned, but advances also occur
when members sense the camaraderie and community nature of the wiki. This team
spirit tends to cause the community to take ownership of problem resolution. Optimal
wiki communities are marked by high levels of volunteerism to work on tasks. In this
environment, project managers happily work with "volunteers," rather than having to
push work onto unwilling or reluctant employees with no sense of community.

Wikis: Safe and Supportive

Wikis also tend to promote more experimentation because wiki team members feel
they are in a safe "cocoon." Members know that if they get into trouble, the community will guide them. For example, a wiki member might be unfamiliar with a
product enhancement or feature. Rather than attempting to solve the problem or
search for an answer, the wiki member can query the community and quickly receive
assistance. Similarly, wikis encourage the basic human instinct to seek safety in numbers. The collaborative tone of a wiki happens even when community members have
never met each other face-to-face, work in different countries, and confront major
time zones differences. It is often extraordinary to see that noncollocated groups that
use a variety of social tools experience social bonding of the same intensity as traditional collocated teams.

Strong wiki communities encourage conversations that enrich understanding and
provide value at the individual and at the group level. As any CEO will tell you, social
interactions don't pay the bills. The reason companies are embracing wikis is the
noticeably improved work environment, productivity, and creativity of employees
who use wikis, all of which can contribute to the bottom line.

To ensure a positive wiki experience for all, companies must define, establish, and
enforce ethical conduct guidelines. Under no circumstances should hostile and aggres-
sive interactions be tolerated on wikis or other social networking forums. A "bully" or

a few disrespectful comments can damage or destroy the trust of the community. The safe and supportive wiki environment must be protected.

Wikis as Data Mines

Collaboration is the most obvious value provided by wikis. However, wikis offer a secondary and perhaps equally important advantage: They generate a wealth of data that can be mined to support other projects and business initiatives. But proceed cautiously. Before engaging in any wiki data mining, employee personal privacy must be carefully protected. Thoroughly document the governance model that maintains the privacy of employees and communities involved in the wiki process. This is a key best practice to preserve the trust of the wiki community. If the company IT team is perceived as a watchdog, intruding on people's privacy in any way, the trust of the community will be broken. Trust takes some time to build, but it is the bond that maintains a thriving wiki community.

The wiki community should always view the IT team as an enabler and facilitator, alleviating pain points and providing an effective platform for communication.

Businesses must respect and comply with privacy mandates that maintain wiki community trust but can still draw great benefit from wiki mining. Respect for employees' privacy and data mining are not necessarily mutually exclusive. But be careful. A few misguided steps from the IT group can easily jeopardize this hard-won trust with devastating consequences to the productivity of a team.

Wiki data can be mined to identify trends and ideas within the business to predict future demand and products. Because wikis are inherently open environments, the wiki communities create a transparency that can reveal the true leaders—not just of a project, but those leaders who have the know-how and are eager to help transform the company into a true—and effective—meritocracy.

Empirical Evidence for Wiki Effectiveness

As we discussed, overwhelming anecdotal evidence points to the effectiveness of Social Age tools like wikis and blogs. And now data gathered within IBM from 2006 to 2008 provides substantial empirical evidence about the transformative power of these tools. The data is provided courtesy of IBM and offers compelling insights into the ways Web 2.0 tools have supercharged innovation and productivity at IBM.

IBM started an innovation project in 2006 with the modest goal of increasing communication channels, improving collaboration, and reducing overall e-mail traffic. Other objectives included increased employee productivity and improved documentation quality for some key projects—specifically to facilitate auditing and root cause analysis. The original success criterion of the project was to have 20 percent of technical employees participate in the new wiki and blog services. By mid-year 2006, the IBM wiki and blog services had been deployed to a subset of early adopters. These new wiki and blog services were called WikiCentral and BlogCentral. Following enthusiastic initial feedback, a full deployment plan was implemented in 2007.

Remarkably, WikiCentral took nearly everyone by surprise as it quickly surpassed 150,000 users in daily volume across all wikis in just one year. Total page views per month (Figure 3.1) reflect this massive adoption. This participation rate, which represented approximately 40 percent of the total workforce, was startling to say the least, and happily far surpassed our most optimistic predictions. These were people who might or might not have collaborated before, but within a year more than 150,000 of them were working together using a wiki.

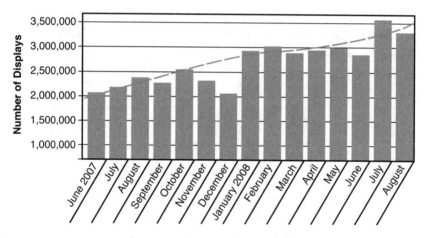

Figure 3.1 Monthly volume of displayed pages reflecting IBM wiki traffic from June 2007 to August 2008.

These results provided initial evidence that wikis are for real and potentially represent one of the most important productivity tools in the history of IBM. Traffic volume on IBM wikis nearly doubled in July 2008 when compared with July 2007 (Figure 3.2). Overall, network traffic (representing unique visitors) on WikiCentral increased by more than 40 percent. Because WikiCentral was intended specifically for business-related collaboration, traffic was uniformly lower on weekends in both 2007 and 2008, as illustrated in Figure 3.2. The slightly increased volume on Sunday was caused primarily by countries such as Israel, which traditionally works on Sundays.

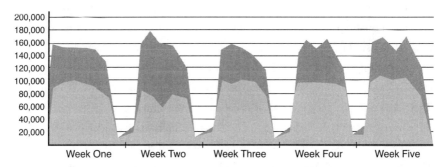

Figure 3.2 IBM Wiki traffic, showing increase from July 2007 (light gray) to July 2008 (dark gray).

Not All Wikis Behave Alike

When the data at IBM was dissected, it was found that wikis established for project collaboration do not all attract the same level of activity. A strong "middle pack" of wikis generated more than 50 percent of total wiki traffic at IBM (see Figure 3.3 for wiki activity in 2008).

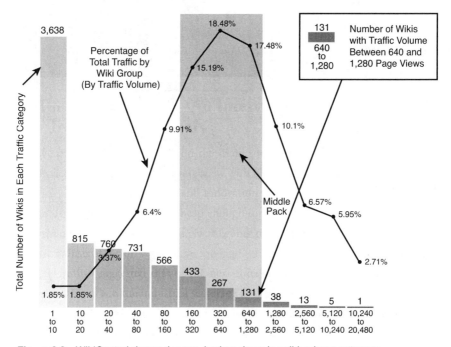

Figure 3.3 WikiCentral demand curve, broken down by wiki volume category.

For example, these middle-pack wikis included 433 wikis that generated between 160 and 320 page views each in 2008 (see Figure 3.3, left-most middle-pack bar). This data point illustrates a tremendous collaborative effort around scores of projects, each of which generated value to the business. When taken in combination with the other data represented by this graph, it is easy to see the advantages of this social networking medium.

Wiki Effectiveness, a Random Example

But that's all just data, isn't it? To actually get a sense of the "buzz" around the wiki phenomenon at IBM, and a sense of the power unleashed by a wiki, a quick trip to WikiCentral is all it takes. At random, I opened one of the top ten wikis on Wiki-Central and found that more than 100 IBMers are registered users of that wiki, across an organization with more than 21 departments.

The "Function Zone" page of the wiki, "…[can be] modified by anyone with knowledge to add or amend." More than 50 topics are currently discussed in the Function Zone, from "Best Practices" to "National Language Support" to "Versioning." This wiki supports an IBM business unit that is global in scope and meeting the needs of literally thousands of customers. And yet despite the incredible size and breadth of this business unit, customers receive products, services, and support more efficiently than ever before, thanks to this wiki.

The 100+ IBMers updating this wiki represent only a small percentage of those who benefit from it. There are certainly many others who access the knowledge and experience contained on the wiki and yet don't necessarily contribute. Keep in mind that our data showed that within a year of the first wiki being established on Wiki-Central, more than 150,000 IBMers were creating, accessing, or updating wikis.

For those who doubt the incredible power of a well-executed wiki strategy, all we can say is, "Can 150,000 IBMers be wrong?"

As I write this, IBM has just published its quarterly results,[2] that not only exceeded analysts' expectations, but which also included an optimistic outlook for the current year. These results come in the midst of a worldwide economic slowdown and deep recession that some are comparing with the Great Depression. Is there a correlation between the success of IBM and the social tools now used extensively by IBMers? As we said at the beginning of Chapter 1, "Dawn of the Social Age," only time will tell. However, at least for now, social tools enjoy great traction across businesses and the trend will continue. Remember, communication and collaboration are vital for business success, and social networking makes it happen!

Wiki Best Practices and Recommendations

- **Education**—Be sure to educate first-time users about wiki processes. If people don't know how to contribute they won't get involved. Create a section in your wiki that covers simple steps to update web pages and an FAQ page.

- **Keep it organized**—Use a simple layout with an intuitive hierarchy to facilitate the categorization of material—wikis can quickly get messy and difficult to navigate without one! Establish the navigation hierarchy early, but be willing to modify it as you get user feedback or as the wiki grows in scope.

- **Templates**—Most people have a very reasonable fear of…the blank page! Building your wiki using templates should alleviate this fear and facilitate the construction of additional content by providing an easy-to-use form. Use templates that support the most common practices and patterns of the wiki community. The templates should support the most common patterns of the wiki community. (Templates also evolve as your wiki grows.)

- **Keep it fresh**—Encourage the community to keep the content of the wiki up-to-date and interesting for everybody. Stale or obsolete material can cause a wiki community to quickly lose interest. A strong contributor can be assigned the task of monitoring new content and checking older content to be sure its "shelf life" doesn't expire! Also, create a process in which requests for updates or information are sent to the main author of a page when they're added; but be sure everyone can see the requests if they care to look. Transparency always encourages increased collaboration.

- **Drive awareness**—Promote the wiki through other media such as podcast, blogs, and social networking tools. Post in other wikis a reference or pointer to your wiki. Don't be afraid to e-mail key contributors, but be careful not to become a spammer!

- **Easy-to-find**—Use corporate search engines to point to your wiki; if your wiki is for public use, access commercial external engines to get the traction you want with customers and suppliers. No one will use your wiki if they can't find it!

- **Have a good index**—List popular documents and topics in a prominent place in the wiki.

- **Leverage the tag cloud**—Add tag and evaluation widgets for easy categorization and evaluation of content within the wiki. A good feedback loop using the tag cloud facilitates a virtuous cycle that creates ever-more-valuable content.

What Are Your Options?

Wikis are powerful tools that facilitate engaged and productive teams, and serve as a strong complement to content management systems and blogging tools. Wikis enable rapid, lightweight content management and collaborative authoring, and, as with most social networking tools, wikis require little technical knowledge.

Commercial wiki offerings include hosted offerings such as Socialtext and Wetpaint. These are among the wiki farms that allow wikis to be hosted by a single provider. Atlassian's Confluence is among the services that deliver similar capabilities and ship with a commercial open source license. (We explore open source in detail in Chapter 8, "On the Shoulders of Giants.") Other open source wiki solutions include MediaWiki, TWiki, DokuWiki, and PmWiki. Each of these offerings has a different focus, so be sure to review technical and functional requirements prior to adoption. Also, hosting your wikis with a third-party provider can save some cost, so be sure to consider this aspect as well.

Forums and Mailing Lists

As with other social tools, wikis didn't just appear one day. Several iterations of earlier technologies eventually evolved into what we know today as wikis. Perhaps the most venerable of these earlier social networking tools are online forums and mailing lists. Although somewhat "last millennium," these tools still have a place to enable grassroots collaboration. Forums enable orderly, web-based discussions on specific topics. Most forum software can be configured with e-mail notification to keep members informed of forum activity.

LISTSERV-type software uses e-mail for member discussions rather than a web browser. Subscription and preferences allow a user to configure levels of involvement. If a LISTSERV is particularly popular, a user might elect to receive the digest of discussion rather than a flood of e-mail for every thread update. Although somewhat "old school" in the world of social networking, forums and LISTSERV provided the foundation for many wiki and blog technologies.

Perhaps because of their maturity, forums and mailing lists tend to be built on open source software. Commercial offerings in the forum space include vbulletin, Clearspace, and Simple Machines Forum. Open source alternatives include phpBB, Vanilla, Yet Another Forum, and JavaBB. Look for web-based discussion forums that include simple user experiences, easy file attachment, and straightforward ability to register for notification of threads of interest. Forums offer a fast, user-friendly, and cost-effective way for employees to share insights and successes and to quickly find answers to difficult challenges.

Mailing list solutions, like many forums, are usually open source or free. An exception is LISTSERV, perhaps the best-known commercial offering. (Despite LIST-SERV's trademark, "listserv" is often used as a generic term for mail list discussion systems.) Majordomo, GNU Mailman, and Sympa are among the most popular open source mailing list solutions. For an easy-to-deploy start in social networking, an open source mailing list can be ideal.

File Management

If dialogue is the core of collaboration, file sharing offers a powerful complement. Discussions around shared documents add to the efficiency and productivity of the creative process. As social networking evolves inside your enterprise, be sure multiple tools aren't enabling similar function. For example, decide if you want files stored with wikis, forums, or some other shared tool. Some commercial solutions unify assets into a common digital library—a master repository—to which all other tools point.

Commercial file sharing solutions are either hosted offerings or customer-deployed. Solutions such as Xdrive, box.net, and ADrive are all popular hosted solutions. For a recurring cost, files are stored securely online and made available to a specific audience.

File folder sharing is also available through many operating systems at no cost, and products such as FolderMaestro and Lotus® Quickr™ offer shared digital libraries as part of workgroup enablement. WebDAV (Web-based Distributed Authoring and Versioning) is a widely used web technology, and an internal WebDAV essentially offers a "shared folder" where employees can share files.

Open source file-sharing options include PHPFileNavigator, Boxroom, and Mindquarry. These offerings enable scalable solutions but without the costs of commercial software. Keep in mind, however, that enabling a true digital library for an enterprise requires a commitment of time and resources, regardless of the technology.

If your business is comfortable using a hosted solution for sharing documents, this might be the simplest online approach. Alternatively, shared folders are often suitable for small businesses. For medium and large businesses, other options should be reviewed. Every solution offers a different set of features, and as with other social networking technology, user content and contributions create the inherent value of the solution.

A Final Word

The heart of any business is the knowledge and experience each employee contributes to the common goal of profitability. As we've experienced first-hand at IBM, and as we've sought to communicate here, wikis are perhaps the best vehicle for unlocking this tremendous potential. They bring together teams of people who contribute relevant skills and experiences to a particular project, and in the process, those skills and experiences are effectively communicated to others on the team. With wikis, the "college of practical knowledge" is always in session, for the benefit of your employees, and for the success of your organization.

In Chapter 4, we explore blogs, a Social Age communication tool that is perhaps even more popular than wikis, and that can also have significant impact on both the profitability and efficiency of your business.

Summary

- Several factors, including societal changes, economic pressures, and increasing complexity, have rapidly accelerated the acceptance and massive adoption of blogs, wikis, and other Social Age tools.

- Wikis are powerful collaborative tools that "pull" information to facilitate communication within communities of contributors. Wikis provide additional value by being a rich data mine for the business to anticipate future demand and new products.

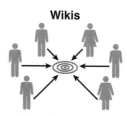

Wikis

- Team Collaboration
- Information Repository
- Generate Ideas
- Improves Team Spirit
- Channel for *Connectors*[3]

- Wikis provide a unique and incredibly powerful way to access, disseminate, and preserve the tacit (experiential) knowledge now locked away in the minds of your employees.

- Wikis follow a unique behavioral pattern. The "middle-pack" wikis generate more than 50 percent of the total traffic. These middle-pack wikis represent the volume generated by collaborating teams constantly updating their wikis.

- Wikis can be augmented with more mature tools such as forums and mail lists to round out collaborative social networking offerings in your organization.

4
Blogs: Your Personal News Outlet

In 2002, Ed Brill, an IBM Lotus Notes® product management executive, was facing one of his biggest challenges as a leader in the IBM Lotus Notes and Domino® organization. Unfounded, negative rumors about the future of Lotus Notes were swirling in the marketplace, and traditional marketing and media weren't effective in debunking the rumors. Ed resorted to a "retail approach," responding directly by e-mail or in person to individual customers as they raised the rumors with him.[1]

Ed quickly realized he had to find a more efficient way to get the word out, so in December 2002, Ed turned to a relatively new social networking tool: He started a blog.[2] By sharing customer experiences, sales wins, and positive press on his blog, Ed quickly responded to negative rumors. He now had a powerful platform that enabled him to quickly quiet the rumors and transform public opinion, allowing Lotus to go on the offensive and get the word out about Lotus's positioning and future plans. Ed's story is just one of countless examples of businesses using social networking tools to improve customer communication and enhance corporate image.

Although fundamentally different from wikis, blogs are another leading Social Age communications tool. Make no mistake—there's a lot of useless junk on many public blogs. Some blogs become magnets for conspiracy theorists or are not much more than electronic personal diaries. On the other hand, many bloggers who would never be published by a traditional press (or have no interest in being published), still have valuable things to say. These bloggers find ample outlet for their thoughts on the

Internet. In many ways, public blogs are a fascinating kaleidoscope of peacefully coexisting thought streams, quietly defending freedom of speech and offering perhaps the ultimate platform for imagination and wit.

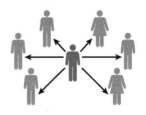

By contrast, business bloggers tend to be a bit more serious in their posting. After all, they have a professional reputation to protect or to build. Business bloggers are often technically savvy and considered to be experts in their area of specialization. They enjoy the process of writing as much as the idea of sharing their knowledge with a wider community. In his best-selling book *The Tipping Point: How Little Things Can Make a Big Difference,* Malcolm Gladwell identifies employees he calls "mavens."[3] Business mavens are the collectors of information in corporations. Blogs provide the perfect channel for mavens to disseminate their collected information for the benefit of others.

Often, business maven bloggers are unaware that they are contributing to a strong and viable "institutional memory" with their posting. Institutional memory is the "collective know-how, experiences, and bits and pieces of culture held by a…group of people."[4] Institutional memory traditionally has been preserved via direct contact between more senior business leaders and less experienced employees. But new technologies such as blogs have opened a channel for consistent communication with the business collective, which serves to preserve the ideology and institutional memory of the organization.

Not Your Father's Company Newsletter

Blogs fill a vital role in the Social Age corporation—they provide a previously unavailable, free forum of expression. By definition, traditional business publications such as newsletters, monthly updates, and other printed materials are self-limiting vehicles for expression. Some companies don't even bother with these publications. For companies that do, articles must be created, submitted, reviewed, and edited before publication. The time that passes while all this takes place might mean that by the publication date, the information is already outdated. The cost of publishing further limits the frequency and length of traditional print publications. Blogs remove these artificial barriers, significantly improving overall business communication.

Another unintended consequence of the limitations of print publications was highlighted in a 2005 article in the *Public Library of Science.* Dr. John Ioannidis argued that although there are few prestigious scientific journals, an immense and constantly expanding pool of contributors clamor to be published in these few publications. In addition, the top scientific journals tend to select only research papers with the most extraordinary claims, which are often disproved after only a few years. The scarcity of scientific journals has created an increasing concern, as argued by Ioannidis, that most current published research findings in prestigious scientific journals are ultimately proven false.[5]

Similarly, when businesses lack sufficient venues for expression, the result can be "innovation stagnation." Based on the demographic of a constantly growing worldwide business community, it will soon be impossible—if it is not already—to limit verbal expression to the printed page.

Blogs are effective, egalitarian, and the least costly method to share ideas within a business and across highly technical communities. And business bloggers who venture onto external blogs might unintentionally even provide free advertising and increased mind share for their company or product!

> *Blogs are effective, egalitarian and the least-costly method to share ideas within a business and across highly technical communities.*

Pushing, Not Pulling

Blogs are among a wide variety of "push" social networking tools. Wikis and forums are by contrast "pull" social tools, encouraging a host of contributors on a particular topic. In the public Internet, blogs and other push social tools proliferate. These tools often integrate technology, social interaction, and the blending of text, pictures, video, and audio. Each social tool is uniquely defined by the varied contributor perspectives and by the creation of shared meaning, as contributors offer the benefit of their stories and experiences.

Goodbye to E-mail with a Blog?

There's telecommuting, and then there telecommuting! Luis Suarez Rodriguez is one of those lucky people who had the opportunity to live in the amazingly beautiful Canary Islands, in the southwest of Spain. Luis is also lucky because he works for IBM, supporting a diverse group of customers all around Europe. And what energy! Luis' enthusiasm is contagious—a conversation with him makes you jump for joy that you might finally have a chance to regain control of your life by using social networking tools.[6] Luis is a full-time "social computing evangelist," avid blogger, and innovator who is widely recognized for his out-of-the-box thinking. His unique attitude toward e-mail, for example, landed him an article in *The New York Times* in June 2008.

Within just a few months, Luis had effectively slashed the number of e-mails to which he had to respond by 85 percent.

Luis made a decision in 2008 about e-mail: He was going to change the way he communicated with customers and coworkers. He would only selectively respond to e-mails and would create a blog in which he would document his status along with the resolution of customer issues. Leveraging blog technology to document his work routine was a simple change, but it created enormous business efficiency for Luis. Every time somebody asked him a question, he would post the response or the solution to the problem on his blog, or choose the appropriate social software tool to accommodate that need.

Within just a few months, Luis had effectively slashed the number of e-mails to which he had to respond by 85 percent. No wonder *The New York Times* gave him room to tell his story!

Using blogs as a communication and collaboration vehicle is a paradigm shift. Sure, you could "cc" a bunch of people with an e-mail, but that just clogs their inboxes. And how many times has an important e-mail fallen to the bottom of your inbox, perhaps never to be seen again? Like Luis maybe you get the same request for information from several people, over an extended period of time. Why repeat the same information over and over when it would be just as easy to post the answer to your blog?

Luis hasn't done away with e-mail entirely and doesn't recommend that you do so either. Instead, he reserves the use of e-mail for personal issues or confidential content that can't be posted openly on his blog. He recommends that when someone asks you for information, it should be posted to your blog. Point the requester to your blog for the answer. This gets them in the habit to look there first for an answer. With a fully indexed, searchable blog, finding information is a snap. The blog is also an excellent place to post documents and make them available to your customers and friends. This strategy eliminates a lot of overhead for both storage and network traffic.

Luis also uses other cool tools such as Google Docs[7] to collaborate with colleagues on document creation and edits. Just as when using the blog to post documents, using collaboration tools for building documents reduces storage, network load, and frustration because the latest version or comments are always available to the community.

When switching to a blog-centric communication paradigm, you also lessen the stress of "mental context switching." Jumping between various desktop contexts creates an unnecessary but real strain on your mind—a strain that is significantly lessened when communication is consolidated in your blog. Finally, the blogger might think that he or she is merely "pushing" information out to readers, but the blog is actually a two-way street. Bloggers receive value when others comment or make suggestions on difficult problems they have trouble with.

Mixed Media

Ironically, while cyber-socializing is exploding in popularity, a similar explosion has taken place in the print publishing world as well, also driven by open collaboration and communication on the Web. A good example of this synergistic transformation is *The Open Laboratory*, an annual publication of the best science, nature, and medical blogs.[8]

This is a noteworthy case because the publishing paradigm was reversed. Rather than publish a book and support it with a Web site, *The Open Laboratory* existed as individual blogs before coming together as a printed book.

Scienceblogs.com first collected a list of the best 50 science blogs, as rated by a community of online scientists. The printed anthology of these 50 blogs, titled *The Open Laboratory*, first appeared in 2006 and was published by Lulu.com. This book was the product of the blogosphere from conception to distribution. It was about blogs, assembled by blogger votes, published by an online publishing company, and promoted through Lulu.com directly to bloggers.

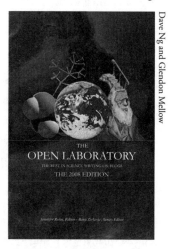

Dave Ng and Glendon Mellow

The success of *The Open Laboratory* was just part of the impressive growth of Lulu.com, and now Lulu.com publishes nearly 100,000 new works each year.[9] Exciting social networking tools on Lulu.com keep authors connected, and Lulu.com leverages their community networks to promote authors' work. *The Open Laboratory* demonstrates that a traditional medium can successfully coexist with and complement a Social Age medium.

At the risk of sounding self-serving, printed books are still an excellent medium of communication and not likely to be displaced any time soon. Publishers of printed books who leverage the Web to increase sales are creating new value for themselves and their customers.

Although maintaining a different focus than Lulu.com, Flickr.com[10] also successfully leverages social networking communities. In addition to providing a storage space for member photographs, Flickr.com sustains a thriving community of photography buffs along with the tools they need to edit, organize, and share their pictures. Flickr.com members take pride in sharing pictures, creating a sense of community that encourages strong customer loyalty.

Many new businesses are now carefully integrating social networking into their business models. With such an approach JacketFlap.com[11] is shaking up the world of children's books. Calling themselves, "...the world's most comprehensive children's book resource and social networking Web site for people in the children's book industry," JacketFlap showcases more than 3,000 published authors of children's books. The site is a magnet for the eyes of educators, librarians, agents, and editors. Jacket-Flap considers itself primarily a social tool for authors and only secondarily a publisher of original work.

Answers: Closer Than You Think

Luis Benitez was stuck. For three days he'd been working on a tricky integration issue at his biggest customer in Detroit. Although based in Puerto Rico, Luis frequently traveled to this strategic customer to provide ongoing consulting and support.[12]

He was almost ready to give up when he turned to his blog. As one of the top bloggers at IBM, Luis often posted to his blog as a way of "thinking out loud" about a difficult problem. Solutions and new ideas sometimes came to him after he saw the problem in print...but this time something unexpected happened. Within a few hours of posting his dilemma on his blog, someone blogged back, "Luis, I know exactly what you're trying to do. I have the answer."

And then the wait began. Luis replied, asking for the answer that had so tantalizingly been dangled in front of him. No reply. Luis watched his blog all that day, but it was not until the next day the answer came.

"I have the answer," the blogger posted. "What is it!" Luis replied.

"Well, I notice you're here in the building.... I can come up to the 27th floor if you want.... I'm down on 25."

Amazingly, the blogger—Bryan Jager, another IBMer—was in the same building, at the same customer. Despite their proximity, Luis and Bryan had never met before that day.

Going around the world for answers, and sometimes finding them only a few floors away—that's the power of social networking!

Blog Traffic Patterns: Empirical Evidence

In 2007, a team at IBM deployed an enterprise blog service called BlogCentral as a way to stimulate collaboration and to create an alternative channel for information dissemination. Later in 2007, the services were instrumented to track unique browser views and RSS (Really Simple Syndication[13]) feed requests. Six months after Blog-Central opened, the creation of new blogs leveled off and the total number of active blogs topped out at approximately 5,000. The traffic to these blogs continued to grow, however, and by November 2007, the average volume to all blogs was approximately 148,000 users per week.

Hot news drives traffic volume on popular blogs just as it does in traditional news media. BlogCentral network traffic spikes were caused by product announcements or organizational changes that generated a flurry of comments on the blogs. Figure 4.1 shows traffic volumes, with lower volumes during Christmas week vacation, and again on the Fourth of July.

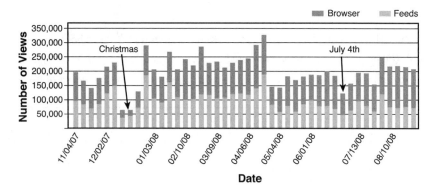

Figure 4.1 IBM weekly blog traffic via browser views and RSS feed retrieval from November 2007 through August 2008.

This study offered some interesting and unexpected findings about IBM blog traffic. Originally, we thought that the more frequently a blog was updated, the more traffic it would generate. After analyzing the data, however, we discovered to our surprise that frequent updates to a blog didn't necessarily generate additional traffic. Instead, blogs that were updated between four times a week and twice a month generated more than 57 percent of total blog traffic.

Rather than a frequently updated blog, a successful blog was one that included clear writing, an interesting topic, and regular weekly updates—daily updates didn't generate any significant additional traffic to the blog. Among our top 5,000 blogs by activity, the majority are updated less than once a month. BlogCentral demonstrates that quality counts in a business blog much more than frequent updates.

Figure 4.2 shows the number of most active blogs compared with the update frequency. The percentage line shows, by blog category, the traffic generated.

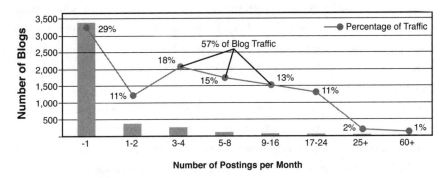

Figure 4.2 IBM blog update frequency and traffic they generate after a new posting, March 2008 through August 2008.

The traffic generated by BlogCentral followed a "long-tail"[14] typical of other social tools (Figure 4.3). The long tail is caused by the large number of user accessing only a few blogs and a large numbers of blogs viewed by a much smaller number of users.

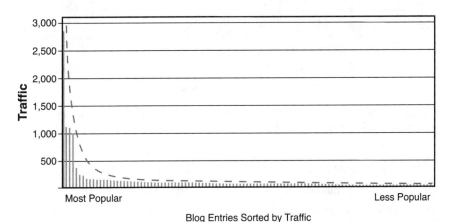

Figure 4.3 IBM blog traffic distribution, which follows a typical long-tail pattern.

BlogCentral is a worldwide phenomenon at IBM, as illustrated by the business region distribution in Figure 4.4. Combined globalization and increased economic pressures were instrumental in worldwide adoption because all regions had equal access to the technology. Little if any local resources were required to take advantage of BlogCentral from any IBM office worldwide. Feedback on the effectiveness of blogs and efficiency gains were likewise not limited to any region. Globally distributed satisfaction surveys were analyzed by region, providing strong quantified evidence that internal blogs generate great value throughout a global environment.

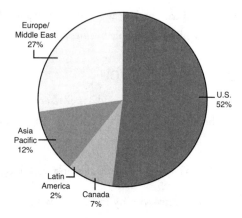

Figure 4.4 Worldwide distribution of BlogCentral users, February 2008 through July 2008.

Business *and* Personal

Ed Brill's blog success, mentioned at the beginning of this chapter, had many other positive consequences beyond just quieting unfounded rumors about the Lotus product. His blog continues to positively impact Ed, the Lotus community, and the Lotus brand. Ed proudly notes that Lotus Notes and Domino have had 16 consecutive quarters of growth. He doesn't attribute all this success to his blog, of course; but by providing a unifying platform for the Lotus community, it definitely contributes to the success.

Although not a company-sponsored IBM blog, Ed's blog provides a face to the Lotus brand with which the community can interact. The blog covers a wide variety of topics relevant to Lotus customers. The posts might be around product announcements, upcoming events, or media coverage of Domino. As important as these business topics can be, people still crave the human touch in their interaction with corporations. Ed's blog bridges the gap perfectly between his corporate and personal persona. He says that because this has always been a personal blog, he includes much more personal information than he would have if it were an IBM-sponsored blog. Ed has blogged about a host of personal issues, from his difficulties obtaining a Brazilian visa, to a review of the restaurant where he had an anniversary dinner with his wife.

Readers might go to Ed's blog to learn more about Lotus, but end up personally getting to know Ed Brill, the man behind the blog. They find out Ed is not just an IBM director but is also the regular guy from Chicago who blogs all about his worldwide travel adventures. As any good salesman will tell you, people buy from other people. Getting to know the people personally with whom you do business helps build trust and loyalty. Blogs create a magical balance when personal stories get intertwined with valuable business content.

Blogging and You

Wordpress.org, Blogger, and TypePad are some of the more popular hosted blog sites, in which anyone can create a blog on any given topic.[15] These sites share some common characteristics:

- **Free**—No cost to create and host your blog on these sites.

- **Comments**—Ability to interact with your audience. Comments can be turned on or off for the site or individual blog posts. Comments can also be moderated, requiring author's approval before being publicly viewable.

- **Profile**—Blog authors create a profile page that describes their background, interests, and expertise.

- **Access controls**—Determine who can see certain posts.

- **Customization**—Ability for a blogger to choose from a wide variety of ready-made themes to personalize the appearance of the blog. Themes control font, colors, and layout. They can provide a mood for your site—corporate, playful, informative, or zany, depending on the purpose intended for the blog.

- **Widgets**—Increase the usefulness of your reader's experience by including widgets or drag-and-drop elements. These can include elements internal to your blog such as search, blog archives, or recent comments. You can also include external feed elements such as Twitter, Flickr, or social bookmarking.[16] (Amazon.com provides easy-to-use widgets that might get you some easy income by linking your blog readers to the Amazon.com retail site.)

- **Embedded authoring tools**—These sites provide their own embedded authoring tool for writing your posts. They provide rich text and photo import abilities and basic formatting controls.

Blogging Clients

The embedded authoring tools described previously are sufficient if you publish one blog or if formatting requirements aren't complicated. If you post to multiple blogs, (for example, inside and outside of the corporate firewall), or if you have sophisticated formatting needs that aren't met by the embedded authoring tools, a blogging client is probably called for.

Blogging clients also provide

- **Blogging while disconnected**—Save an entry you've written offline until you're connected and ready to publish.

- **Saving blog entries**—Blogging clients enable you to save your work in draft mode. When your post is published, a copy is saved in your client. Publishing the post on a different blog at a later date is easily done. This feature also provides portability of your content if you delete your blog or switch blogging accounts.

- **WYSIWYG editing**—Type just as you do with word processing software. No HTML or other coding required.

Popular blogging clients have a few unique features to consider:

- **BlogJet**—Rich feature set and also the most expensive of this list.[17]

- **Ecto**—A native Mac OS X application, offering a more powerful and easier-to-use editing interface than the built-in control panel of your blog.[18]

- **Windows® Live Writer**[19]—Part of Windows Live, Writer makes sharing your photos and videos on almost any blog service straightforward. Publish digital media to Windows Live, Wordpress, Blogger, Live Journal, TypePad, and many more[20] (only available for Windows® platforms).

- **Qumana**[21]—Make money from your blog posts. Use it to insert keyword ads in one click. Exercise choice and control over the ads in your blog posts.

- **ScribeFire**[22]—ScribeFire Blog Editor enables you to easily drag-and-drop formatted text from the Web into your blog, post entries, take notes, and optimize ad inventory directly through the Firefox browser.

Enterprise Blogs

Consider how your company blog or your employees' blogs can provide value to your customers. Companies commonly use blogs to share ideas on upcoming products, at the same time enabling some level of interaction with consumers. Some companies have encouraged employees to blog externally, on behalf of the company, as a way to engage with individuals in cyberspace. When considering blogging for your company, determine if blogging provides value beyond existing formal communication channels. Blogging is a helpful tool if it advances your business or helps set the tone for the business.

Inside a company, blogging can play a variety of roles and offer a host of benefits. With a blog, employees can share their work with a broader population. Strong collaboration starts with common understanding, using a common language and conceptual framework. Individual or team impact increases the more broadly this information is disseminated. Blogs enable distant employees and associates who most likely will never meet in person to create a bond and business relationship that is

Blog Best Practices and Recommendations

It has been wisely observed that you have only one chance to make a first impression. When someone ventures onto your blog, what kind of first impression do you make? The first impression is frequently a key factor to a return visit. When starting a new blog, keep in mind these simple recommendations to ensure a successful and fruitful blogging experience:

- Enjoy writing! That means writing about what you want to write about rather than what you think others want you to write. Blogging quickly becomes a mental exercise that helps clarify your thoughts and direction.

- In this same spirit, be sure to keep in mind a specific theme, purpose, subject, or audience for your blog. The most successful blogs have identifiable themes or offer a particular political viewpoint or technical perspective. Readers will let others know about your blog if it is of interest to a particular community of readers.

- Be consistent with the frequency of your updates. Readers will rely on predictable, regular updates. The most successful blogs are usually updated 2–3 times a week.

- Post comments to other blogs, and use hyperlinks to point your readers to other blogs. Consider having the hyperlinks open a new window; that way your blog remains on the desktop. A community of blogs can quickly build around your blog.

invaluable for the business. We live in a smaller world, and the more connections and relationships we have, the more business opportunities we can enjoy. As with wikis, with blogging tacit knowledge is more easily shared. The discipline of writing also forces people to articulate their thoughts and activities in a way that teaches others, strengthening communication skills at the same time. Finally, blogging *personalizes* the workplace in a meaningful way. The closer you feel to colleagues and associates, the more capacity you can develop to handle stress. In essence, wikis and blogs play a subtle but important part in decreasing stress in the workforce by lowering communication barriers and building relationships, even with colleagues in distant parts of the company.

- Keep it real: *authentic* and *personal*. People want to learn about the person behind the blog just as much as about the professional work you do.

- Advertise your blog in healthy ways. For example, advertise through other social networking tools and perhaps point them to your blog when it has a good posting that explains a solution to a problem somebody mentioned in another blog or wiki.

- Don't blog about everything. (You'd be surprised how few people care about what you had for lunch!) Choose your topics wisely and use common sense. A good guide might be to not to write about things you wouldn't feel comfortable telling your manager. Or your mother!

- Because people don't comment doesn't mean they aren't reading your blog. Be patient and consistent in your posting. In the blogosphere a lurker is not a bad thing; he or she is just another friend you haven't met yet. They'll speak up eventually.

- Offline blogging—Just because your schedule is jammed and there are times when you're "unplugged" doesn't mean you can't blog. Use offline tools such as Ecto, Windows Live Writer, Qumana, or ScribeFire. Compose your blog entries with these tools, and then simply upload them when you reconnect.

Typically businesses are concerned that if employees are communicating freely with social networking, they might violate social taboos or business protocols. This is an understandable fear, but the powerful benefits of enabling this interaction greatly outweigh the potential harm. (A well-thought-out and carefully communicated blog governance policy can help mitigate any concern in this area.) Blogging helps employees feel more connected and is an excellent way to bridge the greater global divides and empower geographically dispersed employees with a common mission.

Commercial blogging tools include external hosted tools such as Blogger, Live Journal, and Lotus Connection Blogs.[23] Open source counterparts include Wordpress and Drupal.[24]

Commercial offerings make it easy to host many blogs on the same service. Lotus Connection Blogs for example, can enable tens of thousands of blogs, allowing a large company to create a vibrant community. Businesses might consider how integrated they want the blogging community to be within the company. Is there going to be a need for an integrated search covering all the blogs? Will the blogging be focused internally or externally? How does the blogging activity support the mission of the business? All these questions have a bearing on the blogging tool ultimately selected.

Commercial offerings allow for a single installation that provides multiple hosting solutions. Products such as Lotus Connection Blogs enable a company to internally deploy and enable the workforce with an integrated set of tools. With little technical knowledge, employees can create blogs around specific topics or publish their thoughts on day-to-day activities. Open source counterparts can enable a similar solution but would require more work. Solutions such as Drupal are the likely best fit, enabling similar blog creation management with lightweight installation. Although not as mature or feature-rich as some commercial counterparts, several open-source alternatives can be considered solid blog platforms.

IT Planning for Wikis and Blogs

IBM's experience confirmed that social behavior associated with blogs and wikis is remarkably different. Corporate blogs "push" information out to a large constituency of passive readers and generate new content from few sources. Corporate wikis, on the other hand, "pull" information from a diverse set of employees collaborating with each other and draw mutual benefit from the interaction and content contribution. Wikis and blogs are, therefore, distinctly different in traffic volumes and network patterns. At IBM, wikis have *30 times* more traffic than blogs.

Because of these differences, the IT demands of wiki technology and those of blog technology are also significantly different. High traffic levels on effective corporate wikis require significantly more IT capacity than most blogs. The resource-hungry, middle-pack wikis discussed in Chapter 3, "Wikis: Bringing the Crowds to You," benefit from dynamic provisioning of software and hardware, which is provided most effectively on highly virtualized servers leveraging cloud computing. (In Chapter 6, "Cloud Computing Paradigm," we explore cloud computing in detail.)

Without careful planning, the heavier demands of wiki traffic can strain your IT infrastructure and your IT team. Successful business transformation using wikis requires exceptional system response time and reliability. The wiki community needs to experience good performance and feel the tool can be trusted. Poor performance or a cumbersome interface can discourage users, and the business benefit of the wiki can quickly be lost.

There are several options for businesses to establish a companywide wiki service: Build it in-house (self-hosted); buy it (outsource the hosting); or rent it. (Many SaaS[25] vendors offer wiki services.) Regardless of the option chosen, the business should maintain control over the taxonomy and overall data on the wiki. That is to say, the basic structure and naming conventions of wikis should be the same across your company. Be sure users feel at home the first time they venture onto any company-hosted wiki.

Socializing Your Social Networking

Some organizations create groups of social networking ambassadors who act as evangelists, promoting the capabilities of the tools through their own use of them and encouraging the participation of others. IBM and some IBM customers have encouraged participation with the use of "merit badges," given to users who attain a new skill or achievement in social tool use. Merit badges might be given, for example, for the first 10 wiki contributions, the first 100 bookmarks, or the first blog created. The badges can be glyphs displayed within the social tools or on e-mail footers.

Social tools will not be embraced by everyone, no matter your adoption strategy. But you need only a subset of your organization to be active, and everyone else can still benefit. If only 10 percent of an organization is tagging information, it can still improve Search for the entire population.

The model Rheinmetall adopted, as mentioned in Chapter 2, "Social Age Organizations," in which tool preferences were offered for several generations of workers in a single portal, might be a good solution as social networking is rolled out in your organization. Sometimes older employees adopt social networking tools more slowly than Generation X or Millenials. Even if these older employees do not contribute directly to the social tools, however, other employees can still benefit from their work experience. For example, a social tool user might communicate with one of the older employees and receive information via e-mail or instant messaging. These communications can be tagged by the social tool user and then contributed to the social systems. This method enables workers with different work styles to effectively interact, while at the same time capturing knowledge in a reusable form for the benefit of all.

As we close this chapter on blogs and other "push" tools, keep in mind that in some ways, blogs create something of an oligopoly, in which most of the production (in this case information content creation) is driven by a few key bloggers. Intentionally or not, these few blogs can set or redefine the culture and pace of the company. Just as in the case of public blogs, business blogs follow a long-tail pattern characteristic of social tools. That is to say, on a graph of usage, only a few blogs (the oligopolists) account for most of the traffic. The rest of the traffic forms a long, flat tail. (Figure 4.3, BlogCentral, shown earlier in this chapter, is an example of the long tail.) With this in mind, be sure to create a corporate governance for blogs and for wikis to maintain an environment that supports corporate goals and to set expectations about what is acceptable.

In Part II, "Social Networks," we provide important guidance about the significant implications of the Social Age for an organization's overall infrastructure and priorities. Deploying Social Age technology without proper planning and support can lead to unnecessary and unexpected challenges.

Summary

- Blogs are fundamentally different from wikis, which "pull" information from the community. Blogs "push" information and provide an important medium for information dissemination not available in traditional print media.

Wikis   **Blogs**

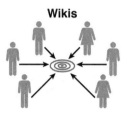   

· Team Collaboration	· Individual Contribution
· Information Repository	· Institutional Memory
· Generate Ideas	· Disseminate Ideas
· Improves Team Spirit	· Builds Personal Reputation and Credibility
· Channel for *Connectors*[26]	· Channel for *Mavens*[27]

- Wikis and Blogs each play different roles in the enterprise and leverage specific contributor skills.

- Blogs follow the classic long-tail demand curve because only a few blogs generate most of the traffic.

- Different traffic patterns on blogs and wikis respectively require careful IT planning before implementation.

5
Tagging and Social Clouds

So now you know we're in the Social Age! We explored some of the trends and innovations that got us here, and you've begun to get a flavor for the incredible power of wikis, blogs, and other Social Age tools in the enterprise. We think you're probably ready for a trip into the clouds.

Social Age clouds are not big, puffy things in the sky from which rain falls. Social Age clouds are really "clouds of knowledge," which incorporate services and information, making both easily accessible from anywhere. These clouds are a key enabler for our smaller, smarter, and more social world. These clouds are why people in the Social Age generation can take for granted that the web page they're looking at is "smart." That is, we now expect the web page we look at to know who we are, what we want to read, and to suggest other web pages, services, or products in which we might be interested. We expect that when information or events change on our favorite site, we'll be aware of it immediately, including receiving proactive notification, depending on our profile.

Early clouds are with us today, and more clouds are rapidly forming to take advantage of the global transformation now underway. Clouds will become even more pervasive and encompass ever-increasing knowledge as more people commit to this medium and increasingly engage in social networking activities.

Social Age clouds are available worldwide and include collective knowledge unimaginable just a few years ago. They can be either "tag clouds" that aggregate social behavior and community interests or "computer clouds" (better known as cloud computing), which we discuss in detail in Chapter 6, "Cloud Computing Paradigm."

At least for now there's not a lot of interaction between various services in these clouds. In other words, open standards are still evolving that ultimately will facilitate the integration or exchange of information with other social tools. For example, perhaps you use a social networking site, and during registration, you were asked to invite your friends from your Gmail or Yahoo distribution lists. Soon these questions will be unnecessary as new standards for data exchange emerge and the maturation of cloud computing accelerates. Driven by market pressures, these open standards and web services protocols will dramatically increase the collective information available in the cloud.

> *Tagging is the action or process by which an individual can label and classify an item.*

Of the two categories—tag clouds and cloud computing—tag clouds are perhaps the most interesting to the average Internet user. Tag clouds are an aggregation of personally created keywords that can be applied to either content or people. You can tag a web page, a document, a video, some new music, a friend's blog, some wiki comments, a book, a collection of bookmarks, or even a person.

Tagging is the action or process by which an individual can label and classify an item. Social networking communities share an enthusiasm for the pastime of tagging, making it the primary driver for the collection and availability of tags. Tag clouds are virtual entities in the Social Age that are aware of community preferences and behavior through the aggregation and analysis of tags.

Folksonomies

In the Social Age, the practice of tagging is an organic process usually referred to as *folksonomy*.[1] Previously the classification of information and objects (whether people or things) was the exclusive domain of the highly specialized science of taxonomy. Now through the folksonomy of social networking, everyone is getting into the act! The primary advantage of communities and especially businesses participating in the exercise of tagging is that it generates a group preference or classification that specifically reflects the needs and desires of the collective.

Folksonomies create a powerful bridge between the individual and the collective, and they differ fundamentally from formal taxonomies. Typical IT taxonomies are carefully structured by specialists to define data dictionaries for databases. IT

Keep in mind that because of the interconnectedness of the smart web pages created through tags, a networking space can consist of many different social networking tools that share the same community interest within a single tag cloud. As the community changes its preferences, the tags will change and the tag cloud will surface other documents and items, making the social space an accurate reflection of common interests and values of the community. The tag cloud allows us to see the relationship among the individual, the collective, and the shared social spaces, as illustrated in Figure 5.2.

By now, you have probably realized the significant value and incredible power of tag clouds for your business. So what is the most effective way to apply a tag cloud to the enterprise? How can tags help improve your business search engine? What tag cloud services are applicable to corporations?

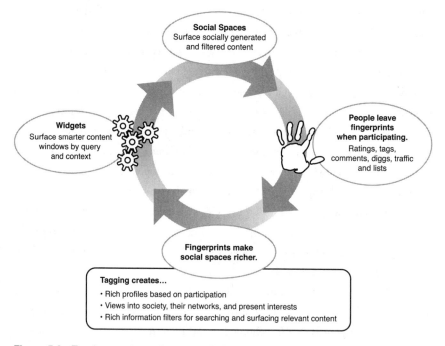

Figure 5.2 Tagging creates a virtuous cycle for social networking.

One of the key benefits of implementing a tag cloud service within the enterprise is the cultural transformation that occurs through tagging. Properly implemented, tagging can make the corporation increasingly people-centric and unleash the collective knowledge and experience of its employees. Just as public tag clouds foster greater understanding through shared interests and mutually beneficial folksonomies, tagging within the enterprise helps build stronger corporate communities and teams. In the enterprise, you can tag documents and internal Web sites to more easily highlight content of interest to specific business communities.

The tag cloud empowers businesses to tune their search engines to reflect the interests and values of the corporation and their communities. This tuning creates efficiencies in information identification that can significantly improve employee morale and customer satisfaction. In addition, as previously discussed, the virtuous cycle is accelerated in your business through a well-established tag system. The tag system helps people find the information most relevant to them and this, in turn, has an effect on the overall web traffic on the most popular pages.

Tagging at IBM

Two years ago at IBM, we designed a cross-business-unit solution called the Enterprise Tagging Service (ETS), which provided common services accessible to IT internal applications to ensure every tag generated was collected in a common data repository. These tags were correlated and made available in many different ways to satisfy specific application needs, regional and local requirements, and the business needs of other internal communities. The ETS team designed a tag aggregation service for applications to publish and consume tag data and a tag analytics program to define how to apply tags in multiple contexts. The ETS framework was well documented and several example widgets were created to enable easy access and attachment of these artifacts to web pages everywhere within the firewall.

Note that tag widgets were created to facilitate adoption of the technology. Again we return to the importance of proper planning and implementation to ensure the success of your tag cloud. The tag widgets should have simple interfaces to make it easy to integrate them into Web sites.

The IBM tag widgets illustrated in Figure 5.3 are easy to implement and can be attached to web documents and applications in just a few steps. We created these tag widgets by leveraging Web 2.0 technologies and then made them easily available to IBMers to customize and attach everywhere within the internal firewall.

The result of implementing a companywide tagging system was an avalanche of participants eagerly tagging all kinds of information. Technical and nontechnical employees participated equally in the creation of new, simple tagging widgets, which they attached to many of their favorite sites and applications. It seemed everyone was jumping into the tagging frenzy. After the establishment of the tagging service, the internal Web site traffic pattern was actually altered by the new tag cloud—nearly 70 percent of the site traffic was related in some way to the ETS redirects. This was a perfect example of the influence a community can have on employee behavior.

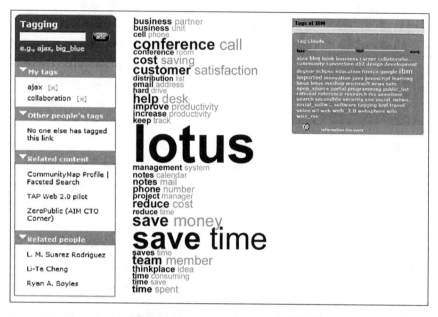

Figure 5.3 (Left to right) (1)"Tagger" widget listing tags based on configurable categories; (2) tag cloud, represented by relative font size, the popularity of the tag, or particular application; (3) tag cloud widget rendering the tags associated with a particular web page or web application.

Expertise Location Through Tagging

For your business, finding information through tagging might not be as significant as identifying someone with the right skills or expertise for a particular job. Tags can help people find each other, and they can help you find just the right person for a job. Because of the large number of participants, the tag cloud serves as a trustworthy source of information about a person's abilities and experience. The tagging process is an excellent way to locate people who have a vote of confidence from the community and recognition for earlier accomplishments. Because this can be such a valuable resource for your business, we spend a few pages discussing some of the Social Age strategies and tools for expertise location. The minds

Alexander Graham Bell, Library and Archives Canada

"Great discoveries and improvements invariably involve the cooperation of many minds."

Alexander Graham Bell

you attach to your environment determine success or failure, since human resources are the most valuable business asset. As Alexander Graham Bell said, "Great discoveries and improvements invariably involve the cooperation of many minds." To get the best outcomes, you want the best minds to be part of your community.

With the incredible volume of easy-to-access information on the Internet, it would seem that finding an expert should be simple enough, right? Unfortunately, because of the complex nature of such a search, standard Internet searches just aren't going to get it done. Unlike other information, expertise location—whether searching for an expert or for an expert answer—remains a vexing challenge, existing as it does at the odd intersection of machine learning and individual identity. Fortunately, traditional communication channels for expertise location—including standard Internet searches—are giving way to dynamic social solutions such as wikis, blogs, and forums, quickly identifying the right person for the job, or the right answer to a problem.

Current corporate structures usually lead to dispersing information and expertise within silos of specialization, and employees working in this structure recognize the limits of their knowledge and experience. So how do we uncover the diversity of perspectives, approaches, and experience that invariably produce higher quality results?

Are We Looking for Experts or Answers?

Web and intranet search has replaced most forms of traditional document research to get immediate insight on business issues and to gather information necessary for decision making. It is often the case, however, that an answer alone is not enough. A recognized authority who can verify the answer—an "expert"—is also required. This is common in customer interactions or when an employee campaigns for a particular point of view to his management team or to an external partner.

An intranet search of company resources for an answer often comes up empty, so using one's business network can be an effective mechanism for accessing the required information. In these cases, we don't necessarily need to find the definitive expert; instead we just need to find the person in our network who can connect us with the expert.

Why Are We Looking for Expertise?

Expertise location often begins with a basic search for the answer to a specialized question. The answer leads to more research, which often leads to the need to consult with subject experts. Among the most frequently mentioned needs for expertise location are

- **Quick, accurate answers**—Perhaps the most popular need, when traditional search techniques have yielded few or conflicting answers.

- **Decision support**—Management needs rapid and deep understanding of an issue or business challenge. Prior experience—tacit knowledge—is invaluable. Collective intelligence can be important here and a consensus might be sought.

- **Team augmentation**—An appropriate person is needed to fill a performance or skill gap.

- **Collaborative innovation**—For accelerated refinement or adoption of an innovation by experienced collaborators.

- **Campaigning or sales**—Influencing business results inside and outside the enterprise with expert opinion.

Because expertise location is either for answers or for experts, many organizations focus first on the simpler of these—answer services—and use this as a first step in the full development of enterprise search services.

Just the Answer, Please!

What's the total energy used by our building site? Who knows how to buy replacement toner cartridges? How do I hire a contract developer? What's the average return on direct-mail marketing for apparel?

Organization-specific research questions like these have a locality and often confidentiality that point employees to an enterprise search, but the questions are often general enough to make searching difficult. So where to begin? The enterprise intranet? The employee directory? Or maybe you should just do what you always do: start calling the usual colleagues for suggestions. Typically an employee will first do just that—ask colleagues. If that doesn't yield a good answer, a broad intranet search is next, with incremental refinements as clues and related information are discovered, leading—it is hoped—to the answer or the expert. Many IT organizations have observed this process and sought to automate the query process and to capture the resulting answers for reuse. This approach has the benefit of building an enterprise-specific knowledge base while gaining a better understanding of the needs of employees. Figure 5.4 illustrates the process flow for answer services that interact with an expertise network.

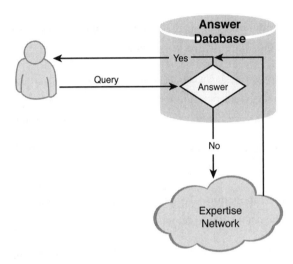

Figure 5.4   The Answer Service process. A user queries the database and either the answer is provided or the query gets sent to the Expertise Network for an answer. If the answer is approved by the user, it can be added to the database permanently.

Automated answer systems typically include a data repository of known answers—product support problems and solutions, frequently asked questions, process documentation, and so on. This data repository is coupled with a search engine and an application that connects acceptable answers to queries. Mature answer systems go one step further—they capture the quality and relevance of answers through user surveys and rerank the search result accordingly.

As might be expected, these automated answer systems work best in contained environments such as on-line product support or for process support in complex enterprise applications. When deployed as part of an enterprise help desk or a business support function, these answer systems can be effective for answering common questions quickly and online. More difficult questions can then be referred for human assistance and, in turn, documented and managed in the automated database.

Several public "answer services" have been created on the Web. General search services such as Ask.com and About.com blend proprietary documentation with web search, while on-call web-based human researchers are available through Google Answers, Experts Exchange, and others. Many enterprises adopted similar intranet-based service desks to help remote practitioners or high-need employees.

As powerful as all these techniques can be for you and your business, social networking takes them to the next level. For example, instant messaging can be paired with an enterprise answer system in which employees volunteer to affiliate with communities or topic groups. When a query is received by the system that can't be answered with the database, the query is broadcast with an unobtrusive notice to the affiliated community. If they have an answer, or just a pointer, they can instant-message the seeker directly. An accepted answer is stored in the database.

A lightweight example of a broadcast answer product is the Lotus Sametime® Skill Tap feature. Similar solutions use an intranet web page coupled with e-mail notification to solicit answers. Social networking also helps identify individuals within the communities to which queries are directed. User profiles in social networking communities are more easily updated through the beneficial synergy created by the answer system. This synergy also enables deeper collaboration and capability discovery.

Deeper Expertise

Studies have shown that we rarely collaborate casually more than 150 feet (50 meters) from our office.[3] It is, therefore, highly unlikely that we will stumble upon the expertise we need through casual contact, especially when deep expertise or extended collaboration with a trusted source is called for. The challenge is to find experts outside your existing network or local environment.

As we said previously, using corporate intranet search tools or directories is an obvious first choice. However, these tools often do not have the content needed to identify the right expert, nor the indexed data repositories that allow us to easily tease out more insight and information. Researchers have found the average enterprise worker spends more than *12 hours per week* searching for information.[4]

Fortunately, in the Social Age, finding answers no longer needs to be so difficult— or time-consuming! In the Social Age, automated profiling is increasingly used to provide an incredibly detailed picture of each employee. Unlike a few years ago, when corporate profiles were not much more than electronic business cards, automated profiling today provides an up-to-date, detailed snapshot of each employee's specialized areas of expertise.

Automating the Profile

In the Information Age, time was perhaps the primary impediment to maintaining current employee profiles. After all, updating an employee profile is a lot like updating a resume. And unless you're looking for a job, why do it? Likewise, what's in it for an employee, who has a million other things to do, to manually update his or her profile? Automated profiling essentially eliminates the burden on the employee for updates.

Automated profiling begins with the collection of as much *published* content as possible for an employee. The content or an abstract of the content is included with the profile, along with a full text search index. The results are ranked based on frequency, linked citations, and timeliness. This step works if employees produce a constant stream of published intranet documents. Unfortunately, this is rarely the case.

The second step is to consider indexing an employee's e-mail and other private content, while cloaking specific details. Linguistic tools can extract relevant keywords while cloaking the context of the private communication. Keywords are then stored in a hidden, indexed portion of the profile, or they can be clustered and placed in the profile. Searches for these keywords or related topics (using the technique of expanded search term with a thesaurus) results in a hit on the target's profile.

Although this technique works well, it has one drawback. Although most companies have a policy that all e-mail and other employee communications are not private, some sensitivity should be exercised with regard to the *perception* of employee privacy. At a minimum, the employee should have the opportunity to edit the keywords to filter out anything they consider nonbusiness-related.

This review of keyword topics, however, places the burden back on the employees to interact with their profiles. One solution is to use subject taxonomies. These are terms relevant to the enterprise, which are used to cluster topics. Based on document or e-mail scanning, a small set of higher-level categories can then be suggested to an employee using these terms. When accepted, the terms would help identify employees with the strongest affinities to a category and would be displayed when browsing or searching for similar content.

Another solution to both the privacy and the efficiency issues is to use a "broker" to gain access to a potential expert. Tacit Software's KnowledgeMail system used text mining of e-mail to determine a user's interests. Then, rather than expose the expert in search results, the system used e-mail to notify the experts of the request. The experts had an opportunity to respond or ignore the request, with the option of revealing their identity only after knowing the identity of the requestor. The KnowledgeMail system solved many of the privacy and control issues but sacrificed the immediacy often required for expertise location. Oracle recently bought the KnowledgeMail intellectual property from Tacit Software and is planning to integrate this technology into the Oracle Beehive for a more robust and secure enterprise expertise location solution.

Early Knowledge Management systems were developed during the Internet expansion of the late 1990s when these solutions seemed not just possible, but inevitable. Although the bursting of the Internet bubble delayed Knowledge Management development, the dawn of the Social Age reinvigorated it in unexpected ways. In the Social Age, it seemed everyone was becoming comfortable with writing publicly. Blogging tools were free and accessible. Wikipedia clearly demonstrated the social value and mechanics of simple collaborative authoring. It was natural that social networking tools began to include shared profile information, initially offered for purely social reasons, but which ultimately extended into business relationships as well.

Protecting Your Experts

One of most common objections to expertise location and corporate social networking is the risk of interrupting or disturbing someone. Many organizations are protective of their experts and alert to competitive recruiting, either inside or outside the organization. Although these objections might seem like an obvious threat, they rarely pose real concerns.

Just making one's expertise accessible doesn't give anyone new privileges with your time. The usual mechanisms of contact control—voicemail, e-mail, instant message, or administrative assistants—are still in force to protect an expert from unnecessary interruption.

As for recruiting, most experts are widely known already within their communities of interest. Recruiters already know how to find your experts; colleagues and customers are the ones who need a little help…social networking *works!*

Getting Social

Having such a rich trove of information available through social networking tools was an exciting turn of events for expertise location within the enterprise. Seemingly overnight, public social networking tools have become commonplace, accompanied by a profound shift in attitude—one's identity, relationships, interests, activities, and passions are no longer private matters but are essentially open to the world. Many businesses leverage this change in attitude and have developed proprietary social tools, using them to gather core information about business and technical expertise.

So does this mean we have finally found the answer for quick, efficient expertise location? Not exactly, but we're building the tools that get us a lot closer. Perhaps the biggest challenge is generational. People in the Social Age generation have used social tools throughout their academic careers and are, therefore, comfortable with the personal transparency of this medium. Although this demographic continues to stream into the workforce, and thus expand the use of social tools in the enterprise, mid-career and older professionals are increasingly getting into the act with business-oriented platforms such as LinkedIn.com. Naturally it will take some time to create the most-efficient solutions for expertise location using this wealth of information. But the content is there, and it will continue to grow at a blinding pace as more people join the Social Age revolution.

Social Bookmarking

To access the wealth of data on social tools, new Web 2.0 tools are continually emerging, often with direct enterprise value. Del.ico.us[5] is a well-known example of one of these tools, which leverages the concept of "social bookmarking." Bookmarking creates a browser bookmark on a web page and applies a tag to the URL. Social bookmarking in the enterprise is a lightweight method of improving "findability" of content and for sharing one's intranet discoveries. Integrated browser extensions make this process unobtrusive and simple. Even when only a small percentage of the enterprise is engaged in tagging, the results are powerful.

At IBM, a small set of early adopters of an internal tagging service called Dogear[6] quickly tagged the majority of important intranet documents.[7] These tags—created by less than one percent of the workforce—proved so valuable that they were immediately integrated into the IBM corporate search engine, improving the company's search by more than 60 percent.

Given the success of document tagging at IBM, the obvious extension—tagging people—was tested. Would employees feel comfortable tagging colleagues? Would the system be abused? What types of tags would be generated? A test version of the popular IBM Bluepages employee directory was the basis of a research pilot called "Fringe," which was used to answer these and other questions. To eliminate potential abuse, person tagging was cleverly designed to reveal the tag author and to allow tag removal by either the tag author or the profile owner. (No abuse has ever been reported to the Fringe team.)

The results of Fringe were a pleasant surprise. Employees used tags for a host of purposes, some expected, some completely unexpected. Tags were used as reminders, as skill labels, and to create quick ad hoc collections of people. In addition to including tags as key search terms, the system was used to create mailing lists, geographic maps of member locations, and a visual relationship map of tag groups. At the conclusion of the pilot, person tagging was included as a feature of the Lotus Connections profile component and has been shown to be an effective social tool.[8] For the adoption and success of people tagging, the process must be seamless and the results must be relevant and easily accessible.

Expert Attention

How do you get the attention of an expert? Sounds like the beginning of a bad joke, doesn't it? Well, when you find the expert, getting their attention can be a whole other challenge. Experts, by their status, have become quite adept at ignoring contacts from people they don't know. With social networking, however, the barriers can start to fall. It is often the friend-of-a-friend who can provide an introduction or whose name you can drop in your approach to the expert. We might be separated from the Queen of England by only six degrees, but good luck ringing her on the phone or dropping by for tea.

Fortunately, many tools have been developed to show the varied social paths to the queen, or for that matter to that solar panel expert you've been trying unsuccessfully to connect with. Although these tools work to connect you with the right people, the ultimate value of these tools are realized only when experts are graciously willing to respond to business colleagues.

Topical Friends

Another social innovation that supports expertise location is *friending*, the explicit and usually confirmed assertion of a person-to-person relationship. Friending is useful in an enterprise to understand the relative strength and diversity of relationships. Although not always conclusive, these factors can indicate influence, working style, and openness to contact, and provide a snapshot of an employee's topical network.

Most friending network features focus on relationships, their quantity and structure, together with some measure of strength.

Text mining tools are emerging as a vital tool to suggest topical relationships. For example, e-mail or other collaboration sources are used to correlate communication with the subject of the communication. The result of this correlation is a network map of someone's interest groups and specifics about frequency of contact. Privacy issues have limited these tools to personal use to reveal one's own network, but they have still proven to be incredibly valuable in many businesses. In time, these topical relationship maps will likely support automated listings of communities of interest on employee profiles. Uncovering informal groups with automated community listings is a valuable extension of the employee profile.

A collection of relationships is referred to as someone's *social graph*. Vendors are eagerly anticipating the day when the details of these graphs can be leveraged to provide targeted service and products. As we discussed in Chapter 1, "Dawn of the Social Age," standardization will accelerate adoption of this technology as it has done to many others. Having an open, standard social graph allows competitors to combat the "lock in" enjoyed today by most current social network solutions providers. Open social graphs can also be a powerful tool for finding expertise, especially if the graph contains specific subjects and strength of the relationship. The graph can reflect the breadth of expertise, as well as relationships within the network. The opinion of someone's resume is one thing. The opinion of someone's peers is something else indeed!

As the use of expertise location goes beyond the corporate firewall, this idea of a topical social graph will gain increasing importance. Ideally the social graph will be built with the same structure that allows Google to predict the best site for any query. The Google Page Rank algorithm correlates a graph of links that others have created using the same search criteria, speeding up the search, and providing the best results. With a similar approach, a verified social graph will quickly and reliably identify the best experts for a given topic query, providing your business with an incredibly powerful competitive tool.

Vendor Expertise Analysis

Exposing capabilities is a further challenge in the area of expertise location. The context has now shifted, and the question is somewhat different: How can I find a potential vendor of services with the skills needed to complete the task at hand?

This is an organization-to-organization challenge, not specifically a question of finding an expert. This challenge is about finding a partner that can ensure success. In the past, vendors met with you in person to demonstrate both the competence and the scale of their capabilities. Today, to be competitive, these activities must take place online. Evidence of the vendor's experience and the dynamics of the proposed team are important differentiators today and are increasingly available through online tools.

Building a relationship of trust is primary in any business engagement, but as business relationships become increasingly virtual, it is perhaps even more critical. Social networking plays a crucial role here; it is a powerful mechanism for establishing trust based on the accumulated evidence of competence, shared values, and reputation.

As an Internet provider of a product or service, the capability of your offerings must first be discoverable. Although advertising can drive traffic to your site, it's your reputation and evidence of accomplishment that keeps you on vendor lists. Showing signs of open collaboration or availability to vendor expertise during the presale period is often a differentiator, especially in markets that cannot sustain direct sales contact. After the sale is made, the customer's ability to get responsive service and support and *build a relationship* with vendor personnel can powerfully enhance your company's reputation.

Open Up!

Business relationships deepen further when internal expertise location tools, such as employee profiles and communities of interest, are open to your customers. Although the thought of opening your enterprise up for internal inspection might seem radical, we believe this level of transparency is inevitable and vital to success in the Social Age. It is certainly possible to be selective about the clients or partners who have access and the extent of this transparency. Serena Software uses a third-party social network as the basis of its intranet,[9] precisely to achieve an increased transparency in operations. Service providers such as TopCoder.com[10] have embraced transparency as their core business model; they reveal almost all aspects of their business processes, current work, and results online as a means to secure the best contract developers.

Although this cycle of building a reputation on responsive customer service is a well-known and obvious business model, the migration to an effective and profitable online model is still maturing. Social networking features, including people tagging, topical connections, and explicit communities, can provide a powerful vehicle for marketing your organization's capabilities.

Participation in social networking activities is also a powerful way for savvy employees to create proof points for their expertise. Tags empower individuals to contribute to their community and at the same time to enhance their own reputation.

IBMer

At IBM we have a self-branding tool called IBMer that enables the creation of a professional identity and reputation. A participant in IBMer builds a personal brand based on a list of skills and experiences, but the corporate community ranks and evaluates each person's skills. Tags are used in this case to create the reputation of IBMers in a completely transparent way. These reputation tags help identify people with appropriate skills and simultaneously serve as implicit community recognition.

An employee tag cloud can also help surface key companywide concerns, differences between divisions, and new company trends and ideas. IBM has a strong business tag cloud of more than 600,000 tags that have helped accelerate innovation by enabling better communication and collaboration across the company. The growth of this tag cloud is illustrated in Figure 5.5.

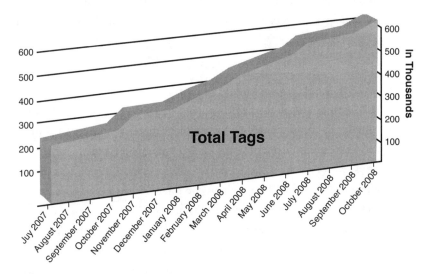

Figure 5.5 Tag Cloud Growth at IBM, July 2007 to October 2008.

Another view of the tag cloud, as shown in Figure 5.6, uses different size boxes depending on the popularity of the discussion subjects. Within each subject box, the document status is shown with color-coded bars. There is virtually no limit to the ways you can display and get business insight from the data contained in the tag cloud.

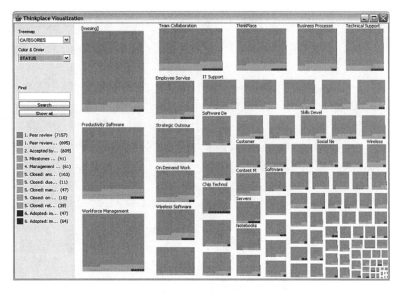

Figure 5.6 IBM researcher Martin Wattenberg's Tag Cloud visualization represents by the size of each square the relative popularity of a tag assigned to a discussion subject.[11]

Every business has different needs and priorities. Tag tools might need to be customized for your situation, but by instrumenting your Web site with a tag tool, you can gain valuable business insights from the tag cloud created by your corporate community.

Summary

- In the Social Age everything is about the "clouds of knowledge" that incorporate services and information, making them easily accessible everywhere.

- Tag clouds encapsulate social behavior and community interests. These tags are user-generated keywords applied to content or people.

- Tag clouds represent the preferences, values, and associations of a community. Tag clouds build bridges between the individual and the collective.

- Expertise location is much more effective through the use of social networking tools.

6
Cloud Computing Paradigm

As we said at the beginning of Chapter 5, "Tagging and Social Clouds," the Social Age has brought us both tag clouds and cloud computing. Having looked at tag clouds in some detail and explored the value of tag cloud collaboration for society, we now turn our focus to cloud computing.

Cloud computing is an amazing style of computing that leverages virtualized hardware in a way that changes the way we think about computing—raising expectations about technology and about the accessibility and availability of information. You are probably asking yourself many questions about cloud computing: Exactly how is cloud computing created and consumed? What are the economic factors that give cloud computing such a powerful competitive advantage? Why is this technology creating so much excitement?

Cloud computing has quietly evolved over the past five years or so and is now at the leading edge of a paradigm shift in the way we think about and use technology. With cloud computing, you no longer need to be concerned about all the devices and connections between you and the applications you need. Plug in anywhere, at any time, and get the solutions you need for your work or personal life.

"Cloud computing...is a style of computing where IT-related capabilities are provided 'as a service,' allowing users to access technology-enabled services 'in the cloud' without knowledge of, expertise with or control over the technology infrastructure that supports them." —Wikipedia, the free encyclopedia[1]

Irving Wladawsky-Berger, visiting lecturer at M.I.T. and long-time IBM thought leader, is perhaps best known as the leader of the team responsible for IBM's Internet and e-business strategies in the mid-1990s. When I interviewed Wladawsky-Berger for this book, he provided an insightful perspective into the irresistible appeal of the cloud computing model. Comparing the services we expect from our car to the services people will expect from cloud computing, he said

> Do you think about your engine when you get into your car? Of course not; you think about your destination. You think about driving. The vast majority of the world could care less about software. Cloud computing has nothing to do with *software* as a service; it has to do with *services* as a service. This is a huge distinction.[2]

The distinction Wladawsky-Berger makes is something we should consider carefully. Such a mind-set epitomizes the mind-set and expectations of the Social Age: Don't bother me with the details; give me easy access to *value-generating services.* This mind-set is diametrically opposed to the Information Age way of thinking about IT. In the past, people focused on servers, networks, applications, and security. All those things cost money, however, which translates to real dollars spent on tremendous energy costs, personnel, and operations.

As we begin to think less about the IT infrastructure and packaged software and more about delivering valuable services to our organizations, we begin to see the brilliance of "services as a service." This is the profound and compelling idea at the heart of the cloud computing model.

As we discuss later in this chapter, don't confuse or equate cloud computing with "grid computing." Grid computing—strings of clustered and loosely connected boxes—represents merely a subset and an enabling technology for the cloud services. Cloud computing leverages grid computing technology, but it is the services on top of the virtualized grid computing hardware that create a new simplicity and ease of use not experienced before.

Although tag clouds provide insight into the interests of a community, cloud computing provides simplicity that enables users to connect anywhere, anytime, via any device, and at an affordable price. Cloud computing offers a collection of ubiquitous services that virtually eliminate the need for complicated, time-consuming application configuration and maintenance. Only the requested service is rendered at an exceptionally low cost and with remarkably high reliability; as Wladawsky-Berger said: "*Services* as a service."

Transparent services and ease of use are the primary values of cloud computing to the end user. Any Internet-enabled device—cell phone, laptop, TV, PDA—can leverage the cloud, enabling a busy, highly mobile professional to save time by retrieving documents and generating transactions from anywhere in the world with just a few clicks.

Cloud computing builds these services on top of a virtualized set of clustered, loosely associated computers. Common examples of computer clouds are Google, Yahoo, Apple MobileMe, YouTube, Skype, Amazon Elastic Compute Cloud (also referred to as EC2), IBM, and other smaller players such as SoonR and Mosso.[3]

It's All About Economies of Scale

Do you visualize cloud computing as a gigantic warehouse full of computers in some unknown location, mysteriously feeding information to the world? As with many misconceptions, there is some truth here. However, cloud computing is much more than just a giant server farm, or 1990s-style managed hosting. Instead, the core of cloud computing is a highly efficient, dynamic infrastructure that ensures essentially uninterrupted services to anyone accessing the cloud.

The primary driver of cloud computing services is the tremendous economies of scale they generate. These greater efficiencies and dramatically lower costs offer a clear strategic advantage compared with single-purpose corporate IT departments. However, the questions then become: How do they do this? How can cloud computing providers, with colossal data centers, create these tremendous efficiencies? Why can they generate IT services at such a low cost?

The answer to these questions is deceptively simple: It is just more financially efficient and energy-efficient to manage a massive number of services through *virtualized* hardware than just a few services on dedicated backend servers, as in the traditional IT model. Twenty-four hours a day, seven days a week, a traditional data center consumes energy, even when data processing is happening at a greatly reduced rate, such as at night or on weekends. Regardless of processor idle time, electricity is consumed and heat is dissipated around the clock. Disks spin, cooling fans turn, and the computer room air conditioner (CRAC) hums along. Due to high idle time, traditional data centers waste massive amounts of energy.

By contrast, cloud computing providers can manage their workloads in a more efficient way, utilizing many different types of virtualization techniques. Virtualization enables the over-commitment of processor units, physical storage space, and memory to help reduce the overall idle time. This means clouds can derive more useful work from the same amount of electricity consumed by most traditional data centers.

Did you just hear the cash register ring? If you're like most companies, a huge part of your IT budget is spent on the infrastructure and personnel required to deliver computing services that could just as easily—*and much more inexpensively*—be cloudsourced.

Consider this comparison. There was a time when power to run a company's machinery was generated locally. In the early Industrial Age, companies typically were located near a river, which provided the energy they needed through a water wheel for the companies' machinery. A substantial operational cost was often associated with maintaining the water wheel and associated infrastructure.... Sound familiar? *An entire department was dedicated to maintaining and updating the power plant of early Industrial Age companies.*

Then what happened? Economies of scale enabled electric companies to generate and transport electricity at a much lower cost than locally generated power. The same is true today for IT services. Economies of scale allow cloud providers to generate a host of services at a much lower cost—*with greater availability*—than traditional dedicated IT departments.

ITs Dirty Little Secret

The commoditization of hardware and subsequent expansion of traditional data centers has led to something of a paradox. A plethora of traditional "computer farms" now sprawl across developed and emerging countries, each requiring staffing and electrical power. The majority of these boxes are grossly underutilized, with more than 85 percent of the computing capacity sitting idle, wasting precious resources.[4] The boxes might have been cheap, but the cost to manage them and supply them with power is anything but cheap! To add to the problem of underutilized capacity created by the sprawling data centers and dedicated back-end servers, the dirty little secret of data centers is that traditional IT is one of the most energy-*in*efficient processes in the world. (Secret, that is, unless you're the one paying the electricity invoice for your company!)

Consider that for every 100 units of energy mined from coal, only *35 units of useful energy is created* and only 33 units of that energy actually make it to the data center. Fifty-five percent of that amount—more than half—is spent just to cool the equipment. The remaining units of energy are used to power the computers, but nearly two-thirds of that energy is lost through heat dissipation. *Essentially this means that for every 100 units of energy taken from a coal mine, only approximately 3 units is used to generate meaningful IT work.*[5]

Figure 6.1 illustrates the grim reality about where 97 percent of our energy is wasted. Compelled by this reality, market forces continue to drive adoption of the "utility" model offered by providers of cloud computing, which leverages green technologies and economies of scale to optimize the production of useful IT work.

How is energy in the traditional data center consumed?

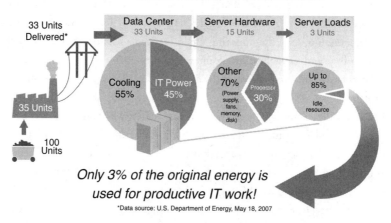

Only 3% of the original energy is used for productive IT work!

*Data source: U.S. Department of Energy, May 18, 2007

Figure 6.1 From energy source to IT useful work, the steps of inefficiency are colossal, as illustrated here.[6]

The complexity and escalating costs of traditional data centers are creating powerful market forces that will accelerate the adoption of cloud computing, maximizing the useful work output per server and lowering the overall cost of IT services. The new generation of IT professionals and CIOs view cloud computing as a strong alternative for achieving business scalability, less business risk with no long-term contracts, and lower up-front costs—a result of the pay-as-you-go utility model for cloud billing. If you are a CIO who has ever signed a multimillion dollar purchase order for new servers, we suspect this resonates with you!

IBM Cloud Case Study

A few years ago, a group within the IBM CIO organization was chartered to facilitate new sources of innovation. The goal was to enable 25,000 IBMers to quickly and easily prototype and deploy new technologies to a community of volunteers in IBM who would test and provide feedback for each innovation. The number of volunteers in the program quickly grew to approximately 120,000 IBMers. It seemed everyone wanted to get their hands on new technology! The program expanded to more than 100 projects per year.

The Challenges

When the innovation program was launched, software and hardware were deployed in the traditional way—manually—a process that proved to be slow, tedious, labor-intensive, and error-prone. A typical pilot team for a new innovation needed one to three months to procure and build the infrastructure. This model required 550+ servers and 15 administrators to support 100+ projects, which meant nearly 500 additional servers were required when the program launched. The challenges of manual infrastructure deployment and increasing operational costs made this an ideal environment for a cloud computing implementation. Cloud computing could be used to automate provisioning, monitoring, and virtualization to increase automation and flexibility of the infrastructure and sharply reduce the amount of hardware and labor required.

Solution

The innovation program represented a near-perfect laboratory in which to leverage cloud computing and essentially reinvent the IT organization that supported the program. Virtualization allowed underutilized physical servers to be consolidated into fewer, more fully utilized servers. The team used the IBM Tivoli® Provisioning Manager (TPM) to provide users with the ability to request servers, operating systems, and storage in near-real-time. Hardware costs were reduced dramatically, as were installation and configuration time. Optimization of resource utilization was facilitated using IBM Tivoli Monitoring (ITM), further contributing to hardware cost-savings.

Rather than the 500+ servers originally scoped for the project, the cloud solution efficiently supported 100+ projects with only 130 servers—370 fewer than planned! The reduced hardware footprint also led to a significant reduction of administration costs. Valuable labor resources were then available to work on other high-value activities.

The cloud model *reduced total operational costs by nearly 85 percent*, and the cost-savings was instrumental in funding new development, business investments, and acquisitions.

Cloud Computing Layers

With an understanding of the significant economic advantages of cloud computing, you might wonder how all this happens. What are the components of cloud computing, and how do they all fit together? Where does virtualization come in? Perhaps the best way to think of cloud computing is in terms of three layers—the physical layer, the network layer, and the services layer.

The physical (hardware) layer is heavily virtualized, enabling the cloud to maximize hardware usage by easily swapping workloads and moving them around as needed. This virtualization and highly efficient workload management minimizes idle time. The second layer, the network layer of cloud computing, links many loosely coupled computers. The computers are addressed as part of the same network, even if the physical boxes are located in different parts of the world. You can think of this as network virtualization.

The third layer—the services layer—is perhaps the most important. The services layer encapsulates all the hardware and network dependencies so that the user sees only a simple business interface—only the applications needed to perform required daily tasks. These services are now ubiquitous because of the simplicity and elegance of the cloud computing model.

The layers of the cloud computing model are illustrated in Figure 6.2.

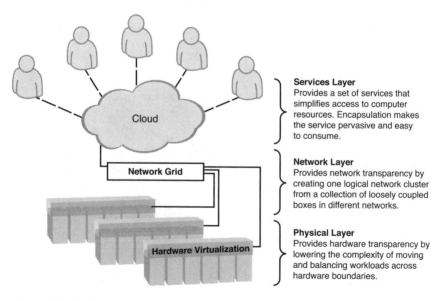

Figure 6.2 The cloud computing model.

WWW: More Than We Asked For

The massive telecommunication cables that constitute the World Wide Web (WWW) provide the network on which cloud computing depends. Data centers are distributed around the world to minimize network latency to their target markets, enabling us to connect to any computer regardless of its location. This network is a literal globe-spanning collection of cables from various telecommunication companies, frantically laid down to over-capacity during the dot-com boom of the late 1990s. In some ways, these huge, over-provisioned "pipes" were something of an embarrassment for a few years and led to the demise of more than one company—they built it, but no one came. Simply put, the bandwidth offered far exceeded demand, driving revenue down, and companies out of business. In the Social Age, however, all that has changed. This worldwide *uber*-infrastructure now provides the massive network capacity needed to support the insatiable Social Age appetite for video games, YouTube, and many other high-bandwidth social tools to which we have become accustomed.

Care to find out just how massive this network is? Take a look at www.caida.org and prepare to be dazzled at the great tools this site offers to analyze your network infrastructure. Use some of CAIDA's virtualization tools to see the way networks connect through the primary global network. Figure 6.3 shows how UUNET connected the world. In the 1990s, UUNET was one of the largest network carriers and was acquired first by WorldCom, and then a few years later its network assets were acquired by Verizon Communications. These transactions epitomize the consolidation that has happened throughout the telecommunications industry.

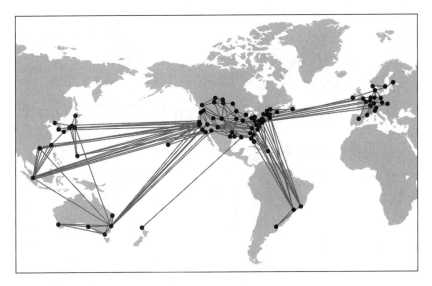

Figure 6.3 Data from CAIDA, UUNET Connections.

Virtualization: Just What You Need

The key to cloud computing is to obtain an effective virtualization process through the various layers of IT infrastructure. Virtualization is nothing new. It has been a proven part of IBM mainframe computers since the introduction of the IBM VM family in 1972. Two factors, however, served to propel virtualization as a key enabling technology in the Social Age.

First, massively parallel processing machines increased the complexity of operating systems, creating a variety of difficult challenges. These challenges drove innovation in the simplification of computer interfaces and resulted in the creation of the virtual machine solution called the *hypervisor*. The hypervisor runs on top of operating systems and disassociates hardware from software services. Second, the commoditization process mentioned earlier has pushed virtualization features from high-end servers into lower-cost computers. VMware[7] is a hypervisor development company, whose founding charter was to create an alternative to high-end operating system virtualization solutions and drive further efficiencies in backend servers. Another recent newcomer in the virtualization space is Xen,[8] with technology based on open software that can be used under the GNU[9] license agreement.

With services-oriented computing and the IT clouds to support it, computing cycles and resources will increasingly move away from connected client devices (client-server architecture). The reliability and availability of the cloud and its underlying IT directly translates to the increasing availability of the services in the cloud. The core values of reliability, availability, and efficiency that are central in current enterprise data centers apply equally, or even more critically, to cloud computing.

A Mainframe Pedigree

Since its inception in the 1960s, the heritage of mainframe computing is one of large-scale, highly efficient resource sharing among a mixed set of applications with no-excuses levels of reliability and integrity. This is in stark contrast to the classic distributed system architecture that has dominated data center design for the last 20 years. In a distributed architecture, each server is typically dedicated to one application set, with multiple boxes needed for workload growth. Occasional system outages are expected on a per-application basis. Mainframes, on the other hand, are designed and intended to host a consolidated set of workloads of all types. Two components in today's mainframe ecosystem make it suitable for cloud computing initiatives: the IBM z/VM® hypervisor and the ubiquitous Linux® operating system.

As we've said, virtual machines (VM) have been commercially available on mainframe systems since the early 1970s, and noncommercial versions of IBM's VM product have been available since the mid-1960s. The significance of this historical perspective is that virtual machine technology has been a fundamental part of mainframe architecture for years. The z/VM hypervisor distinguishes itself by allowing users to host hundreds of copies of operating systems on a single copy of z/VM. The security and integrity of each hosted operating system is managed by the whole system, not just the z/VM software layer.

This attribute makes the mainframe attractive for a cloud computing infrastructure because it is ideal for applications such as data analytics that require massive overcommitted memory.

Consolidation of workloads also translates into energy cost-savings. Some Linux-on-z/VM clients have enjoyed an 80 percent reduction in floor space and energy consumption compared with the distributed computing model. These operational characteristics are invaluable in a cloud environment in which users want their systems and applications online and ready immediately after they click the Configure Now button.

Cloudsourcing, Not Outsourcing

Unlike the traditional outsourcing approach, the cloud computing model provides standard services that can be accessed through common open protocols such as web services. In traditional outsourcing models, customers give up control of the IT infrastructure but demand preservation of their proprietary business processes (the "Mess for Less" value proposition).

Unfortunately, efficiencies and cost-savings gained in the mess-for-less model are often diminished by the lack of standardization and the cost of proprietary application maintenance. Social Age companies are becoming acutely aware of the increasing need for rapid, nimble transformation in the face of new business challenges. Embracing cloud computing and transforming business processes to the most-efficient expression can drastically reduce operational IT costs. Cloud computing creates a flexible alternative for businesses that cannot sustain ever-changing IT requirements.

In his "IT Doesn't Matter" article in the *Harvard Business Review* in 2003, Nicholas Carr famously predicted that IT departments will eventually disappear.[10] We respectfully disagree with Mr. Carr and believe that Social Age IT departments will indeed survive and will focus on core competencies that cannot be duplicated by generic cloud computing services. The commoditization of computers and computer services doesn't mean that the value provided by the IT department is diminished. On the contrary, IT groups will embrace cloud computing to reduce overall IT costs, while acquiring additional services to complement their core competencies. Rather than rendering IT departments obsolete, cloud computing will simplify and accelerate the transformation of IT departments.

The IT department of the Social Age has a fundamentally different charter than the IT department of the Information Age. Instead of painstakingly managing a hodge-podge of applications and hardware, Social Age IT professionals will be developing a diverse skill set focused on leveraging social networking channels and cloud computing services. They'll mine marketing data, derive intelligence from communities, and focus on business process optimization and employee collaboration. Perhaps most importantly, they'll manage innovation programs to accelerate the business transformation and keep the business in a leadership position.

Cloud Computing Lexicon

Virtualization: Software between the hardware and the operating system, known as the "hypervisor," which isolates the application from the physical box; examples include VMWare Hypervisor and open source Xen. Virtualization allows you to move applications to different hardware images without the application even "knowing." Applications are called "virtualized" when they can be isolated to a hardware instance in this way. A current limitation of this technology is that these software solutions only work within a single hardware platform. To date there are no platform-independent hypervisors.

Grid: An application that strings together many servers with different network addresses into a single logical network cluster. Here, we virtualize the network rather than the hardware. On a grid, servers can be addressed as part of a single network, even when they are distributed around the world. The World Community Grid™, with more than 400,000 users, is a great example of a grid. Community members share part of their computer idle time to the benefit of research projects such as cancer, human genome, HIV, and others. (http://www.worldcommunitygrid.org/)

Cloud Computing: A set of virtualized hardware that is clustered in a network and provides automatic provisioning of software and hardware through services. The pervasive nature of these services is the greatest value-add in this evolution of IT. Cloud computing has created a simplified model that enables a transparent consumption of resources anytime, anywhere in a completely virtualized way. In cloud computing, consumer-ready services are friendly and easy to use.

IT Transformation Under Way

In addition to increasing virtualization of services, the Social Age is a time when traditional "geeks"[11] are slowly losing operational control of the corporate infrastructure. Market forces, including tremendous power inefficiencies, are driving companies to lease IT services through cloud computing—a much more cost-effective alternative to the traditional data center model. As a result, IT departments in the Social Age will transform themselves from IT infrastructure guardians to centers of business transformation. They'll leverage social networking intelligence and become a sponsor of innovation programs for the business.

As previously discussed, cloud computing providers will be able to provide low cost IT services because of two important competitive advantages: lower energy consumption optimization using economies of scale and green technologies, and virtualization technologies in the cloud that will be used to maximize hardware usage and minimize idle time.

As businesses continue to embrace the cloud computing utility model, the marketplace will push for more standardization and increasingly pervasive services. With cloud computing we'll soon be connected everywhere and be able to communicate with our communities and customers at any time without having to worry about the IT services that support us. Interoperability of services on cloud computing will enable seamless communication across the rich variety of social tools.

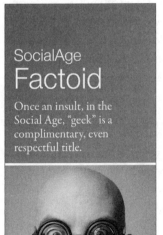

SocialAge
Factoid
Once an insult, in the Social Age, "geek" is a complimentary, even respectful title.

IT groups that embrace cloud computing will also have to think strategically about how to leverage their internal and external social networking communities. In the Social Age, even non-IT business units will be able to create and maintain their own IT solutions. These newly empowered groups, who will be using the latest collaboration and social networking tools, will need to be included in the planning by the IT group. Finally, the Social Age IT group still needs leadership. What does that look like? Well, for an answer we turn to the Social Age CIO.

The Social Age CIO

In the past, IT organizations controlled costs by controlling solutions and by minimizing the number of applications they had to manage. Until recently, the chief information officer had a simple charter:

• Keep costs down.

• Keep everything running.

The Social Age, however, calls for a fresh look at traditional approaches. Increasingly, the CIO is considered a strategic player in the corporation. CIO decisions now touch all parts of the corporation in a much more meaningful way than they ever did before. The CIO of the Social Age, rather than a chief information officer, will become in many ways the chief *innovation* officer and will take a more active role in the strategic transformation of the company.

Several questions are raised in this context: What is the role of CIOs in the Social Age? How can CIOs leverage the cloud? Should the IT organization trust non-IT groups to create their own solutions in the cloud? What is the control point that ultimately delivers the best efficiencies to IT? What about social tools and communities inside and outside of the company?

The answers to these questions can be complex and will vary company-to-company. In general, businesses benefit first by leveraging cloud computing in their IT strategy. In this new paradigm, it is vital for the CIO to be ready—and willing—to relinquish some level of control. He or she must not only trust the cloud, but also trust emerging social communities and allow non-IT groups with good business insight to build and maintain their own business-unit-specific applications.

Many options are available to the CIO to encourage non-IT groups to contribute to the IT assets of a company. For example, corporate data and applications services can be designed and offered as a "business utility" by leveraging web services. By careful documentation, the services can be made accessible to everyone in the company. This creates a self-service model, lowering overall IT development cost.

Some CIOs may resist a community approach to IT because they suspect it will result in "spaghetti" code, and may even create an array of essentially similar applications they'll need to maintain. Fortunately, nothing could be further from the reality of the Social Age IT environment. In the self-service model the "control point," for cost reduction purposes, resides on the web services, and not in the number of IT applications that are generated reusing cloud services.

In this kind of Services Oriented Architecture (SOA), the services are heavily used and reused by a variety of IT applications. SOA services can be used as a control point for IT groups to maintain common services. These can include access to databases, backend transactions, Web 2.0 widgets, connectors to legacy applications, and other valuable and reusable services. SOA and cloud computing complement each other since this combination brings everything as close as the nearest web service.

The key factor for broad acceptance of reusable IT assets is a transparent process making any application available to anyone within the company. Good documentation, including easy examples of how to use the data and services, within the SOA framework, will encourage adoption.

At IBM, my team "primed the pump" by creating some Web 2.0 "mashups."[12] Using web services, they created several mashup applications collecting a variety of corporate data, from different data sources, as well as data from outside the firewall. These applications became popular and promoted the use and creation of more Web 2.0 applications.

> *The Social Age is about a fundamental rethinking of everything we've done in IT for the past 25 years.*

CIOs are discovering the usefulness of social networking tools and the power of communities to create and maintain solutions to lower IT cost. The CIO of the Social Age embraces cloud computing to lower the IT infrastructure cost. He or she builds an IT self-service model that leverages the power of communities and encourages non-IT groups to build their own applications, reusing well-defined services available in the cloud.

Final Thoughts

The Social Age is not about just wikis, blogs and Facebook. *The Social Age is about a fundamental rethinking of everything we've done in IT for the past 25 years.* There are unprecedented challenges in the traditional data center—power inefficiencies, excessive downtime, and escalating personnel costs, all in the context of an increasingly mobile, highly demanding workforce. IT professionals and CIOs of the Social Age will be prime movers in transforming enterprise IT departments. This new generation sees cloud computing as an obvious alternative to the traditional data center model. Using the pay-as-you-go utility model, cloud computing offers scalability, less business risk with no long-term contracts, and better cash flow with sharply lower up-front costs.

In many ways, the massive changes in the way the Internet is used in the Social Age calls for massive changes in the way we execute IT strategies. Increasingly, it is an organizational imperative to deliver "*services* as a service."

Everything else has become secondary.

Failing to implement a visionary combination of social tools and cloud computing strategies will certainly jeopardize the best laid plans of any Social Age organization.

Cloud Benefits

- Scalability
- No long-term contracts
- Ease of management
- Lower cost
- Utility model pay-as-you-go
- Available anywhere, any time

In Chapter 7, "Social Media and Culture," we look at some software development strategies that make extensive use of social networking principles. We also look at the ways new media and social tools have changed human communication, interactions, and culture forever.

Summary

- Cloud computing provides hardware and software services via an abstraction layer of virtualized boxes. Virtualization enables the over-commitment of processor units, physical storage space as well as memory to help reduce the overall idle time. This means clouds are able to derive much more useful work from the same amount of electricity consumed by most traditional data centers.

- The grim reality is that 97 percent of our IT energy is wasted. That is, for every 100 units of energy taken from a coal mine, only around 3 units is used to generate meaningful IT work.[13]

- The energy crisis and market forces demanding IT cost efficiencies will accelerate the adoption of cost-effective cloud computing by traditional IT organizations.

- Cloud computing providers will compete based on how well they leverage "green technologies" and economies of scale to optimize the production of useful IT work at lower cost.

- The CIO of the Social Age embraces social tools and sees his or her role strategically, as an enabler and facilitator of the IT group as well as non-IT business communities. Cloud computing provides new freedom and alternatives for CIOs.

7
Social Media and Culture

Not too long ago, it seems, we drove to our nearby office, performed our job responsibilities for the civilized hours of 9 to 5, and then returned home to spend time with friends and family. The lines between work and home were clear: business was business and personal was personal.

All that changed with the acceptance of telecommuting, flextime, work-from-home positions, and the always-on connectivity of mobile devices. Traditional lines between business and personal are nearly gone now. A paradigm shift, to be sure, and one that social networking takes one step further: Your entire persona, both personal and professional, can now often be found in one online profile or blog site.

So how does this transparent and unified existence benefit you as a professional? Quite simply, those online personal tidbits enable people to get to know you better. Sure, you focus on business during a sales call. But perhaps just as important, you want to know the person, too. As I once heard a top salesman say, "People buy from other people."

That little saying becomes more profound the longer you think about it. To learn about the people you're doing business with—and for them to learn about you—there are few methods as efficient as social networking.

Social Media

Social media is a term used to describe a wide variety of Internet-based tools—also known as social networking tools—for sharing and discussing information. Social media typically integrates technology, social interaction, and the blending of text, pictures, video, and audio. Each social medium is uniquely defined by the varied contributor perspectives and by the creation of shared meaning, as contributors offer the benefit of their stories and experiences.

Social networking tools and sites for business are abundant. They range from general interest sites such as MySpace and Facebook, to niche sites like Covestor[1] (investors) or LinkedIn (professionals) that appeal to specific areas of interest. Shared among these sites, however, is the ability to publicly connect with others who share an interest in a particular area, and the ability to e-mail and instant message privately within the site.

Although social networking might be a relatively new phenomenon, the concepts behind the technology have been around since humans first lived in community. Human interaction—exchanging information, advice, and cooperative work—has been going on for thousands of years. In his recent book *Basic Instincts—Human Nature and the New Economics,* Peter Lunn said, "Highly complex social exchanges between non-relatives take place in every human culture, including the last few hunter-gatherer tribes."[2] But now, thanks to orders-of-magnitude advances in technology, we are no longer constrained by geographic location or cultural barriers.

Perhaps most profoundly, our social circle has likewise enjoyed a similar advance through social networking. We do not necessarily personally know those with whom we network socially. We've often never met (and might never personally meet) those with whom we interact, and we don't need to. Instead, our social and professional circles have expanded to include not only those whose telephone or e-mail we have in our Blackberry, *but also to anyone in the connected world who shares our interests, aspirations, or expertise.*

The choices in social networking can seem overwhelming to anyone who first ventures into this world. But you need to use these tools—to stay competitive, to stay current, and to gain priceless insights from the ongoing cyber-conversation. A look at some of the choices most widely used today and their potential use in your business is a good place to start.

Twitter

Leveraging the trend toward language devolution first seen in text-messaging (you know: CUL8R, LOL, and so on), Twitter  is a micro-blogging site. No windy e-mails here; you have 140 characters to answer a simple question: "What are you doing?"

At the beginning of Chapter 4, "Blogs: Your Personal News Outlet," we learned about IBM Lotus executive Ed Brill's blog success. Ed's use of social networking tools extends beyond blogs, and the personal touch he brings to his customers is strengthened significantly through his use of Twitter:

> The point on good relationships cannot be underscored enough. People sometimes ask me why I think Twitter is so valuable…. [I] learn a lot through what others are talking about, and it helps me get a clearer picture of names in the industry. One fine example [recently] took place at [a] customer luncheon in Sydney. Someone stood up to ask me a question, and he started by telling me that he was @hollingsworth on Twitter, who had been giving me restaurant recommendations for the last few days in Sydney. Knowing who he was and that he was a Twitter user was helpful in answering his question, because it gave me an opportunity to mention TwitNotes, the Twitter plug-in for Lotus Notes 8. Our connection was immediately stronger despite having never met in-person nor even so much as heard [his] name before.[3]

In Chapter 1, "Dawn of the Social Age," we talked about the cost of communication and about the way communities expand as communication costs decrease. Ed's experience is typical in the Social Age. Someone he never met before in person, who lives on the other side of the world, feels comfortable addressing Ed as a personal acquaintance when he finally meets him.

If you tell this story to someone born before 1950, don't be surprised if you get a shake of the head and a comment like, "Too much for me" in response. But even many pre-boomers are starting to get into the act when it comes to social networking. Grandparents are beginning to realize Facebook and other social tools are an easy way to keep up with what's going on with their children and grandchildren.

Joining the Conversation

If you go to the main page of Twitter and read the public timeline, you might feel like you've just walked into a party with thousands of strangers. Everyone is engaged in a lively conversation, and you might feel compelled to try to listen in to each one. It quickly becomes apparent, however, that although some of the conversations might apply to you, others clearly don't.

Perhaps you notice a conversation that prominently mentions the company you work for. "@Bob685" is frustrated with tech support or with the latest software update. How valuable is it for you to listen in on that conversation, or perhaps join it? Wouldn't you want the opportunity to find out what's wrong and how you could fix it? Or perhaps you're part of the creative team of a television show, and you notice that "@SusanHouseFan" is giving an opinion on last night's episode. Television rating systems are by their nature one-dimensional; personal and detailed feedback like that offered by Susan provides much more valuable information.

The real power of Twitter is using Search to narrow your cyber-eavesdropping to those conversations that are relevant to your field, skills, interests, or organization. Usually in one second or less, Twitter uses key word search to retrieve all the recent (and not-so-recent) conversations you're interested in. These conversations connect to other information or other people that can provide incredibly valuable business intelligence. When you establish a Twitter network, you can even use a tool called "Mr. Tweet" that analyzes your network and suggests other "tweeps"—another name for Twitter users—you might be interested in following. Mr. Tweet's "bio" says, "Who are the influences and followers you are missing out on? Follow us to get personalized suggestions of who should follow!"

In today's business world, which increasingly seems to move at the speed of light, who couldn't use a personal assistant like Mr. Tweet?

What Should I Tweet?

Used as a business tool, we think you now understand a little of Twitter's tremendous value. If you're a technology specialist, what you had for lunch is probably a lot less interesting to your tweeps than the information you have about the latest beta patch. What else are you working on today that's going to help your tweeps? Did you just read an article about the latest gadget that makes your job easier? Tweet it! Did you find a new way to configure an application? Tweet it! Even if you're tweeting primarily business topics, don't feel that you can't share personal tweets. The best tweeters understand the important, if sometimes delicate, balance between personal and professional information.

The nature of Twitter is one of immediate and constant interaction. Tweets are posted so frequently that if you blink, you'll probably miss them. But that's okay; you don't have to respond to everything. Unless you're directly messaged with a comment or question ("DM" in Twitter-speak), you don't have to acknowledge any message. Glance at Twitter from time to time, or use Search to follow the topics and conversations of interest.

On Twitter, as the old saying goes, there are no strangers, just friends you haven't met yet. Don't hesitate, for example, to use the @reply feature to reply to "strangers" if you see them talking about something of interest. Even if they don't follow you, they'll see your @reply on their Replies page. They'll also spot your reply if they monitor Twitter for references to themselves. Twitter @reply is a great way to make informal, topic-centered connections.

As with any powerful new technology, a host of third-party applications are available to extend the capabilities of Twitter. Use a search engine to search "twitter tools" to find out more about products such as itweet.net for live updates to a web page and twhirl.org, that allows you to interact more easily with the stream of Twitter updates.

The many uses for this seemingly trivial social networking application can quickly become apparent to you, but there are three key areas Twitter can help you as a business professional:

- **Grow your network.** I once heard someone describe Twitter as a "stupid easy way to connect with people and grow your network." Click the Follow button and you connect to a potentially worldwide network of like-minded people. "[Twitter is] not just news and links," said Andy Piper, a consulting IT specialist at IBM, "it's awareness of where those people are and what they are looking at that matters to me. It's also important, I find, to be diverse in the choice of who to follow. My network has expanded far beyond [just] IBMers."[4]

- **Get smart!** Are you kidding? In many ways, Twitter lets you walk around all day with CEOs, industry analysts, editors, and technical specialists, and eavesdrop on some of the most knowledgeable conversations you'll ever hear. These thought leaders are on Twitter, sharing their insights and knowledge in bite-sized portions. Shouldn't you be listening in? Or even contributing to the conversation?

- **Stay competitive.** There's time, and then there's cyber-time. Knowledge travels today in cyber-time, so the only way to keep up is to be "plugged in" at all times. Twitter can help you stay informed about the latest research, product launches, or market trends as they're happening, providing you with tremendous competitive insights.

LinkedIn

We should have known the days of the business card were numbered the first time we saw someone "beam" their contact information to someone else's PDA. Remember

those stacks of business cards in your bottom drawer, neatly sorted alphabetically and bound with a rubber band? Sometimes you found time to enter the information in your database, sometimes you didn't. Then, inevitably, the day arrived when you needed to contact one of those people. You couldn't remember his name, and you spent half an hour flipping through all the business cards to jog your memory. You met him at MacWorld; he was wearing a blue Hawaiian shirt. You think his name was Barry. Or was it Gary?

And then LinkedIn arrived. Today your "so-last-millennium" request for a business card is likely met with a blank look. "I'm on LinkedIn" is now the standard reply. LinkedIn virtually eliminates the need for business cards, while offering incredibly detailed personal and professional profiles that provide you with powerful business intelligence. LinkedIn users have the option to provide work history, professional and personal recommendations, and even upload a profile photo. If you're good with faces, but not names, this is a huge help!

Don't think of LinkedIn, however, as merely an electronic replacement for business cards. As a social networking site, LinkedIn allows you to take these relationships to the next logical step. You can stay in contact with colleagues through LinkedIn status updates sent to your e-mail account, and third-party plug-ins allow you to customize your online persona. You can also grow your network by automatically seeing LinkedIn "connections." You might think you have only 50 people in your professional network. However, LinkedIn tracks *connections of connections*; meaning that even if your 50 contacts have only 50 contacts each, you're already connected to 2,500 people. You can quickly request introductions within the extended network by simply tracing your connections. Talk about "degrees of separation!"

LinkedIn Groups allows members to gather virtually around a particular topic, brand, or event. Hundreds of Groups are available for everything from software professionals to trade shows to groups of employees from a particular company. Groups can poll members with discussion items or share news articles. LinkedIn

...even if your 50 contacts have only 50 contacts each, you're already connected to 2,500 people.

Groups provide professionals with a great way to share their knowledge or publicize their skills.

Personal Branding and Social Networking

In October 2008, Laurisa Rodriguez was in a difficult spot when her job at IBM was eliminated. She had 30 days to either find a new role inside the company or begin an external search. The good news was that Laurisa had a worldwide community of 400,000 colleagues in the IBM organization, any one of whom might connect her with her next job. The challenge was to reach as many of these people as possible in 30 short days. What would be the most efficient way to get the word out about her skills and background and her track record of success? In the Information Age she might have been limited to mass e-mailing or using the telephone to reach out to her network.

Fortunately for Laurisa, she was a Social Age expert and regularly contributed to social networking sites both inside and outside IBM. Laurisa quickly crafted a blog post clearly stating her situation, skills, and a link to her resume, which she posted to an internal social file-sharing site. She asked those who wanted to help her to join her LinkedIn network and perhaps even write a recommendation. Within hours of her post, IBMers from around the world had commented on the blog post with words of encouragement and job leads. Within a few days, Laurisa's LinkedIn contacts had doubled (doubling at the same time the number of secondary connections, of which there were already several thousand).

Multiple recommendations from IBM colleagues and business partners appeared seemingly overnight on Laurisa's LinkedIn profile. Surprisingly, some of the rec-ommendations came from individuals Laurisa had never met face-to-face, or even directly interacted with on any level. Laurisa's dedication to a fundamental principle of social networking—provide value to the community to receive value—paid off handsomely as she quickly landed another position at IBM.

Facebook

The fastest growing demographic on the social net-working site Facebook is users 25 years of age and older. Originally a college-student-only phenomenon  (the site started at Harvard University in 2004), Facebook quickly became a world-wide phenomenon and now has more than 150 million users![5] During registration, a variety of tools enable you to easily grow your network of contacts. This feature helps business people easily stay in touch on both a professional and a personal level. People tend to go where the crowds are, and Facebook provides a tremendous advantage to reach people with similar interests and backgrounds.

Much like LinkedIn, Facebook also has a status update feature that enables you to broadcast a short message to your network when you make changes to your profile. Professionals use this feature to communicate about projects, job postings, or even business trips. It's an effortless way to stay in contact with colleagues without having to contact each of them individually. Increasingly, there is a movement toward consolidation of social networking platforms. In this case, if you use Twitter, you can have it update your Facebook status automatically.

Facebook is also an application platform, so developers can create applications to share among friends. Fan groups—for instance fans of a product, person, or event—can also be created. One health food company created a Facebook application to motivate its customers to participate in healthy challenges, such as trying a new recipe or fitness regimen. Users can invite their friends to participate and track their results. The company promotes its healthy lifestyle philosophy and simultaneously builds product loyalty. Customers feel involved not only with the company, but also with a community of friends who share the same healthy goals.

Companies are even going so far as to create fan sites around their product, store, or brand. For example, an international retail clothing chain has a Facebook fan site where it communicates regularly with members about everything from holiday sales to new store openings. Users of the site can take a virtual tour of the store via video. Customers can even try on the latest fashions in a virtual online dressing room.

Facebook fan sites, however, aren't just about pushing information out to customers. Facebook allows customers and company reps to exchange ideas, perhaps even discuss where to open new stores. Discussion boards on Facebook encourage customers to share their enthusiasm for upcoming fashions or make suggestions for outfits. Facebook users even upload photos of themselves shopping in the store or wearing their latest purchase.

YouTube

To borrow a term used by Malcolm Gladwell in his bestselling book of the same name,[6] it seems a "tipping point" was reached by YouTube in the midst of the 2008 U.S. presidential elections. Whether people were watching a candidate speech, tracking down a scandal, or submitting a question to a live presidential debate, it seemed the whole world was suddenly on YouTube.

YouTube allows anyone to upload and share with the world a video on virtually any topic. Have a neat card trick that you've already shown all your friends? Why not upload it to YouTube so the whole world can enjoy it? Do you enjoy creating music, but just haven't been able to get the attention of a big-time record producer? A 20-something musician named Tay Zonday composed and recorded a song called *Chocolate Rain* that to date has been viewed 33 million times on YouTube.[7] What music exec wouldn't sell his or her soul for that kind of commercial play? (If you haven't seen *Chocolate Rain* yet, fair warning—be prepared to have the catchy melody dancing in your head for the next week!)

In this context, it might be reasonable to ask what business value we hope to gain with YouTube. Well, first, YouTube is a common way to establish a communications channel—literally. A YouTube channel gives an individual or company a centralized location to share videos related to their brand. Access YouTube and type in the name of any large corporation to see the way this technology is exploited. For example, the Ford Channel currently has 121 videos on YouTube.[8]

Catching a virus is usually a bad thing, whether in your sinuses or on your computer. For a video on YouTube, however, a virus is not a bad thing at all. Tay Zonday's *Chocolate Rain* video quickly "went viral," as it was passed through e-mail, blogs, and other social networking forums. With an advertising budget of $0, Zonday's song became a worldwide hit and landed him appearances on *Jimmy Kimmel Live* and *Good Morning America*.[9] Easy-to-use widgets allow you to quickly embed YouTube videos on your blog and even automatically update a section of the blog with the latest video from a particular artist or company, while increasing the "contagiousness" of a cool or helpful video.

In 2009, British singing phenomenon Susan Boyle enjoyed a YouTube turbo-boost similar to Tay Zonday's when she first appeared on the television show *Britain's Got Talent*. A complete unknown, and at 47 an unlikely pop star, Boyle wowed the *Talent* audience with her performance of *I Dreamed a Dream* from the play *Les Miserables*. Through viral distribution of the video, a worldwide YouTube audience quickly became convinced—as *Talent's* judges were—that Boyle was the real thing. YouTube carries numerous versions of her performance; the number of combined views of these videos to date is approximately 100 *million*.

Zonday's and Boyle's performances are similar to thousands of other videos that currently stream on the World Wide Web. As shown in Figure 7.1, there has been a significant shift toward traffic from Social Age tools such as YouTube and Facebook.

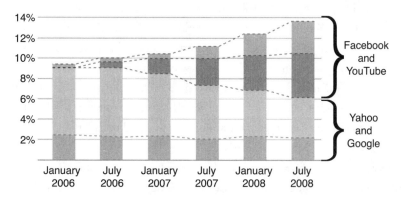

Figure 7.1 Internet traffic's shift from traditional portal search sites to social networking sites.[10]

Value of Social Networking Tools for Professionals

Now that we're aware of some social tools and networking sites, let's look at their professional value to individuals and some of the ways companies can use these tools to grow their business.

- **Sharing information:** Sharing information inside an enterprise can be difficult. As discussed in Chapter 4, most organizations determine what can be published and by whom. Processes control everything from initial submission to final publication. This traditional top-down approach takes time. In the Social Age, where information can literally travel around the world in minutes, companies need to adopt methods to share information just as quickly.

What's your business challenge? Spreading the word on ways to overcome a common sales objection? Alerting a user base to a discrepancy in a technical manual? Sharing information about a competitor with your worldwide sales team? Quickly sharing any of this information saves valuable time for you and your colleagues and provides a competitive edge. E-mail won't get the job done quickly enough, and besides, e-mails quickly drop (often unread) to the bottom of our e-mail box.

Social networking allows this information to be shared informally and efficiently. By collaborating and participating in forums, blogs, wikis, and social bookmarking, employees have an outlet to share this valuable information. Sales consultants can easily blog about overcoming a common sales objection. A techie can correct a documentation discrepancy through a product documentation wiki. A marketing rep can share information on a competitor by adding a link to the social bookmarking repository.

With social networking tools, employees can share information with the people they know, but more importantly, they can share information with people they don't know!

• **Making employees smarter:** "Intelligence isn't owned by any individual company," said Adam Christensen, IBM social media specialist. "Grounding happens by public conversations. It requires honesty."[11] Companies that encourage the use of social networking tools, both inside and outside of the corporate firewalls, have employees who work smarter, and are thus increasingly well-grounded.

Ongoing virtual focus groups offer the opportunity for employees to speak honestly about their work, and they provide a forum to engage regularly with customers and business partners. Actively listening and participating in these types of conversations helps employees better understand customer needs and expectations. By knowing who their counterparts are in other companies, they can also be up-to-speed with the overall marketplace. Together, social networking can produce an increasingly smart workforce.

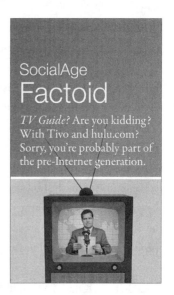

SocialAge
Factoid

TV Guide? Are you kidding? With Tivo and hulu.com? Sorry, you're probably part of the pre-Internet generation.

Social Networking: An IBM Business Partner Perspective

Two years ago, Keith Brooks, an IBM business partner and former Lotus employee, started what ultimately became one of the most popular Lotus LinkedIn groups: Lotus Software Professionals. Keith used the group to form a community of individuals interested primarily in Lotus Software technologies.

"I thought it was a good way to meet others, find a job, maybe some projects," said Keith. "What it became was a very robust group with some of the [best-known] Lotus people, inside and outside of IBM...."[12]

Different business professionals interested in Lotus Software use Keith's site. Some are IBMers, some are customers, some are business partners, and others might be just fans of Lotus products. A discussion feature allows members to interact with each other on topics ranging from technical support and troubleshooting to job searches.

Keith also uses his blog to share his knowledge and experiences with potential clients. He has been chided by some who tell him he's giving away his knowledge for free. Keith doesn't see it that way. "The blog has brought in leads," he said. "Clients have contacted me because they were researching a topic and found an article on my blog."

Keith also monitors Twitter for Lotus references. He uses the search function to catch tweets of people commenting on their experiences with Lotus. Twitter's interactive and random nature allows him to reply to these comments and a productive business conversation often ensues, which has sometimes led to client engagements.

Because of his use of LinkedIn, Twitter, and blogs, Keith has grown his network of business contacts. He now has a large, ready-made network to which he can market new offerings.

In many ways, Keith is the classic Social Age entrepreneur, leveraging all the tools, while simultaneously building valuable personal and professional relationships. "I have connected myself to over 4,000 people on LinkedIn," Keith said with obvious satisfaction. "There are always possibilities to grow and expand the [number of] people you touch and thus can help or work with down the road."

Social Tools: Business Impact

Regardless of which social networking tools or sites you choose to use, first identify your goals. Do you want to connect with existing customers? Grow market share? Get feedback on new products or service offerings? What do you want to *do*?

And what do you want to get out of your new relationships? You won't be interacting as a faceless, monolithic corporation. You're talking with people and building *relationships*. Remember what that veteran—and very successful—salesman told me: "People buy from other people."

The social networking medium requires a fundamentally different attitude and tone than earlier unidirectional communication. No longer are companies allowed to make "pronouncements" and hope the market simply accepts what they say. The social networking community has the opportunity to react, both positively *and* negatively, to your message. And believe me, they will! These responses in large part can't be controlled.

> *No longer are companies allowed to make "pronouncements" and hope the market simply accepts what they say.*

Use of Social Tools in Marketing Campaigns

Let's look at a traditional marketing methodology and see how social networking plays a role. There are five fundamental actions you must take to effectively leverage social networking on the Internet, as illustrated in Figure 7.2:

Figure 7.2 Steps to monitor the Internet conversation to effectively leverage social networking in your marketing campaign.

- **Monitor the market conversation**—Listen to the market conversation for insights into your current position.

- **Identify and engage**—Identify and engage key influencers who are influencing the market conversation around your brand, product, or service.

- **Maximize distribution**—Maximize distribution and impact of key digital marketing assets.

- **Empower advocacy**—Build and foster brand loyalists and empower them to advocate on behalf of your brand.

- **Understand the impact**—Measure your tactics.

Monitor the Market Conversation

At this moment, people are engaged in discussions about your brand, product, or service. They're blogging about their interactions with your customer service department. Or they're creating an online review of your latest product. Or they're tweeting about the product line in your stores. Or they've created video how-to guides about your product on YouTube. People will talk about your products whether you want them to or not.

Happily, these are usually public conversations to which you're free to listen. So why not have a listen? By listening you can exploit one of the most important aspects of social networking. Listening provides you with the following value:

- To understand the good, the bad…and the ugly opinions of the marketplace about your product, service, or brand

- To hear not just the words, but the tone and impact of that conversation

- To begin identifying areas of opportunity for shaping the conversation and to gather valuable market intelligence

> *People will talk about your products whether you want them to or not.*

How to Listen

It's all out there: all the conversations and comments and ratings about your company and your products. How do you decide what to monitor? There are companies that exist just for this reason—to monitor your brand for a fee. Are you a large company that needs sophisticated trending and impact statistics? Using an outside company might be a good choice.

If you have some basic monitoring needs and are on a tight budget, you can find good, no-cost, or low-cost monitoring tools online. With these tools you provide key words or phrases such as your brand name or an industry buzzword. These search tools bring you customized content based on your search criteria, on demand. Here are a few of the most popular "listening" tools:

- **Technorati**—In addition to providing a search engine for key words, Technorati provides real-time ranking of the 100 Top Blogs. These rankings are categorized by authority or number of fans. Authority is defined by number of times a blog is externally referenced. Number of fans refers to individuals voting by "favoriting" a blog on the Technorati site.

- **Google Alerts**—Select a key word or phrase to monitor. Choose to monitor web pages, blogs, video, Google groups, or a combination of all four categories. Results can be delivered either to your e-mail account or to a feed reader.

- **Twitter Search**—Monitors tweets for a particular word. This is particularly useful for getting a feel for what people are talking about—the "buzz"—at any particular moment. You can also drop in to observe conversations between individuals.

- **Bloglines**—An online site to easily subscribe to the most popular blogs in a variety of categories. Bloglines is a combination of feed reader, blog publishing tool, and search engine. Searches can be quickly converted to a feed and added to any feed reader. After you populate your preferences, Bloglines can suggest additional content you might not be aware of and add it to your customized content.

- **Google Blog Search**—Similar to Google Alerts, this tool searches only blogs. It also offers categories such as Business and Technology, which provide the most popular blogs for those categories at any given moment. Searches are provided in feed format for easy subscription.

- Other similar sites include Blog Pulse, Newsgator, and YackTrack.

RSS (Really Simple Syndication) feeds on these sites enable you to subscribe to them in a feed reader of choice, bringing you up-to-the-minute updates from each site.

No magic formula tells you what to listen to. Some of this will be done through trial and error, based on your needs. If the results aren't what you expected, consider modifying your search or update criteria. You'll begin to get a feel for which sources are worth listening to. You'll quickly identify a community of like-minded individuals, and the authoritative and influencing voices.

Identify and Engage the Influencers

After you invest some time into uncovering the buzz around your product, service, or brand, you can begin to recognize the influencers. These people continually appear in your feed reader. They're the tweeters that provide comment-stimulating topics. Join in the conversation. Nowhere is it easier to engage with others than in a social media environment. Even introverts come out of their shells when they're safely participating from the comfort of their homes or desks. Influencers want a discussion, they are passionate about their community, and they crave engagement. Comment on their blog, or respond to a question on twitter. Join the conversation; perhaps you'll become an influencer as well!

It is vitally important for you to identify and engage with the influencers. Here are a few of the reasons why:

• To understand and establish each influencer's relative impact on the market conversation

• To strategize ways to engage influencers through social media capabilities

• To establish enduring and mutually productive relationships with the influencers

• To empower their advocacy for your product or capability

Social Media on a Financial Services Web Site

Banco Popular de Puerto Rico, the largest commercial bank in Puerto Rico, has embraced social networking to interact with its customers. They host a lively blog called *Mi Banco*, in which they announce new products, ask the customers about services they'd like to see in the future, and provide a basic level of customer service.[13] What makes this blog work in a business environment? *Mi Banco* follows basic blogging guidelines including clear identification of authors, comment feedback from the author, and frequent posts.

Including a bio of all the bloggers on *Mi Banco* helps the readers know exactly who they are interacting with and what their roles are inside the company. The authors write with authentic and expert voices about the area of business they handle. This vital to helping customers feel they are interacting with someone who is listening to their needs and who has the power to take their ideas forward and act on them.

The readers of *Mi Banco* are also enthusiastic with their comments. One post on the *Mi Banco* Web site recently received more than 500 responses! The *Mi Banco* blogging team makes sure every blog post is read, and authors actively monitor the comments and respond to all questions in a timely and concise manner. This, in turn, helps promote usage and readership of the blog. When customers and potential customers feel they have a voice, customer satisfaction and customer retention increases.

Mi Banco authors post regularly. Readers know the blog is a vital part of Banco Popular's business and receives respectful attention inside of the company. Similarly, Banco Popular also has a Twitter id to promote its services and financial products.

Social Networking and Brand Loyalty

A highly specialized team of marketing, communication, and legal specialists have traditionally taken responsibility for protecting a company's image and reputation. Brand loyalty has always been the product of a series of carefully crafted messages written by these specialists. Consumers had no choice but to trust and believe what was said by the company, whether that was a product description, service agreement, or marketing message. Thus the proverbial advice: *caveat emptor!*

With social networking, however, much of the traditional brand creation and preservation model has undergone dramatic changes. In a world where people can freely interact with each other about practically every product, service, or company, they no longer need to rely on the word of the company. People have always trusted their friends and word-of-mouth much more than corporate advertising. Now, social networking has exponentially increased the number of "friends" and "mouths" we have to listen to. At the least, consumers now habitually check product reviews before buying anything online.

What Do You Lose by Not Implementing Social Tools?

In spite of these benefits, some companies are still apprehensive about allowing their employees to participate in social networking. Firewall blocks are not uncommon. Concerns range from fears of lost productivity to socially inappropriate comments. Clearly, management might be concerned about employees interacting directly with the public, or identifying themselves as company employees. This is a valid concern and should be addressed with corporate social networking policies that are clearly communicated and carefully enforced. But there must be a level of trust in the people you hire if you hope to tap into the tremendous power of social networking. A refusal to join in can carry significant costs for a company. This question is perhaps best considered from each perspective.

From an employee standpoint, a company's refusal to join the social networking movement means that employees are largely disconnected. However, humans are social; they enjoy and benefit by interacting with others. Consider that your employees have probably already formed groups on Facebook, LinkedIn, or MySpace because they share the common bond of employment by your company. What are common questions we ask when we meet someone for the first time? "What do you do for a living?" "Where do you work?" Social networking lets us answer those questions and share the common victories and challenges of our place of employment.

Employees might also sense a lack of trust from their employer if it blocks access to social networking sites such as Facebook or LinkedIn. The employee wants to think he is being judged by his performance and contribution to the company, rather than by the amount of time he spends on a social networking site.

From the company's standpoint, when it fails to exploit social networking tools, it is probably limiting its ability to inform and engage with customers. It is also missing out on conversations currently taking place about their brand and their company. As I said, people talk about your company in cyberspace whether you like it or not. Wouldn't you like to know what's being said? If your product or store has a fan site on Facebook, wouldn't it be important for someone in product management or customer relations to know first-hand what your customers think of your newest product?

By not embracing social networking, your company also faces the real risk of appearing—and actually being!—out-of-touch, irrelevant, inflexible, "last millennium," not-with-it, and as not listening. Depending on your product or service, this combination could cause lasting harm to your business and your brand. Without social networking, you're potentially missing out on opportunities to share your message, product, service, or brand via a powerful word-of-mouth method. After all, isn't it an axiom that more people trust word-of-mouth than any other type of advertising?

In Chapter 8, "On the Shoulders of Giants," we review how the social networking mind-set provides tremendous benefits in the area of software development and generates a wealth of vibrant open software communities.

Brand Transparency and Blogs

As the Internet has shifted toward a participatory environment through blogging and other social networking tools, some care should be exercised, particularly with regard to marketing and brand position. In the Social Age everyone has a voice, which means that a single negative blog post about a product—especially from a known source—can be amplified in the blogosphere and diminish the effectiveness of even the best marketing campaign.

Recognizing this challenge, many organizations have found that the best response is to embrace the Internet's modes and culture. A Social Age organization must demonstrate transparency and honesty, admitting mistakes when it makes them and addressing them quickly. Even with nothing to hide, it pays to proceed thoughtfully in this area because trade secrets and competitive issues might be in play. If handled properly, such transparency might become a key resource to demonstrate your organization's superior capabilities.

Summary

- Social media is a term that describes a wide variety of Internet-based tools—also known as social networking tools—for sharing and discussing information.

- Twitter, LinkedIn, Facebook, and YouTube are well-known examples of social media, each of which can empower your social networking efforts significantly.

- Professionals benefit in a variety of ways from social networking, including ease of information sharing and becoming smarter about industries, competitors, and customers.

- Social tools are about enhancing your social effectiveness—"People buy from other people."

- Easy-to-use widgets that allow you to quickly embed videos, tags, and other features to your social Web site create a contagious cool effect. This has ignited a shift in Internet from traditional portal search sites like Yahoo to social networking sites like Facebook.

- Social tools can be used effectively in marketing campaigns through effective monitoring of conversations related to your product or company. You can easily find basic monitoring tools at no-cost or low-cost such as Technorati and Bloglines. These tools can monitor phrases such as your brand name or an industry buzzword.

8
On the Shoulders
of Giants

In the context of the profound changes we've already discussed, it should come as no surprise that software development in the Social Age has changed as well.

In a 1676 letter to his rival Robert Hooke, Sir Isaac Newton talked about the importance of earlier discoveries by his predecessors: "If I have seen a little further it is by standing on the shoulders of Giants."[1]

Newton's comment applies as much in our day to open software as it did to the discoveries he described in his brilliant *Principia Mathematica*. In the world of open software, building on the work of others is a fundamental principle. Collaboration, sharing of ideas, and discrete contributions made by a group of individuals produce powerful results—often rivaling and surpassing those produced using traditional software development methodologies.

Sir Isaac Newton
Painting by Anfenee Waller at MCMS (1889)

What Is Open Software?

Open software does not just refer to the traditional concept of open source but refers to the *process and methodology* of creating software collaboratively. The collaboration might be completely open to anyone who wants to participate or it might be driven by a smaller subset of contributors with similar interests or experiences. For example, a corporation can start an open software project across multiple organizations and include external contributors such as partners, ISVs (Independent Software Vendors), customers, and academia. The outcome can be kept as part of the intellectual capital of the corporation or made publicly available through an open source license agreement. As with other software creation, open software consists of two major elements: Development and Distribution.

- **Open collaboration development methodology**—Open collaboration occurs at many levels, from sharing ideas and concepts for a project, to sharing code that has often been constructed following an agile methodology. The drivers for collaboration vary, but the core of the methodology is a symbiotic relationship between the leaders that started the project and the collaborators. A successful open software engagement is one in which everybody wins and recognition is insured because of the inherently transparent development process. Many enterprises have recognized the value of collaboration and social tools and create their own solutions using open collaboration. Even when the resulting code is not made publicly available, these corporate open development initiatives leverage great minds across the business, resulting in the best possible product.

- **Open source distribution**—If you want your hot, new solution accepted broadly, what better way than to give it away! Later in this chapter, we look at some high-profile examples of open source distribution. Essentially this method of distribution is the bread-and-butter of many companies, especially startups that leverage the LAMP software stack—an acronym for Linux, Apache, MySQL, Perl/PHP/ Python, and lately could also include Ruby. Using LAMP, a host of consortiums, companies, and technical communities create software that is made available for free. Keep in mind, however, that just because software is in the open source community, it doesn't necessarily mean that it was created in an "open collaboration" methodology. Code is sometimes made available in the open source community as a defensive strategy to blunt another company's competitive advantage, or when a company goes out of business. In some cases, software is made available as open source because the original creators need assistance from the community.

For example, a startup company might have the resources to create a solution that works with ten devices, but there are another 200 services from five different software platforms and vendors that could benefit from the solution. By making the code available to the open source community, the members of the community can help create additional extensions to support new services. A good example of the way companies have leveraged this concept is Jaiku—a micro blog service similar to Twitter. Google acquired Jaiku in October 2007, and went to work diligently to integrate the tool into their Google app engine. A few months later the entire JaikuEngine was declared open source under the Apache License 2.0 and is now available on Google Code Project, where anyone can use it and run their own JaikuEngine instance. Although Google will no longer actively develop the Jaiku codebase, it was smart to make it open source, because now it can benefit from the contributions of thousands of passionate developers. These contributions ensure the services remain vibrant with new service extensions.

With an understanding of the two elements of open software—development and distribution—we turn our attention to the virtuous cycle of development at the heart of open software. The common tools of the LAMP stack and the collaborative power of social networking (wikis, blogs, and forums), which facilitates open development, combined with the boundless energy of dedicated programmers, have converted open software into a powerful business strategy. Geographically separated communities of programmers (including the best minds in a particular technical discipline) can collaborate to improve open source code, each for their own reasons. Financial pressure to bring a solution to market quickly might drive one company, whereas market pressures to lower the cost of overall IT solutions through reuse of software might drive another. For some open communities, it seems there is just a pragmatic recognition that Social Age collaboration is here to stay and that proprietary platforms are often just relics of an earlier technological age.

The Virtuous Cycle

Combining open collaboration methodology and open source distribution creates a potent virtuous cycle. The cycle begins with a great idea that addresses a problem or customer pain-point.

Prototyping by the originator of the idea—whether an individual or team—is next. In this step, the value of the solution is validated and credibility is established. With the confidence gained from approval by their peers, innovators might publish a paper about their idea and findings. The technical community reviews, evaluates, and critiques the idea, often using public forums, wikis, or blogs. Additional ideas emerge from the discussions, and eventually, a strong technical leader emerges in the community. This leader typically has great technical insight and charisma and is frequently a community connector. He or she takes the lead to create an open source project to build a new implementation.

The company or team that built the first implementation will sometimes make the code publicly available with the hope that it will get assistance from programmers in the open source community. As the community starts collaborating and

An Open Source Success

Elias Torres is director of engineering at Boston-based Lookery, a user-targeting service company. Elias is also an enthusiastic participant in open source communities, especially those focused on distributed and collaborative systems projects.

Elias Torres

"Open Source communities are an excellent vehicle to grow your technical abilities," Elias said, "because of the freedom you have to experiment. The collaboration and support provided by other users and developers in the community is a great encouragement."

Because open technology is free, Elias said that companies using open source projects can focus resources on their core business rather than on building solutions "from scratch." These companies add value and innovation by carefully combining software and hardware. They create reliable and profitable products and services.

Elias noted that there is a welcome abundance of information available on the Internet when evaluating open source projects and their technologies. Use cases, competing product analyses, tutorials, bug archives, and mailing lists are all available. Perhaps most importantly, you can quickly—and directly—contact project authors.

Highscalability.com, for example, is a great place to learn about the best architectures and software to build scalable Web sites. Prepare to be dazzled by the amazing amount and quality of information freely available, not only on highscalability.com, but also on any Web site focused on open source.

Open source and collaborative software development are a new mind-set in software; they are part of a cultural revolution that is enabled and driven by the incredible power of social networking.[2]

building code together, more synergy is created. With time the "long tail" of contributors, along with a passionate core team of programmers, can often create a better implementation.

With a new open source implementation now available, programmers use the open source community to generate more reference implementations that fit their industry and solutions. Collaboration generates many code examples and a wealth of educational material. Relevant forums, wikis, and blogs become a testament of the project evolution, technical decisions functionality, and problems encountered along the way. The virtuous cycle keeps progressing and augmenting the value provided by the open source community, as seen in Figure 8.1.

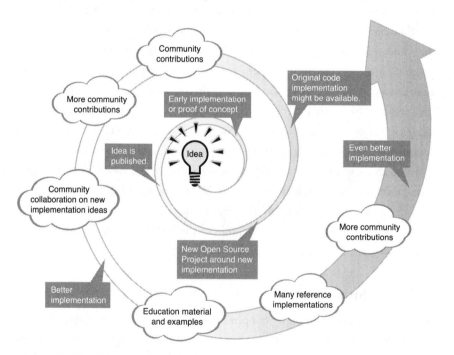

Figure 8.1 The virtuous cycle of open source.

At the heart of a successful open source project are good collaboration tools that enable communication, social interaction, and tracking of source code. Traditional Source Control Management (SCM) systems, such as CVS (Concurrent Versions Systems), don't fit well with the dynamic aspect of open source, in which the software code is modified and forked constantly by many people loosely linked by collaboration tools. Linux is an example of a large open source project that experimented with alternative SCM approaches. In 2002 Linux used BitKeeper to track the operating system kernel changes but finally moved to Git, in June 2005, as the official tracking system for Linux.

Git was designed and implemented by Linus Torvalds (best known for his contribution to the Linux kernel), who had the idea to create a distributed SCM. Git differentiates itself from other traditional SCM in that it was designed for open source collaboration; with Git, forking and merging are greatly facilitated. Git also maintains ancestry on the history of prior branches and makes possible keeping track of changes across many source trees. Better yet, it minimizes bottlenecks by enabling multiple replicas of the code via "pull" and "push" capabilities. These capabilities help contributing programmers have the source code in multiple, decentralized locations that harmonizes with the way in which the community works. The Linux kernel has thousands of line changes every day, with thousands of programmers around the world contributing to the code. This dynamic rewrite of the Linux code actually generates a completely rewritten kernel every couple of years. Another key factor contributing to the success of an open source project is the quality of the community that supports the effort. The community needs a strong leader or core team to establish good communication and attract a variety of technical skills. The open source community leaders not only contribute back into the community with changes, but they also create work streams to explore alternatives and use their influence to gain acceptance. A great example of this kind of leadership, and of the virtuous cycle, is the Apache Software Foundation. The goal of Apache is to teach a small group of developers, who work on open source projects, the best way to grow, communicate, and collaborate efficiently to make the project a success.

LAMP Lights the Way

Among the best-known examples of open source software are the Linux operating system, Apache web server, mySQL database, and interpreted programming languages such as Perl and PHP. Referred to as the LAMP stack, these are usually installed on Linux servers and capable of running on most operating systems. The technology industry has rallied around the LAMP stack as a viable alternative to more complex and expensive commercial solutions.

Most web applications today require the dynamic presentation of end-user-submitted content. The LAMP stack supports the development and deployment of such systems, offering a solid operating system, fast database, integral programming languages, and an increasingly popular web server. Some of the most popular Web sites today were built completely on an open software platform, with custom software riding on top.

Open software, however, goes beyond the idea of open source. It is best considered a superset of open source—applying the principles of working out in the open, supporting standards, designing for integration, and planning for extensibility to commercial solution development. This is a profound departure from traditional software development, where a small number of stakeholders drive the vision and requirements for the development team.

A myriad of other applications might enjoy significant benefit from a more dynamic, communal approach to software design and creation. Open software demonstrates the possibilities of team-developed software and the culture change required to do it well. In many ways, open software aided by social tools can be seen as an industry revolution and establishment of a new mind-set. It is this new mind-set, coupled with financial pressures and a desire for standardization, which will push further adoption of open source and collaboration development processes.

Dynamo

Even if you don't shop at Amazon.com, you probably go there (as we do!) to compare prices or read merchandise reviews. But what's behind the scenes at this incredibly fast retail Web site? Tens of thousands of servers linked together around the world all working with no failures, right? Wrong! At Amazon.com, the systems are failing constantly. With tens of thousands of servers, avoiding system failure would be impossible. The key to Amazon.com's "always on" service is to effectively and transparently manage failure. Werner Vogels is the Amazon.com CTO and mastermind of the cleverly designed Dynamo solution, which runs on Amazon.com core services, providing this "always-on" level of service. In an October 2007 paper, Vogels and several key technical leaders of Amazon.com described Dynamo and the strategy behind this key-value storage system.[3]

This paper was a great milestone in software development because it made the intellectual property available to the technical community. This sparked great interest and development activity. Immediately after the paper was published, many technical and thought leaders began creating improvements and ideas for implementations. Many LinkedIn engineers got involved in early implementations that resulted in a new open source project called Project Voldemort.[4] LinkedIn is now one of the supporters of this open source community providing resources to contribute to the code and—it is hoped—gain influence in the direction of the open source project.

Jay Kreps, senior software engineer at LinkedIn, is the leader that created Project Voldemort. Jay drives and inspires the team; he provides the strong leadership required to ensure a successful open source project. Project Voldemort is a compelling example of the virtuous cycle of open software at its best. In this case, powerful technology concepts moved from Amazon.com to the dynamic creativity of the open source collaboration environment.

Hadoop

Google was selected in 2008 as the best global brand by *Business Week*.[5] And no wonder; who doesn't make regular use of this powerful and appealing technology? Google is, of course, a good—some would say the best—search engine, accessing massive data on thousands of servers, but there's a not-so-secret ingredient that drives the Google business.

That ingredient, called "MapReduce," was described in a 2004 paper[6] by Google's Jeffrey Dean and Sanjay Ghemawat. This technology reduces and manages large data sets and is at the core of Google's success with search engines. Dean and Ghemawat's paper described in detail the MapReduce structure and implementation. After it was in the open technical community, this paper inspired incredible creativity for the best way to enable large-scale, parallelized computations across large computer clusters.

Shortly after the publication of Dean and Ghemawat's paper, open source advocate and search specialist Doug Cutting stepped up to the task of creating a new open source project. Hadoop was the result.[7] The Hadoop project charter was essentially to create a new, open source implementation of MapReduce. Yahoo quickly saw the value of using the open source community to help improve its search technology. It supported Hadoop development by hiring Doug Cutting, who now is dedicated fulltime to leading the Hadoop community. Yahoo has benefited the Hadoop community effort and uses it to improve some of its services.

Open, but Not Free

Open source software equals free software, right? Well, not so fast. In the early years of the Internet, when open source was first on the scene, it was heresy to suggest that software could one day be "free." Proprietary commercialization of software was dogma in the technology business. After all, when a company spent millions of dollars developing an application, didn't it have the right to reap the rewards of that effort? Didn't it have the right to shrink wrap, at the cost of a few dollars, a couple of CDs and a user manual and sell it for hundreds of dollars to recoup its investment?

And what about intellectual property? Recall the browser wars of the late 1980s and early 1990s when Netscape and Microsoft® battled it out in the marketplace and later in the courts. It was in this context that the power of the people first began to be felt in the realm of open source software, and we started to hear the term "Linux" everywhere we turned.

Just because the operating system and development languages were free, however, didn't mean the applications wrote themselves. There is a cost to anything that contributes value and, with open source, the cost is usually not monetary in nature. Consider the key attributes of open source software and their related costs:

- **Transparency**—The source code for the entire solution is made available for anyone to download, inspect, compile, build, use, extend, and redistribute.

  Contributors work out in the open, creating an interesting and public peer pressure to deliver good code. In the early days of television, a children's program closed with the host looking through her "magic mirror" at the camera and saying, "I see Bobby, and I see Jane, and I see Eric...." In the world of open source development, the magic mirror is held up to every developer; and that developer's work is subject to intense peer scrutiny—and comment! Delivering solid code and frequently updating an open source application carries a nonmonetary cost of time, attention, and uncompromised personal commitment to the development community.

- **Diversity**—The core development team is often diverse, representing individual and institutional views. This means that the requirements for a given solution are not controlled by any one owner. Leaders emerge in open projects, but primary responsibility is sometime distributed across a few diverse individuals. Meeting the needs of a broad user base means a price must sometimes be paid in terms of compromise and flexibility with individual requirements.

- **Commitment to collaborate**—Finally, open source software is developed in a highly collaborative fashion. If the seventeenth-century poet John Donne had been cranking out open source code in 2009, he might have said, "No developer is an island, entire of themselves." Effective open source teams need to be constantly engaged in dialogue, as with a traditional development team. As we said, open development increases the pressure of the team to deliver to the best of their capabilities. And because the collaboration extends to anyone who wants to contribute, bugs are more easily identified in this context, and code extensions and patches can be more efficiently surfaced.

Taken as a whole, these three characteristics of open source software highlight perhaps the primary cost of this important resource: One individual or one organization cannot control the evolution of the open source product. The primary means of influencing development is through contribution, which means businesses must dedicate development resources to an open project—not just a wish list.

Although software might be available through open source at no *monetary* cost, the risks and investments are still important considerations that must not be overlooked by the would-be open source developer.

Creation and Cocreation

In the Social Age, collaborative open source development is not just for developers. As we might expect, collaborative development now extends to end users as well.

In an earlier age of software development, the opinions of users, if not distained, were certainly often minimized. "We know what consumers want," was the self-confident assertion of many developers and decision makers. In the Social Age, however, such an attitude has increasingly been shown to result primarily in lost customers and dwindling market share. When consumers are given a voice through the power of social networking, development cycles are enriched through meaningful and relevant user feedback. Features aren't added just because a developer thinks they're neat; they're added because they meet or exceed the expressed expectations of the target user.

Here we return to the tremendous power of the virtuous cycle, executed most efficiently in the context of social networking. How do we know what consumers want in their software? With the combined power of open software and social networking, *they tell us!*

In addition, when solutions are designed and developed collaboratively, there is shared investment and recognizable satisfaction when the product addresses the specific concerns of a contributor. Open source development moves beyond the logistics of code sharing and management; it moves us to a model of cocreation. This is a model that thrives in an environment of openness, collaboration, and the acknowledgment of interdependence in achieving success.

IBM Lotus Sametime 7.5—Open Collaboration

As early as 1999, IBM's innovation labs were leading the way in open source development. Working with the enterprise instant messaging product Lotus Sametime, innovators explored integration with other IBM products and the use of publish/subscribe messaging as a means for unique collaboration. Although Sametime is not specifically an open source application, the development methodology—including intense user feedback—was quintessential "open" and provides helpful insights into the process.

The Sametime 7.5 development team had an existing Sametime user base to leverage for feedback and testing during the development of the upgrade. There was also an enthusiastic, knowledgeable community of early adopters for Sametime 7.5, which embraced and helped develop other innovation projects at IBM through the Technology Adoption Program (TAP). Although ultimately a resounding success, the Sametime 7.5 development process was not always smooth. Growing pains were felt as early adopter feedback was integrated with the typical software development process.

"It was difficult—painful—to the team to receive such negative feedback so early," said Sametime development team leader Konrad Lagarde.[8] "One thousand people in a week [testing] the alpha 1 was bigger than we thought. A lot of developers were not paying attention initially to the bugs that were found in the [alpha 1 and 2] releases. Alpha 3 and 4 is when we hit 5,000 [users], and the development team was starting to see the impact of their work—and starting to fix the bugs and really pay attention to things. [At one point we were managing] 2,100 bugs in bugzilla!"[9]

Because of the tremendous synergy between the user community and development team, in the course of six months, the Sametime 7.5 team ultimately released nine alphas and four betas. This is only meaningful when one considers that a milestone in typical, traditional software development is one beta *per year!* But the business result of open development was clear: Leveraging the collective intelligence of the early adopter community dramatically shortened the software development cycle, while simultaneously returning a much more usable product.

As we said, this success didn't come without a price. Change and growth can be stressful but are also usually deeply rewarding. Moving from a single beta per year in traditional software development to three, four, or even five betas in open development can certainly create stress points. Specifically the Sametime 7.5 development team faced a different kind of stress, arising from the requirement to act on and incorporate near-real-time customer feedback. As Sametime development team leader Lagarde said,

> There was a lot of churn for the team, and a lot of stress, but we saw a reality in how the product was really improving. We could validate things directly with our customer, [which] is incredible. They could vent, they could be honest, [they] could receive builds to show [that] what they were saying was being addressed—real time, on demand and immediately.[10]

Just how successful was the Sametime open development project? Before the first copy shipped to a customer, more than *50,000* enthusiastic early adopters at IBM had upgraded from Sametime 3.1 to Sametime 7.5 as their regular instant message tool.

As he reminisced about the experience, Konrad Lagarde said it perfectly: "Good software is not designed by committee; but it is validated by a community."[11]

The Culture of Open

The move to open software is a cultural movement at most organizations, an evolution of sorts, in much the same way the Social Age is an evolutionary advance from the Information Age. The evidence that open development is embraced by commercial enterprises can be seen in the drive to standardization in the context of service oriented architecture (SOA), and in the integration of existing open source as the basis for commercial offerings.

There is undeniable power in approaching solution development with an open software mind-set. Done properly, open development attracts diverse talent from outside the formal walls of an organization, who both benefit from and contribute to the solution. Which developer wouldn't benefit from having more eyes on the code? Any developer will tell you that addressing challenges and issues as early as possible is always a good thing. Less-seasoned developers can be educated on how to best approach software engineering challenges. Finally, empowering the development community, even in a traditional business, and democratizing the creation of a solution, efficiently distributes responsibility and ownership. The result is high morale and shared commitment to accomplish more.

Leadership is distributed in open development and, just as in any democracy, a few individuals help guide others to achieve the collective goal. The open software methodology is a conscious approach to create better software solutions by lowering the center of gravity or decision making to the team doing the work. This is a substantial departure from the traditional organizational hierarchy, where decisions are made at the top by managers or project managers with limited knowledge of the intricacies of the code. The loosely connected network of the open software community is a substantial business advantage over traditional software development.

Business Value Through Open Source

Open software transforms the proprietary nature of traditional solution development. For decades, consumers were confronted with the carefully shielded black box of commercial software development. Who knew how the solution worked? The attitude seemed to be, "You don't really need to know, do you? It works, doesn't it?" And when modifications were needed for specific purposes, the black box seemed more like a black hole.

With the growing popularity of open source, however, the computer code is open to essentially anyone. The reuse of the code is, therefore, much more likely, and the resulting solutions much more broadly adopted. The dawn of the Social Age brought a new mind-set that increases usage of open software solutions, lowering costs, and accelerating time to market, as illustrated in Figure 8.2. This is one of the powerful drivers for leveraging open software to deliver business value, but there are other ways it can transform your business as well.

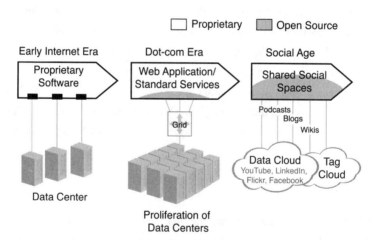

Figure 8.2 Open software is a key enabler in the evolution of IT from legacy data center to cloud computing.

Open Development and the Globally Integrated Enterprise

To understand what it takes to succeed as a globally integrated enterprise, the open software movement is a good place to start. Leveraging the many advantages of open software development is critical when managing and facilitating communities that cross geographical and organizational boundaries. Global development is not about simply hiring developers in an emerging market, as you might do at your domestic locations. Instead, global development means successfully extending the capabilities of your existing team to the places it is needed and using the talent best able to deliver on the specs. The technologies and mind-set used to successfully drive open source and open software apply to successfully building global development teams as well.

Enablement at Reduced Cost

Mature open source software has often been developed by dozens of developers and includes generally applicable features and functions. For example, most server-based open operating systems, such as Linux, come with e-mail services, which enable a company to provide the capability without custom development.

The cost of supporting an open solution is different than its development—usually less. A more readily available and affordable skill set can be used to run and support a developed product.

Participation is one of the key costs of open software and one of its major benefits. Genuine participation in development communities can strengthen the team and align specific business goals with the overall solution. In some cases, open source software is even adopted as the foundation for commercial products and services. Some commercial open source licenses for proprietary products ship with source code for ease of integration and extension. Three examples of this trend include the IBM HTTP Server, Drupal content management, and Sun Microsystems' MySQL database.[12]

IBM HTTP Server

The IBM HTTP server has long used the Apache web server as its foundation. IBM contributes developers to the Apache web server community, but more importantly it ships the software as part of its WebSphere[13] product line. Through participation and extension, IBM can provide a feature-rich web server that integrates tightly with its other products, specifically IBM WebSphere Application Server.

IBM's focus and development is not in changing the underlying web server—that's handled by the developers participating in the Apache community. Instead, IBM focuses on extending the web server as the basis for an integrated solution that is simpler and more fully featured.

Drupal

Drupal is an open source content management system (CMS) with a vibrant development community that has transformed the core solution from basic Web site building to a feature-rich collaboration platform. A few years ago, a small startup, Acquia,[14] began offering commercial products, services, and support for Drupal. Acquia packages the core Drupal engine and includes select extensions from the development community, along with its own modules.

In many ways, Acquia acts as a bridge to the open source community for its customers, ensuring the publicly available extensions have a high reliability and a well-defined release schedule. Two modules included with Acquia's distribution enables it to understand the usage of its Drupal distribution and notify customers of updates. Formal support rounds out Acquia's services, providing hesitant businesses confidence with an open source platform.

MySQL

In 2008, Sun Microsystems purchased the company that held the copyright for the extremely popular open source MySQL database. With 11 million installations, MySQL is simpler to use than many commercial counterparts. MySQL—the "M" in the LAMP open source software stack—offers enviable low maintenance and is included by Sun as part of its overall software and services portfolio.

IBM HTTP Server, Drupal, and MySQL highlight real business solutions using open source as a foundation. In many ways, open software is a natural fit with commercial opportunities because the focus of the community is on the best possible software development. In the example of Acquia, its presence actually solidifies and matures the image of the Drupal offering. Open source software can enhance a product portfolio—and a bottom line—and can often be delivered as a competitive differentiator.

Innovation Accelerator

Innovation in the software business can be tricky, especially in the context of open source. In cases where the product distinguishes a business—for example Adobe's Photoshop—open solutions are not viable options. Adobe is certainly aware of open source GIMP (GNU Image Manipulation Program) but is unlikely to use or contribute to the GIMP code. On the other hand, a company that is focused on Linux-based video manipulation might see GIMP as a complementary asset, especially if the feature is not a competitive differentiator. Where the goal is innovation, rather than a specific development platform, open source software can be a powerful innovation accelerator.

Innovation results from thoughtful design and experimentation and is crucial for distinguishing any business from the competition. To experiment—in products, processes, or services—a well-established business builds on established platforms, which accelerates innovation by providing a foundational starting point. Future innovation for competitive advantage will happen not in making adjustments to the base but in radically rethinking the capabilities on top of that base. Although this approach is most easily seen in product innovation, process and service innovation follow the same pattern.

Prototyping is a common activity in innovation and requires a design (in reality or on paper) using existing known elements. Often the process of prototype design creation and testing yields invaluable lessons and seeds ongoing improvements and transformation. Open source software facilitates and accelerates prototyping, leading more quickly to the ultimate goal—innovation.

Consider the Drupal example. With Drupal, a business can construct a content management system similar to the Acquia distribution as a way to enable Web 2.0 experiences. Perhaps a key business driver for the company is to understand user experience when searching for information. Innovating with Drupal offers distinct advantages. First, the basic capabilities already exist—content management, user registration, and so on. Second, extending the platform is easily done with PHP, a popular and easy-to-write development language. Third, the company's proprietary search engine can easily be integrated with the platform, creating a rich test environment. These three factors focus development on the business goal of understanding the way users search for information and the way searches change over time.

Leveraging open source and open software as the basis for accelerating innovation is a powerful, relatively painless approach to solution development.

Agent for Change

In the context of the open source movement, open software involves a set of principles that can drive transformative culture change in an organization. Consider the three attributes previously noted in open source software:

- The source code for the entire solution is made available for anyone to download, inspect, compile, build, use, and extend.

- The core development team is often diverse, representing individual and institutional views.

- The software is developed in a highly collaborative setting.

Wouldn't every business benefit from having more of these traits throughout the organization? When encouraged as a cultural shift, traditional behaviors can change in the context of a more open-minded approach.

First, self-motivated teams allow management to refocus on the overall organizational vision and act as a sounding board, rather than overseeing day-to-day operational execution. Power is shared in this model but so is responsibility. Operational teams in this setting are not only self-motivated but also embrace increased responsibility for the outcomes and success of their work.

Second, the traditional management team begins to value diversity in building its teams. Diversity introduces new thinking and ideas; it acts to stabilize the team's self-interested activity, exploring reasonable alternatives—a sort of check and balance. The group benefits from the variety of thought, while management gains from a team balanced through individual selection rather than top-down command and control.

Third, moving work into public forums highlights the responsibility of each individual to the shared goals of the group. Management supports an overt shift in sharing work products, as it does with software development, inviting critical thought at every step of the process.

For management, there's a trade-off in this scenario. It gives up a level of operational control, but gains—or regains—the roles of visionaries, diversity mavens, and high-performance culture czars, while retaining the ultimate power of veto. Such behaviors can take time to adopt, even with progressive teams. For a time, there might be some adjustments to the new freedoms and the increased emphasis on results, rather than on process and hierarchies.

Applying the attributes and behaviors of grassroots organizations to formal business can be a powerful by-product of the open source movement, where the focus is not on software development but on culture change.

Open Source Software Business Challenges

Open Source Software has created many business opportunities, but there remain notable challenges in leveraging these solutions. The legal issues of open source and its potential impact to the business are not widely understood. The community nature of the development environment presents another issue. A community is not an enterprise, and the specific challenges of business use are sometimes ignored or minimized in this setting. Likewise, an individual company doesn't have veto power in the community. Despite committed participation, a company might find it is outvoted by the community when it comes to the future of the solution. Finally, open source software is still software, which means there will always be bugs. Let's consider these issues in greater detail.

Legal Obligations and Issues

Copyright laws generally give authors an implicit copyright for their work, but they can also often register their work for public and legal recognition of rights to their work. For example, in the United States, these rights include reproducing the work and creating derivatives based on the original work, among others. When deciding whether to work with someone else's creation, be sure to consider the copyright holder and the restrictions of the license.

Sorting out individual copyright is best left to experienced legal counsel, but for those who choose to go it on their own, there are public licenses that define what others can do with the work. Examples of public licenses include Creative Commons, GNU, Apache, and BSD. Each license has different characteristics, which permit, prescribe, or restrict specific actions.

Legal issues tend to be the primary reason many organizations prefer to work with open source that is represented by other companies, such as IBM, Sun Microsystems, and others. Fully understanding your legal rights and obligations—preferably with the guidance of an experienced attorney—is a necessary first step when considering open source development.

Certainly Not Custom Software

Open source software is often the product of small groups of individuals that share a common vision. As development teams grow, design, and implement, decisions are often dispersed. Fragmented solutions or bloated software can result. Although this can happen in any large software organization, open source is particularly challenged in this regard.

In addition, enterprises often require specific performance, scalability, and distribution characteristics from their software—requirements sometimes absent from open source solutions. Standard corporate architectural and development practices are largely unknown to open source communities. This can mean these solutions are difficult to adopt and integrate into existing formal development environments. Considerable planning and potential participation in the open source community are sometimes required to successfully leverage open source for a specific business need.

Participation Doesn't Mean Control

Participation can be a key to influencing open source projects, but participation does not necessarily mean control. If there are organization-specific capabilities that are incompatible with the goals of the open source project, those capabilities might need to be developed outside the community. Control also cannot be exerted by a business when it comes to the longevity of an open source community. There is no formal agreement that ensures the developed product will exist in the future, and no guarantee that the community will remain intact. Participation is clearly a line of defense for a community that dissolves, but it only partially addresses the risk. The vitality of the community is a critical part of evaluating the maturity of an open source project.

Software Is Software

With all the wisdom gained in his decades in the computer business, Fredrick Brooks, Jr., soberly reminds us that software is software, and all software has bugs; including—we're sure he'd agree—community-developed software. Despite the potentially increased number of people reviewing open source code, bugs will always be part of software development.

> *"...Our ideas themselves are faulty, so we have bugs."*
>
> Frederick Brooks, Jr.,
> *The Mythical Man-Month*[15]

Content Management Systems (CMS)

Content management systems (CMS) are extremely powerful tools enabling people with limited technical skills to author, review, publish, and manage web content. Popular commercial CMS products include Fatwire, Vignette, Interwoven, Adobe Contribute Publishing Server, and Lotus Web Content Management. In this space, the open source options outnumber commercial offerings 2:1. Wordpress, Joomla, and Drupal are popular open source CMS tools. Web content administration and authoring is done with these tools through a web browser, so changes to the site appear instantaneously. By comparison, with traditional static content replication systems, changing even one word on a Web site might take hours and involve half a dozen people.

CMSs are the foundation for building much larger communication and collaboration spaces. Some CMS systems, such as Wordpress, are best-known for their blogging capabilities. Joomla is known for traditional web content and site creation. Drupal offers a far more complex set of tools that integrate many capabilities into a single platform. When compared with commercial offerings, these open source tools are extremely lightweight—typically "one-click" installs.

Support for custom business processes and workflow management are the reason for the complexity of most commercial CMSs. Open source content management tools are great for small and medium businesses that are not as concerned about rigorous, auditable transactions.

All the open source packages mentioned here offer custom themes enabling you to match your business' design standards. The more specific the requirements, the better the technology fit. Understand the role of open source in your environment and plan accordingly.

A Closing Thought

Open software is another manifestation of the powerful collaboration possible using Social Age tools and methods. Whether a small group of developers gathers around a specific project, or a worldwide team collaborates on a major corporate initiative, open software provides the necessary development framework to make it happen.

Summary

- Open source tools push against the traditional hierarchical nature of organizations and focus on people connections.

- Open source is merely a subset of capabilities that support grassroots-style workforces. As businesses continue to grow beyond local borders, the flexibility of their workforce and the technology that enables them will be a major success factor.

- Keep in mind that free is not always free of expenses. The costs of a commercial offering should always be compared with the costs of "free" open source solutions. The axiom "You get what you pay for" applies in the world of open source and in the commercial software market.

- Smart selection and application of open source tools, based on your business goals and culture, can enable your workforce in profound ways. Incremental introduction and careful future upgrades of these tools help ensure success. Even if you end up with a commercial offering in a particular area, open source is an excellent way to determine if a specific capability will catch on.

- Creating and enabling the grassroots culture in your organization, using open source technology as a starting point, is one of the most significant ways to generate growth for your business in the Social Age.

9
Social Brain and the Ideation Process

The dense, seductive aroma floods your brain as you open the door. Your senses come alive as you hear the milk being steamed by the *barista* and the grinder at work on another batch of Sumatra. You still haven't figured out why they call the small size cup "tall," but you decide it doesn't matter. You're just here for the coffee.

Some would argue that Starbucks has achieved a bit of coffee perfection with its powerful, exotic-sounding brews. Perhaps, however, you have an idea about improving on that perfection. If you do, why not let them know? It's easy enough to do at mystarbucksidea.com.

Mystarbucksidea.com is one example of an exploding trend in the corporate world today—to explore and act on ideas from a community of interested volunteers to grow and more effectively compete in a rapidly changing world. Competition today, as any business person will tell you, is fiercer than ever. Accelerated globalization and advances in technology drive companies to constantly seek innovative ideas that differentiate them from the competition and allow them to respond quickly to changing business dynamics. And growth—perhaps even survival—depends on constant innovation.

But where do innovative ideas come from? Your top management? R&D? University research? These are good choices, but, as shown in Figure 9.1, the executives who responded to a global CEO study overwhelmingly identified their employees, customers, and business partners as the top sources for innovative ideas.[1]

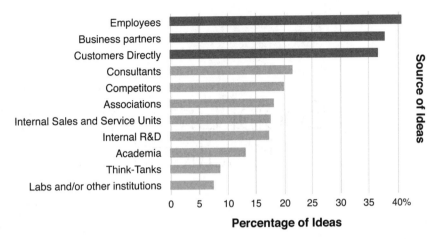

Figure 9.1 The best business ideas and innovations come from employees and business partners, according to a 2006 survey of CEOs.

Before moving away too quickly from this bit of information, consider that these survey results represent a profound *reversal* from historical precedent. If this survey had been taken 50 years ago, or even 30 or 20 years ago, the results might have been the opposite of those shown in Figure 9.1. The consequences of relying on internal R&D only, or on the brainpower of a few C-level executives, can perhaps best be seen in the disaster currently unfolding in many companies today. While other, more nimble companies were busy improving their products and bringing to market what their customers were demanding, many industrial-age companies were focused on "business as usual." In the Social Age, smart companies have discovered that tapping into the collective sentiments and innovative thinking of their customers, employees, and partners is indispensable to long-term success. Without social networking, such access to the collective mind can be possible, but it is difficult and expensive. Now, with wikis, blogs, forums, and other social tools, the incredible power of the thoughts of all these constituencies is literally at our fingertips.

The Social Brain and the Ideation Process

To fully appreciate the incredible power of social networking for driving innovation at your business, we need to look first at the power of the many minds that make up our social networks. In earlier chapters, we reviewed the tools and patterns of social networking transformation that have reshaped our world—making it more informed, connected, and smarter than ever. The Social Age, however, is not about wiki servers, blog interfaces, and survey results; the Social Age is about *human connections*. People want to connect with other people. Social networking tools are merely the conduit through which people connect.

As with any technology, much good can arise from the instantaneous information, increased social connections, and open collaboration available in our world today. A socially networked world can foster increased cultural understanding, peace, and growth. In the Social Age, perhaps more than ever before, people and businesses have an extraordinary opportunity to use social networking to collaborate, generate new ideas, and bring to market the innovations that will drive the next wave of economic and societal growth.

Maximizing Your Innovative Mind

Behind all this unprecedented social interaction is the miraculous human brain. From the brain arise all new ideas and social impulses. Great minds are constantly thinking of ideas to make a better world and about ways to translate those ideas into new innovations and products.

It has long been understood that some environments are just healthier for the human brain. Environments—especially work environments—that challenge us and foster our creativity bring out the best in us. By contrast, organizations that don't foster creativity just as quickly waste this tremendous resource within each employee. "Use it or lose it" is just as true for our brains as it is for our muscles! Exercise your brain regularly and it becomes agile, quick, and resilient. Corporations that encourage social networking activities and social tools for collaboration not only reduce the degrees of separation between their employees, but also provide a work environment that can be conducive to reducing mental stress and generating new ideas.

Social neuroscience describes patterns in the brain related to controlling motor skills and instinctive social needs. As early as the mid-19th century, when German physician and physiologist Emil Du Bois-Reymond (1818-1896) first identified the relationship between electrical current and nerve function, we recognized there is something unique about the human brain.[2] As we explored further, using breakthrough technologies like magnetic resonance imaging (MRI),[3] it became apparent that our brains are what make us social animals. Further, these studies have helped us understand there is a division between the unconscious and conscious mind. While we spend years training the conscious part of our brain through formal education, job training, and our cultural and social environment, it is the unconscious mind— the part of our brain we can't consciously manipulate—that gets leveraged in many unexpected and productive ways.

This unconscious brain appears to have some cognitive patterns built in that are shared by all humans. Emotions and visualization of objects, for example, happen in the same part of the brain regardless of your gender, race, or social background. Exciting new neuro-technologies use these standard signals to essentially "read" our brains. As we said before, MRIs can pick up these signals, and now these new devices are programmed to pick up on some of our basic instinctive thoughts. As much as we think of ourselves as unique—and we are—a large part of our brain has been standardized by the process of evolution. With our growing understanding of the amazing functioning of the brain, incredible technology advances are already beginning to appear.

Thought-Based Interfaces: Fiction or Reality?

Previously only a science-fiction writer's dream device, Emotiv Inc.'s EPOC neuro-headset, based on noninvasive electroencephalography, leads the way in *thought-based* interaction with computers. Leveraging the things we know about the electrical activity of the brain, along with the incredible processing power of today's computers, Emotiv claims that EPOC can, at a relatively sophisticated level, read the brain electrical activity (thoughts) of users and their physiological responses. For the first time, this capability allows interaction with computers in a more human way.

"Why do we fly people thousands of miles for a meeting, instead of opting for a much less expensive phone call?" said Tan Le, Emotiv's president and cofounder, seen in Figure 9.2. Answering her own question, she said, "Because there is so much more to human communication than just the voice. Body language, posture, eye contact—all give us valuable information about our relationships. EPOC allows us to begin interacting with our computers in similar ways."[4]

The potential impact of EPOC and similar technologies in the Social Age is profound and perhaps a little unsettling. For example, a gamer can use EPOC to move his avatar through a virtual world. Or by generating a high level of excitement, the gamer can invoke superpowers in his avatar. Le said that a group of children Emotiv brought in enjoyed playing with a computer wizard game using the keyboard and joystick. The children were then given the EPOC neuro-headset and again asked to play the wizard game. The children described their keyboard and joystick experience as "manipulating the wizard." When using the neuro-headset that enabled them to move the wizard with just their thoughts, however, the children commented that they *were* the wizard. As Emotiv is demonstrating, by removing computer interfaces and going directly to the neuron wave messages, a deeper sense of participation in the computer game is enabled.

The ability of our thoughts to control computer applications promises to have incredibly positive benefits in areas beyond just gamers who look for a totally immersive gaming experience. Music, art, market research, and prosthesis and robotic control in medicine are among countless applications that can benefit from thought-controlled computers. Devices such as EPOC, and the things these devices can tell us about the highly predictable functioning of our brains, will have profound implications for social networking tools.

Figure 9.2 Emotiv founder Tan Le with EPOC neuro-headset.

Genographic

We gain great insight into the predictability of human social behavior when we understand the incredible "standardization" of the human brain and, more importantly, of our subconscious mind. As a recent landmark study helped demonstrate, our brains have a great deal in common, whether we're from Kenya or Kalamazoo.

If you want to be a part of the Genographic project, you can still order a kit like this one at www.nationalgeographic.com/genographic.

In a research partnership between the National Geographic Society and IBM, DNA samples from thousands of people around the world revealed the reason we're all "wired" the same—we all have the same parents! The Genographic study, which I had the privilege of leading on the IBM side, concluded that all modern humans descended from a small group of a few thousand people, who lived in east Africa around 70,000 years ago (see Figure 9.3).

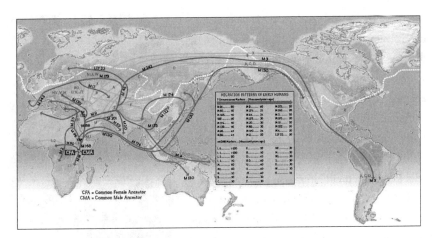

Figure 9.3 Genographic map tracing the origins of humans to two common ancestors in sub-Saharan African (CFA and CMA).[5]

The reality is we all come from the same place in a long and beautiful evolutionary path. Social contact and interaction is primal, and part of what makes us human. We need this interaction; and in the Social Age, this primal instinct is expressed very clearly in social networking.

Ironically, the extensive and highly productive interaction between teams from IBM and the National Geographic Society actually helped demonstrate the reality of this social instinct.

The Social Age spirit of collaboration that began with the Genographic project in 2005 continues today as Genographic researchers increasingly use blogs to work even more efficiently. Above all, the Genographic Project demonstrates—beyond any shadow of a doubt—our common ancestry. It is this common heritage that helps explain why our brain's electrical patterns, physiological responses, and social instincts appear to follow a common blueprint across cultures. Today, the Genographic Project continues to release new findings and to offer everyone the opportunity to learn more about the way they fit into the "family of man."

The Collective Brain

Each of us have approximately 100 billion nerve cells (neurons), interacting with each other via tiny electric charges, in a process that solidifies memories, drives reasoning, and mediates social behavior. Every brain is unique; the external surface of the brain folds in distinctive ways for each of us, reminiscent of fingerprints. That's right—you're as unique as you always thought you were!

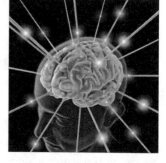

Now imagine what happens when you connect your brain activity to the brain activity of many others. You quickly create a collective value that is far greater than the sum of its parts.

In the Social Age, we face an unprecedented host of challenges and projects of global scope, with profound implications for society: global warming, economic uncertainty, population growth, and political upheaval, among others. Many, if not all of these challenges are already being studied, often guided by new social tools.

Engineering's Grand Challenge is a collaborative effort sponsored by The National Academy of Engineering, currently under way among the best scientists and engineers in the world (Figure 9.4). The Challenge's objective is to generate new proposals to solve some the thorniest problems in the 21st century.[6] As the Grand Challenge demonstrates, nonprofit organizations, academia, and businesses are all exploiting the power of social networking to generate ideas that will make the world a better place to live.

Figure 9.4 The National Academy of Engineering Web site for the Grand Challenges for Engineering.

Social Networking and Brain Chemistry

The brain is an electric machine that processes both physical and mental stress in the same way. An emotionally abusive environment causes your brain to release *cortisol*, referred to as the stress hormone—the identical compound produced by your adrenal cortex under physically painful conditions. Cortisol lowers your immune system, increases your blood pressure, and decreases bone formation. Perhaps not surprisingly, cortisol also reduces thinking capacity.

MRI studies provide hard evidence that social pain and feelings of unfairness appear in the same location of the brain as physical pain—the brain doesn't distinguish between them.[7] Similarly, the National Institute of Mental Health's Thomas Insel and Stanford University's Russell Fernald point to growing evidence that suggests that social isolation and social separation are health risk factors comparable to well-known risk factors like smoking and obesity.[8]

SocialAge
Factoid

Not exercising your brain? You're losing 85,000 brain cells a day!

Do a crossword puzzle. It can help!

By contrast, positive, supportive social interactions cause changes in the adult brain similar to the changes brought on by feelings of love and admiration for an exquisite artwork or good food. Feelings of meaningful social contribution and connections at work provide a sense of stability and security that *releases* stress, limits the production of cortisol, and thus increases the ability of employees to think. Are you a runner, or do you enjoy a good workout? Then, you've probably experienced the opposite of stress hormones: *endorphins*—the natural pain reliever. Produced by the hypothalamus and the pituitary gland, endorphins are experienced during pleasurable events, excitement, and strenuous exercise.[9]

The formula to lower cortisol and raise endorphins is simple: lower stress in the work environment, which ensures a workforce that functions at optimal mental capacity to outpace the competition in generating new ideas. A collaborative and friendly work environment helps employees be more productive, think more clearly, and be more satisfied in their work.

Scientists have discovered that a lack of mental exercise is one of the main culprits for declining mental agility as we age.[10] Just like muscles, brains need exercise! And what better place to exercise our brains than at our place of work, doing the thing we do best? Social networking with others helps you exercise and use your brain in ways you never thought you could, across all parts of your company. (See the "Maximize Your Brain!" sidebar.)

Corporate Army Knife

Train your brain to be alert and sensitive to changes around you and to the market forces that can radically change the way your business works. Think of your brain as a Swiss Army knife to which you continually add new "blades" and "tools" of education or experience.

An employee's success depends on his or her ability to constantly think, quickly adapt, and stay in front of market forces that can affect your market and your business model. Merely lowering costs by working hard and continually improving existing processes is not necessarily the way to succeed in today's light-speed business environment—cost-savings can take you only so far. Many companies recognize this and look first at their innovation processes for answers. Here is a real brain exercise: Create innovations that reinvent your business model or that create new products that *beat the competition.*

Perhaps the best way to encourage innovative thinking is to establish a formal process that encourages employees to come up with new ideas and rewards employees who contribute ideas that are most helpful to the business. Empowering your employees to collaborate in business transformation efforts and idea generation helps create a team atmosphere and sends a strong message to the rest of the organization that the business values out-of-the-box thinking. We take a deeper look at ideation in the next section, and in Chapter 10, "Social Innovation," we explore the important components of a formal innovation process.

Maximize Your Brain!

- **Search for activities that exercise your brain**—Start new projects, create new products for your business, brainstorm to solve problems.

- **Maintain low levels of stress hormones**—Avoid toxic work environments and stressful situations. If you're in a job that's not conducive to your continuous skills improvement or compatible with your temperament, or is not open to your ideas, maybe it's time for a new job!

- **Maintain camaraderie with coworkers**—Be part of the *solution*, creating a welcoming and friendly working environment.

- **Increase your social networking activities**—This can expand your circle of influence and generate an increased sense of security and belonging.

- **Increase endorphins in your brain**—Run in the morning or lift weights after work. (Check with your doctor first!) Physical exercise reduces stress hormones in your body and releases endorphins that help you think more clearly.

- **Stay focused**—Challenge yourself through personal goals and compete against your own goals—not against the goals of others. Looking forward to the accomplishment of a goal keeps you focused.

- **Get your Zs!**—The brain needs at least eight hours sleep to recover; constant sleep deprivation can lead to an exhausted brain.

Social Ideation in the Enterprise

As we've already discovered, social software, such as wikis and blogs, is the ideal enabling technology to gather, share, and act on a wealth of innovative ideas from diverse participants across organizational and geographic boundaries. In the second half of this chapter, we look at several companies that have mastered collaborative innovation by using social software to drive their ideation process.

What Is Social Ideation?

Ideation occurs when individuals or groups generate ideas, concepts, and hypotheses that can be explored or acted upon. Ideation is about thinking abstract thoughts that apply to a specific situation.

Typically, ideation is a formal, facilitated process of limited duration generally referred to as brainstorming sessions. Although these traditional sessions can generate great ideas, ideation is most valuable when it is *ongoing*. An open, collaborative, online ideation environment is ideal for this purpose. When targeting a specific topic or problem, however, an "ideation event" of limited duration might be the best choice. For this purpose, IBM sponsors ideation "Jams" that engage our employees, customers, partners, academics, and other industry experts. We look at Jams in more detail later in this chapter.

Business Benefits

Social ideation is a collaborative process that transcends organizational silos and geographical and cultural differences. As we explored in Chapter 3, "Wikis: Bringing the Crowds to You," when large numbers of individuals collaborate, from diverse backgrounds and areas of expertise, the results can be amazing. Experts from all parts of the business collaborate to enhance the original idea and build on it, often taking it into different, even more innovative directions.

Companywide ideation initiatives offer a host of benefits, such as cost-savings, process improvements, productivity enhancements, innovative business model changes, new areas of opportunity, and ideas to enhance employee well-being, among others. Extend social ideation to include customers and partners, and you can identify customer satisfaction improvements, quickly address unmet client needs, and capture unique business opportunities. Finally, social ideation not only captures innovative ideas but can also help speed them to market.

Social software that provides a collaborative platform accelerates the ideation process along with your company's business agenda. Forums, wikis, blogs, microblogging, social tagging and bookmarking, social ratings and reviews, and file-sharing tools can all facilitate social ideation.

As we mentioned at the beginning of this chapter, mystarbucksidea.com ("MSI" to its community) allows consumers to provide suggestions on ways that Starbucks can improve its coffee or its stores. The community votes on and comments on favorite suggestions. The mission of mystarbucksidea.com is to help Starbucks connect with its customers and in a way to cocreate the future of the company.

MSI has four key components—Share, Vote, Discuss, and See. Each of these steps promotes a virtuous cycle of discussion, interaction, and ultimately action that benefits both customer and brand. From the day it was launched, MSI has been a hit. In less than six months, nearly 75,000 ideas had poured in (no pun intended!), many of which were acted on by Starbucks.

InnoCentive

Crowdsourcing as a concept came to be more widely known after James Surowiecki's *Wisdom of Crowds* was published in 2004.[11] But some com-

panies had been practicing the "crowds" concept well before then. Pharmaceutical giant Eli Lilly launched InnoCentive.com as an in-house innovation incubator.[12] The company originally used the site to post problems that its employees had been unable to solve, and from the beginning the site saw positive results, immediately helping Lilly solve more than one-third of the problems posted.

InnoCentive has since evolved into its own independent company and now serves as a global, online marketplace where organizations in need of innovation can tap into a global network of more than 160,000 of the world's brightest problem solvers.

InnoCentive brings together "seekers" of answers to problems and "solvers," those crowd-sourced experts around the world who provide possible solutions. To incentivize registered solvers, seekers offer significant financial awards for the best solutions. InnoCentive has an eight-year track record of success and to date has paid out more than $3.5 million in awards to more than 300 winning problem solvers.

ThinkPlace

From the earliest days of IBM, founder T.J. Watson recognized the importance of employee participation in the innovation process. This participation began as a simple wooden box, labeled "IDEAS," into which employees could drop their suggestions. Eventually this rustic—and somewhat inefficient—system morphed into the agile, socially networked ThinkPlace, an always-on ideation portal, open to all employees in more than 2,000 locations and 230 countries worldwide. Participants can submit ideas, comment on the ideas of others, add to ideas, rate them, and follow the progress of an idea.

ThinkPlace goals include

- Provide a single, consistent global management system for innovation that supports the management of new ideas.

- Create a culture in which collaboration and interaction across silos is considered an essential element of innovation.

- Educate employees on your company's approach to innovation.

- Reward innovators and innovative ideas in tangible, visible ways.

Successful Ideation: An End-to-End Process

More important than having good social ideation tools is having an effective end-to-end innovation *process*. Identify the problems and challenges to solve, as illustrated in Figure 9.5. Then leverage social software to generate and collaborate on ideas, provide incubation and prototyping support, furnish programs to validate the ideas, and document the value realized, and finally, to reward contributors.

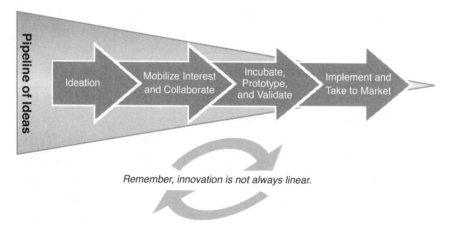

Figure 9.5 Workflow from ideation to market introduction.

A unique, critical role in any successful ideation event or site is that of catalysts. Catalysts are volunteers from all parts of your organization who work with idea submitters to help them get visibility for their idea, access incubation resources, prepare business cases, and introduce others to their idea. IBM Program Director Paul Baffes created the catalyst role at IBM and spoke about its importance in maintaining innovation momentum:

> Catalysts are a key part of the "engine" that drives innovation. Their role, as the name implies, is to act as an extra boost to help idea submitters get their ideas moved forward.... Catalysts are facilitators that help make connections, offer advice, bridge gaps, make introductions, and generally become a partner for idea submitters.

You might want to consider doing as we did at IBM, and reward catalysts for successfully facilitating numerous ideas and helping to recruit and train other catalysts. We offer the rank of Master Catalyst to those who reach certain performance benchmarks.

By the end of 2008, 19,000 ideas had been submitted with more than 150,000 employees participating, and more than 1,000 IBMers volunteered as ThinkPlace catalysts. Ideas adopted and documented for business impact were highlighted as "wins," and to date more than 500 of these wins have resulted in millions of dollars in business value for IBM. Value is realized through cost-savings, productivity improvements, revenue growth, and employee well-being.

Jams: Social Ideation Events

> "Jams have helped change our culture and the fundamental way we collaborate across our business." —IBM chairman and CEO Sam Palmisano

For nearly a decade, IBM has used Jams to capture the collective voice of IBM (Figure 9.6). These companywide brainstorming events have become a management tool of choice for business collaboration and enterprisewide transformation. Jams use Web 2.0 technologies to provide a social ideation environment, along with processes that elicit ideas from a large number of diverse participants around a specific topic. Data mining is used during and after a Jam to discern key themes for action.

IBM's Jam Program Office director Liam Cleaver commented that Jams share some of the characteristics of crowd sourcing. "They are a way to reach out online to a broad group of people to help solve a problem," he said. According to Cleaver, Jams go one step beyond crowd sourcing because "...we go out across a whole enterprise or industry. It's a defined population helping to solve a business problem tapping into their collective smarts and passion for the topic."

At their core, Jams are "innovation events." They are a powerful engine for change across an entire organization, during times when the collective brainpower and support of a defined population is critical to the success of a new strategy or vision. "Jams are a business tool," said IBM senior manager Kristine Lawas. "They're not a free-for-all social networking experience. The user experience of a Jam is deliberately orchestrated so that everyone has an equal voice."

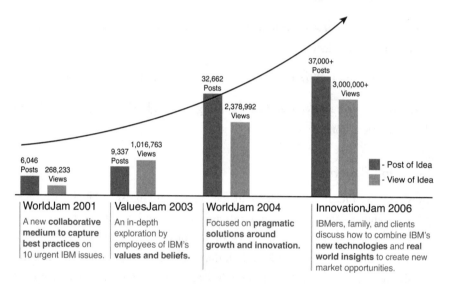

Figure 9.6   The interest and effectiveness of Jams have consistently increased at IBM.

Anatomy of a Jam

The time-limited nature of Jams, typically 72 hours of intense global collaboration, creates a sense of corporate excitement or "buzz" that drives participation. The online event, however, is only the culmination of a period of focused preparation. Depending on audience size, a typical Jam requires between 6 and 16 weeks of preparation, followed by 1 to 3 weeks for post-Jam analyses. As with any event, the communication and marketing of the event (intent, desired outcome, schedule, and so on) is critical to the Jam's success and to the adoption of the post-event ideas and plans.

A successful Jam is typically organized around three to four strategic topics with collaboration taking place in corresponding forums. Each strategic area is moderated by a senior leader who helps guide the discussions and refines or refocuses it as needed. Consider using real-time text mining and analysis tools created to analyze comments and synthesize them into key themes, visible to participants in theme clouds. Other features, such as online polls, can help connect (and re-connect) users with the event.

Four key elements are common to every Jam:

- **Online collaborative discussions**—For audiences ranging in size from a few hundred to hundreds of thousands

- **Innovation events**—To capture the pulse of the group or solicit specific ideas to critical business issues

- **Jam hosts and facilitators**—To guide participants to build on each other's ideas

- **Real-time text analyses and data mining**—To highlight emerging trends and synthesize actionable results

Jamming Benefits

Jams are powerful catalysts to kick-start the innovation process and highlight strategic issues and challenges. They can transcend culture, language, and geographic distance to harness the collective knowledge of the organization. A rich store of priceless ideas and comments are available both during and after the Jam, which can uncover key themes and hot topics. Prioritizing this data and using it as an ongoing source of ideas offers tremendous long-term benefits.

Social Ideation Best Practices

- **Executive buy-in**—Get visible commitment from senior leadership for the social ideation process from idea submissions to idea adoption and rewards.

- **End-to-end innovation**—Establish an innovation management *process*, addressing all steps from ideation through adoption.

- **Advance budget commitment**—Identify available investment resources, not just for Jam costs, but also for prototyping and adoption.

- **Maintain cultural focus**—Provide participants with motivation, trust, and shared rewards.

- **Tools**—Make online enablement tools easy-to-use, open, engaging, accessible, and integrated.

- **Peer evaluation**—Provide for evaluation that includes rating and tagging.

- **Catalysts**—Help idea submitters move promising ideas forward.

- **Communicate-communicate-communicate**—Establish guidelines for participation and success stories. Follow up with participants and be sure to thank them for their participation. (Good communication also encourages business leaders to adopt ideas.)

- **Quantify results**—Create a methodology to quantify the value of ideas: cost-savings, employee well-being, revenue growth, and so on.

Summary

- People want to connect with other people. Social networking tools are merely the conduit through which people connect.

- Great minds are constantly thinking of ideas to make a better world and ways to translate those ideas into new innovations and products.

- Social networking connects the amazing power of individual brains to create a collective value that is far greater that the sum of its parts.

- A favorable work environment is the key to innovation. Feelings of meaningful social contribution and connections at work provide a sense of stability and security that *releases* stress.

- Ideation occurs when individuals or groups (in the case of *social* ideation) generate ideas, concepts, and hypotheses that can be explored or acted upon.

- Social software that connects people, locates experts, and provides a collaborative platform that accelerates the ideation process along with your company's business agenda.

- Jams are powerful catalysts for change across an entire organization, during times when the collective brainpower and support of a defined population is critical to the success of a new strategy or vision.

10
Social Innovation

In earlier chapters, we established that innovation is a key byproduct of collaboration. As we also demonstrated, innovation is not just about technology, business models, or policies but also about *social* innovation.

Social software is at the core of this innovation, enabling us to create and support new social structures as a way to explore, develop, and adopt new ideas. Establishing a culture of innovation depends on effective communication, strong relationships, and increasing levels of trust. The right social tools can make a tremendous difference to the innovation process and the pace of business transformation.

The challenge for a business leader is to scale the effect of social software beyond individual value, to provide lasting benefit to the organization, and to the broader economy. In a 2008 IBM study that included more than 750 executives from around the world, collaboration was identified as key to fostering innovation and growth.[1] The challenge is making it happen. In Chapter 9, "Social Brain and the Ideation Process," we discussed the role of social software in the ideation process. In this chapter, we move to the next step, to explore the ways social software can drive innovation and technology adoption, including specific guidance on bringing social innovation to your organization.

Creation of an Innovation Community

Social networking communities are not about the tools but about the people. Tools are just that—tools. That's why I called this book *The Social Factor* and not *The Social Tools.*

The challenge for businesses today is to create an effective, collaborative environment for innovation, leveraging the incredible power of social networking. Great ideas and great innovations come from the minds of *people*, and socially networked innovation programs are a vital means for empowering people to effectively collaborate in an ever-more-complex world. A successful innovation community ensures that wikis and blogs are not only social venues, but that they also measurably advance the objectives of the company, including the growth of the bottom line.

Above all, the mark of an efficient innovation process is that everything is as easy as possible. Nurture innovators by encouraging them to submit ideas they believe will be of interest to the community. Respond quickly to innovator submissions, using a formal evaluation process that includes an interview and an overview of the innovation program. Be specific about the obligations of the innovator and what the innovator can expect from the innovation community.

Three primary functions are vital to any effective innovation program (see Figure 10.1). In whatever way possible, remove roadblocks to the process of innovation. Employees are too busy with other priorities to struggle with systems—or people!—who stand in the way of their innovation. Second, make wide use of social tools to ensure that innovators can easily reach early adopters and receive feedback on their innovation. Finally, get people excited! A weekly newsletter (or biweekly if you're short on time) provides a regular reminder about new offerings on your innovation site, along with success stories about innovations that graduated from the program and are now saving time or producing revenue for your company. Consider promoting your innovation program through an organized campaign that includes low-cost giveaways such as ID belt clips and pens with the logo of the program.

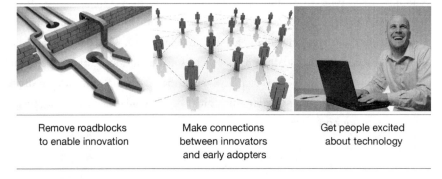

Remove roadblocks to enable innovation	Make connections between innovators and early adopters	Get people excited about technology

Figure 10.1 An innovation program leverages technology and social networking to nurture and encourage innovation.

By leveraging your IT infrastructure and innovation program, you can quickly and efficiently move ideas from abstract concept, to concrete proposal, to prototype, to solution. Innovators should have access to the entire innovation community to test their ideas and receive feedback to improve their solutions. In many ways, an innovation program feeds on itself as ideas are shared across the community.

The "innovation factory" concept, shown in Figure 10.2, illustrates the way an idea is transformed by an innovation community into a prototype. The prototype is evaluated by the community, which provides additional feedback to refine the solution. After several iterations, the solution can be deployed externally. Customers and Independent Software Vendors (ISVs) provide feedback to better tune the solution for the intended market. Finally, the solution can be packaged as a software offering or deployed internally to a production environment.

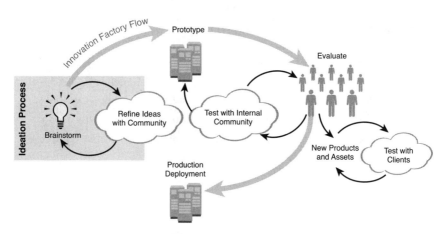

Figure 10.2 This figure illustrates the Innovation Factory Workflow to harvest innovation across your business. This workflow extends from the ideation process to the hardening of an idea into a new product or IT efficiency into the production environment.

The innovation team that supports all this activity should include experts in consulting, project management, technology and infrastructure, marketing, communications, and design. Eliminating the barriers to innovation is the primary focus of an innovation program. Although the combination of an innovation Web site and the team's vast range of expertise will remove practical barriers for participants in your innovation program, the availability of IT hosting for the program might pose a different set of challenges. To overcome the infrastructure challenges cost-effectively, a dynamic and elastic cloud infrastructure environment should be designed for the innovation program, as we discussed in Chapter 6, "Cloud Computing Paradigm."

Innovation Program Roles

- **Innovators**—Innovators want to make things better. They're dissatisfied with the status quo. They want to see real change, and they're driven to contribute to that change. They are highly technical and lead the creation of innovation.

- **First adopters**—Not everyone can be first, and not everyone wants to be. First adopters are a group of hard-core adopters. They're more tolerant than most people of buggy code, and they see the value in giving feedback on the first alpha version of the latest technology. Although innovators are driven to create, first adopters are driven to test. By completing quantitative scorecards and stimulating discussion in wikis, first adopters are leading the pack helping to accelerate innovation.

- **Early adopters**—A technical community that is willing to try new, relatively stable technologies. They're passionate about testing technology and new solutions. Most importantly, they want to give feedback to innovators directly, suggesting ways to make their solutions better. Early adopters' voices and opinions are strong, and their feedback is invaluable to improve new technologies.

Innovation and Technology Adoption Process

Building on the innovation factory concept, innovations begin with a proposal describing the new concept and the value to the business. The evaluation team then reviews and gathers additional information about the proposal. At this point, the evaluation team might act as advocates or mentors, gathering technical resources to support the innovators, obtaining IT resources, and fostering communities to support the evaluation of the new concept.

The innovation process is composed of several phases:

- **Initial value assessment**—The first-adopter community collaborates to provide qualitative feedback. Innovation concepts are assessed in this phase for potential value delivered, weighed against a risk assessment based on past experience.

- **Early adopter feedback**—If the offering passes the first step, it is handed to a literal cast of thousands, representing the business' internal early-adopter community. This group installs, uses, and tests the limits of the new application, providing feedback through forums and wikis. The innovation team aggregates this feedback and compiles usage statistics, user satisfaction details, and other metrics.

- **Value proposition**—In this phase, the innovation community uses a value assessment to evaluate the solution, which is then combined with the early adopters' feedback. A "value number" and a general assessment relating to the offering is the result. This result can lead to the graduation of the offering to become a formal product, a product enhancement, or a part of the internal IT production environment.

- **Graduation**—Graduation represents the movement of an innovation into the next phase of its lifecycle. When an innovation demonstrates, through metrics and assessments, that it has clear business value, the innovation program provides a conduit to extend the reach of the innovation to the business units. Each innovation might be different in scope and overall strategy, so graduation is also relative to the solution. Some move quickly into production, whereas others might continue for a time in the program until a product plan release is fully developed.

Innovation forums, provided as an integral part of the program infrastructure, yield invaluable insight, user comments, and ideas about each offering. Forums provide a centralized repository in which to gather information relating to software defects, device issues, usability problems, and features not initially considered by the application development team. It is the social interaction between the early adopters who use the code, and the innovators who put forward the solution, that results in a continuous refinement of the application.

The innovation factory process encourages the harvesting of new ideas, but the value to the business occurs only when innovators effectively interact with early adopters to make use of the innovation. When this synergy occurs, value flows to innovators because they gain the insight of passionate users who understand the business pain points and opportunities. The innovation factory process includes the generation of an idea marketplace where innovators are encouraged to share ideas and assets that can accelerate the innovation process. The production cycle is also significantly shortened because an audience of early adopters always stands ready to test and provide feedback for the innovators.

Businesses benefit from well-defined innovation programs because they can help accelerate the identification of new technologies that can generate new business opportunities. At the same time innovation programs can generate quantifiable return on the investment (ROI) through improvements on delivery time and product quality. Social tools play an important role for innovation programs because employees become more productive and engaged with their ideas when the community expresses interest in the new concept. Figure 10.3 illustrates the value of an innovation marketplace to innovators and early adopters.

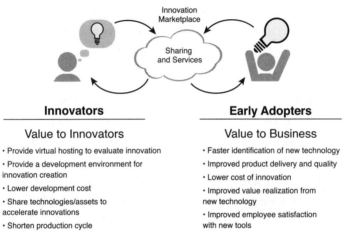

Figure 10.3 Innovation programs provide value to innovators and early adopters and can ignite your business with new ideas and products to keep you ahead of competitors.

Managed Anarchy

To bypass some of the bureaucracy associated with project plans and the formal waterfall development process, I instituted a "managed anarchy" process (see Figure 10.4). This process allowed multiple competing ideas or implementations of an idea to be developed simultaneously and battle each other. Management did not select solutions, but instead the community was the final arbiter. The "knowledge of crowds" proved to be an effective means to accomplish better innovations in less time, by leveraging community feedback early in the process to correct costly mistakes. This process provided concrete feedback to innovators, and even when their solutions were not selected for graduation, the process provided a helpful educational experience.

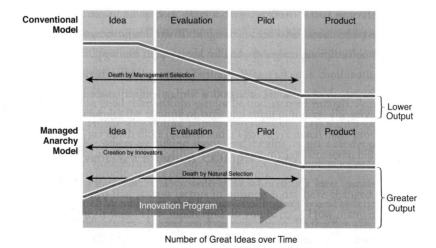

Figure 10.4 Advantages of Managed Anarchy over traditional waterfall development process are illustrated here. When teams compete, and are free to express ideas through social tools, more innovation is generated during the evaluation process. The result is a greater number of new products and production efficiencies.

Many companies' product teams have recently recognized the value of innovation programs as a way to run their internal pilots or supplement their beta programs, and several high-profile software products have been brought through this process to take advantage of the innovation community.

Managed anarchy is also an excellent process for sharing niche applications (also called situational applications[2]), and tools that service the "long tail" of business requirements. This long tail of requirements usually falls outside of regular application development efforts. Teams with needs for specialized tools or information usually remain dissatisfied with formal production solutions created by IT organizations because their needs remain unfulfilled. These kind of situations are typical of software needs represented by the right side of the "long tail," where software has low volume demand but nevertheless generates great value to its users. This niche application market of "situational applications" focuses on rapid construction of "just good enough" tools to meet a wide array of transient business needs, rather than trying to discover the next great innovation. A great illustration of a situational application is the Genographic Project discussed in Chapter 9. The initial focus of that project was on meeting transient business needs the scientists had for gathering DNA sampling, but the result was an elegant and useful solution for a project that has spanned several years.

Technology Adoption Program, an IBM Case Study

As we consider the factors that are vital to an effective innovation program, we need to acknowledge that although communication across the enterprise is crucial, different communities have different needs. To be well received by the target audience, some innovation activities call for customization and fine-tuning. For example, I started an innovation program at IBM in 2004 called the Technology Adoption Program (TAP). Its primary target was IBM early technology adopters, and the program was heavily tilted toward an audience that was assumed to be technically "deep"—the IBM "geeks."

To keep the technical community engaged, however, and to extend the program to others, we created a biweekly newsletter that highlighted projects in the program. We created a dynamic infrastructure for nurturing innovations, which was easily accessible by anyone within the company—any time, from anywhere and, most importantly, for free!

This infrastructure was the IBM Innovation Cloud, which helped lower the barriers for innovation projects that might otherwise have been starved for resources. At the same time, we exposed innovation projects to a large community that helped uncover new value for the business.

By providing a simple process for innovation, within 1 year more than 70,000 IBMers were participating, and by November 2008, the TAP innovation community had grown to more than 125,000 active participants (Figure 10.5). This was more than one-third of the total IBM workforce, representing every business unit, division, country, and job role. Although extremely diverse, this group had something in common. Each member of the TAP community was passionate—passionate about innovation and passionate about driving culture change and delivering business value.

Investments in TAP offered significant savings to IBM because the community used and reused components of various solutions. A combination of new Web 2.0 technology and new social tools enabled more software reuse by many innovators, which translated into reuse within IT solutions. An innovators' library of these components grew steadily, and now totals more than 250 assets (see Figure 10.6). This library is the main sources of asset reuse for new IT applications and other applications within the company.

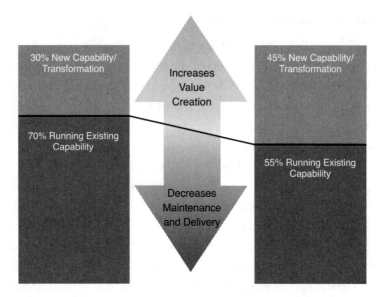

Figure 10.8   Transformation is an investment paradox shift, in which greater investment in innovation and less on run-time capabilities create greater efficiencies. Over time, increased innovation and transformation investment creates higher value and business growth.

Monetizing Social Networking

The incredible power of social networking in the enterprise has been dramatically demonstrated at IBM. We hope these lessons are helpful if your organization is in need of a business case. If you are in the processes of creating a business case for social networking tools, it is vital to articulate the value of social software to gain support for its implementation. This can be done in several ways:

• Usage metrics to capture social software adoption trends

• Success stories to provide anecdotal evidence of value

• User survey data to demonstrate improved productivity and usefulness

• Social network analysis to demonstrate the impact of improved relationships on problem solving and organizational efficiency

Supporting Your Sales Efforts

Perhaps not surprisingly, IBM found that the use of social software improved the sales organization's communication, leading to enhanced team performance. Specifically, these tools helped identify areas in the sales process that needed some improvement. For example, shared community spaces allowed teams to identify customer needs faster and tap into the team's knowledge of previous client interactions. Previously, this kind of knowledge was locked in the memory of a few salespeople, but the usage of social software freed up valuable institutional knowledge. Tools such as wikis, jams, blogs, mashups, and virtual meetings helped the IBM sales force create sales collateral material like demos. They also identified prospective opportunities faster and created effective sales strategies more quickly. Social tools are especially helpful to sellers and technical support personnel because of the large number of people with whom they interact. A survey of the IBM sales community included more than 20,000 participants and revealed interesting patterns about the perceived value of social activities, depending on job role (see Figure 10.9).

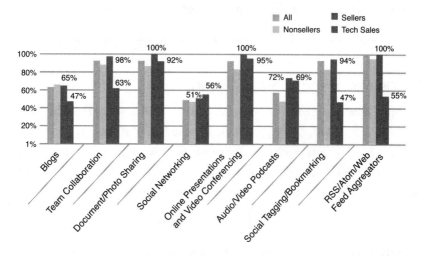

Figure 10.9 Survey results of IBM sales workforce on the impact of various social tools, categorized by job function. In November 2008, participants were asked to rank and quantify productivity increases due to social tools. This is a great example and proof point of the tremendous positive influence social software can have on the productivity of a workforce.

What Is the ROI of Social Software?

Interviews with literally scores of CIOs and CEOs, along with extensive surveys within the IBM IT community, allowed my team at IBM to quantify the significant business advantages available through social tools. These advantages were categorized in three distinct areas—productivity improvements,

> *"Social Software makes it easy to consume someone's knowledge without consuming their time"*
>
> Gina Poole, IBM VP Social Software Enablement

IT cost reductions, and revenue increases. Improvements to the businesses were consistently realized within 6 to 18 months of deployment (see Figure 10.10).

Social Tool	Improve Productivity	Reduce IT Cost	Increase Revenue
Wikis	29%	18%	16%
Blogs	12%	5%	6%
Podcast	8%	6%	
Social Networking	12%	4%	6%
Tagging	20%	6%	6%
Syndication/RSS	12%	4%	4%
Mashups	8%	6%	6%

Figure 10.10 ROI on social software investments measured by IBM CIO experience and several CEO/CIO surveys.

Innovation Programs: Critical Success Factors

With a solid understanding of both the methodology and ROI, there are some central principles that can help ensure the success of your technology adoption and innovation program:

- **Social networking**—Not surprisingly, social networks are key to technology adoption and innovation within your organization. Recruiting early adopters will help encourage others in the use of social tools. As these social software pioneers make their presence and expertise known and explore ways to promote their reputation as trusted sources, others will follow. Tools such as expertise location, profiling, and reputation tools can also help seekers and contributors quickly connect, accelerating the innovation process. Goals identified at the beginning of the innovation program should be tracked using performance and achievement metrics (for example, number of participants, number of wiki contributors, and so on).

Executive Perspective

In an interview with Steve Mills, senior vice president of the IBM Software Group, we gained some insight on his mind-set and views on social software. He has a laser focus on what delights customers.

"Talk to your customers and find out if social software is providing value to them," Mills said. "The stories and anecdotes start to build a pattern and a profile," said Mills. "Communicating the success stories broadly will allow followers to use the stories themselves and take advantage of the capabilities. And you will begin to create a payback formula that's very real and significant to the business."

"The business problem we're trying to address with social software," Mills said, "is the effectiveness and productivity of people within an organization." In this case, Mills pointed out that this effectiveness and productivity is tied directly to "the deep knowledge and understanding of how to make the company run every day." Mills said that this knowledge, "...sits with the people involved in all aspects of how the business operates."

The knowledge Mills refers to is not the kind of knowledge that is necessarily found in operational manuals or classes or procedures. Mills pointed out that the complexity of running a business can be dealt with only through the sophisticated, accumulated knowledge and understanding of its people. "This collective understanding," Mills said, "powers the business' operations, its innovation, its revenue. And these are all human endeavors."

In the case of IBM, Mills said, "Social software delivers value from people sharing information, sharing facts, sharing understanding—and finding each other when the moment of truth occurs.... That's what every company needs to do all day, every day."

Mills also talked about the underlying structure of social software, which facilitates the collaborative thinking needed to run an enterprise. "Social networking and social software provide an infrastructure," said Mills, "a surrounding set of tools and capabilities...that you combine and recombine to bring the organization together to capture…cumulative knowledge and understanding. That's the magic you're trying to tap into, and where technology can help."

Perhaps most significantly, Mills observed that corporations are at something of an intellectual inflection point because of social software. "My goal," he said, "[is] to create a 'virtual genius.' A virtual genius is the result of connecting the knowledgeable people in the organization [worldwide]…so any person, regardless of what country they're in, or what client they're dealing with, can tap into the knowledge base and essentially lift their own knowledge and understanding to more effectively serve and support the client."

"We don't force people to use social software tools," said Mills, but "to choose not to use [them] means you're cutting yourself off from the best knowledge and best experts in the organization."

- **Transparency**—The free flow of information across the enterprise and the creation of a level playing field for all employees and customers are central to the concept of transparency. Transparency can transform companies into true "meritocracies," where recognition and advancement is based primarily on productivity and maximizing value to customers and stakeholders. This transformation naturally creates a more productive environment. Customers benefit from transparency by getting better products, less costly solutions, and better integration. Perhaps most importantly, customers experience increased responsiveness to product suggestions and requests. Increased transparency benefits employees, raising their visibility to management and their social community. This philosophical change gives employees the freedom to act on new ideas and increases collaboration across the organization. Provide the tools needed for employees to freely share their ideas, but also have the process that supports and encourages innovators to create and act on their ideas. By providing tools to encourage transparency, management nurtures a culture that is supportive of innovation.

- **Support structure**—Social tools, IT infrastructure, and budget are the three pillars of a successful innovation program. Ensure the selected social tools fit into the existing workflow and integrate with other IT systems. Social tools support the creation of social networking communities, which are crucial for generating new ideas relevant to the business. With the appropriate and properly budgeted

IT infrastructure, innovative ideas can more easily flow from socially networked teams. Without a nurturing support structure, employees with good ideas might become discouraged following on with their ideas or simply won't get started because the inertia is too strong. To encourage innovation, lower barriers wherever possible.

A Word About Budget

As we've said, innovation programs should have their own budget and IT infrastructure, separate from the production environment. Many CIOs have asked me, "How can I replace current processes with streamlined methods that leverage new technology?" In many ways, this is like asking how to change tires on a moving car. The reality is that it is difficult to change a process within the same infrastructure where a legacy application runs. The first time the new process fails (and it will fail because it is new and not as robust as the legacy system), the innovation project will be killed. For this reason alone, a separate innovation environment is crucial.

Similarly, securing an "innovation budget" and an "innovation IT infrastructure" effectively isolates the relatively fragile process of innovation from the market forces of the business. Think of the innovation budget as a small venture capital investment. You're using this budget to fund the best ideas for a defined period to demonstrate to the company the value of focused innovation. The budget can fund resources, pay for services, and mitigate risk. The innovation IT infrastructure deploys innovations separate from the production environment to avoid conflicts and potential instabilities. Cloud computing can be a great setting for innovation programs. IBM, Amazon. com, Microsoft, Google, and many others provide cloud computing options that minimize capital expenditures and support the structure for innovation programs.

Mature technologies have an advantage when it comes to procuring a budget—an identifiable ROI. Innovation programs, by definition, lack the hard numbers that can justify a specific budget. As we said, viewing the innovation program budget as venture capital makes it easier to get started. Some disruptive technologies can take two years or more to mature before being seriously considered as a replacement for legacy technologies. A separate investment for innovation provides the cushion for innovation programs to prove themselves, rather than being terminated prematurely.

A Closing Thought

Innovation is hard work. Time and money need to be focused on the effort if transformational change is going to happen. An innovation budget helps pay for key resources to devote 100 percent of their time to the innovation to ensure the success of the project. For an innovation program to be successful, teams don't need to be collocated. Instead, good social networking tools enable collaboration and a strong sense of community across the team, without regard to geography.

The challenges of today's economy and the global nature of business require us to think in fundamentally different ways about success. With appropriate attention to innovation, particularly in the context of social networking, we can ensure that our businesses remain profitable and consistently ahead of the competition.

Summary

- The Technology Adoption Program at IBM had a fast adoption rate of less than three years. More than 125,000 IBMers joined the innovation program and transformed IBM business processes and business.

- Innovations are best generated within an innovation factory workflow to harvest innovation across your business, from the ideation process, prototyping, and evaluation to deployment.

- Free your organizations to think out of the box and achieve the impossible by embracing an innovation process that is based on the Managed Anarchy model instead of traditional waterfall methodologies.

- Encourage participation in broader collaboration by acknowledging that your business has neither a monopoly on good ideas, nor all the smartest people in the industry. Adoption of social software changes attitudes and helps break silos.

- Use social tools to foster social networks within the business to transform your corporate culture into one that embraces innovation. Embracing change and innovation can energize your employees and accelerate business growth.

- The amount of investment allocated for transformation is a good barometer of the future success of a business. For meaningful transformation in the Social Age, a reasonable balance is to allocate 45 percent of the IT budget to innovation and new capabilities and 55 percent committed to running the existing infrastructure.

- Innovation programs measure ROI through cost reduction metrics and reduced time-to-market for new products. The IBM TAP program provided an estimated ROI of above 50 percent.

- Key success factors for innovation programs include appropriate implementation of social networking tools, business transparency, and a support structure.

11
Social Economy

The service economy we see all around us is the result of a 300-year socioeconomic revolution. In Chapter 1, "Dawn of the Social Age," we traced the path that transformed a rural society, driven by an agricultural economy, into a manufacturing society driven by the Industrial Revolution. This revolution happened through massive economies of scale, which were the results of automation and standardization.

These industrial efficiencies opened opportunities to create and offer services that provided higher economic returns than those obtained through manufacturing. Services soon became both an important differentiator and a key growth element for many businesses. In the United States, more than 60 percent of the population today works in service-related businesses, and this trend shows no signs of slowing with a GDP services component that is expected to reach almost 80 percent by 2011.[1] World GDP, which was approximately $52 trillion in 2008,[2] is expected to grow to $82.5 trillion by 2013[3] with continued growth in the services component. In fact, the services component of the GDP has grown steadily since just after World War II (see Figure 11.1).

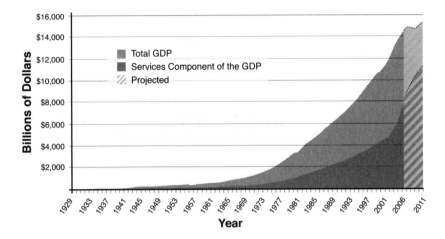

Figure 11.1 The service component of the GDP has become more than 43 percent of the total U.S. GDP in the last 40 years. Data from the U.S. Department of Commerce.[4]

In the Social Age, services businesses stand to gain the most from an environment that will be dominated by innovations in services models and offerings. In this chapter, we explore the financial implications that are upon us in the Social Age and the ways social networking and technology adoption are affecting GDP. We see how leveraging social networking tools within the organization and using external social networks as a powerful new marketing channel can invigorate services businesses to grow and increase their market share.

The Strategic View—An Interview with a Technology Visionary

We gained valuable insights on the trend toward an economy dominated by service industries during our interview with Nick Donofrio, retired IBM senior vice president of Technology and Innovation.

"To make enough things cheap enough for the nine billion people that live on this planet," Donofrio said, "we're going to need fewer and fewer people in the industrial sector."

Donofrio suggested that of the next three billion people, few of them are going to work in the industrial sector, or in the agricultural sector. He said the vast majority of the next three billion people are going to work in the services sector. Manufacturing and agricultural sectors have become extremely efficient and are able to produce more goods, he said, at higher quality and lower cost that everyone can afford.

"We need fewer people in those industries," Donofrio said, "because they are very efficient. It's the tyranny of large and small numbers. The services sector has got to get much more focused and it's got to get much more productive, because it's got all of us in it....This services economy is where seven billion out of nine billion people on this planet live and work."

Nick explained that success factors in business today have changed. In the Industrial Age, it was, "How much land do you have?" "How many factories do you have?" "How much can you produce?"

Now success is determined by the answer to only one question: *"How much do you know?"*

Nick's insights were an important reminder that education, effective communication, and social networking will be key success factors in the Social Age.

"The whole idea of social networking is to gain *democratization* of technology," Nick said in closing. "It's all about making us more productive."

Technology Adoption and GDP Correlation

Even in the face of a linear acceleration in technology adoption, the GDP of developing countries continues to lag the United States. Countries such as South Korea, Japan, Singapore, New Zealand, and Australia, for example, have surpassed U.S. rates of cell phone adoption, but they still lag in per capita GDP growth.[5]

In an interview for this book, Harvard University professor Diego Comin talked about the wealth of data he's gathered that demonstrates a correlation between technology adoption and GDP growth. But although we might expect there to be a direct correlation, Dr. Comin's research demonstrates that GDP grows *more slowly* than the rate of technology adoption.[6]

Other factors must therefore be at play here as well, and I believe at least part of this divergence can be explained by the degree to which an economy is driven by social networking. The effect of social networking between organizations within a country was examined by Dr. Effie Kesidou[7] in her study, "Local Knowledge Spillovers in High Tech Clusters in Developing Countries." Dr. Kesidou defines local knowledge spillovers as "the externalities that are the result of the inability of one firm to retain the economic returns of its innovation activities."

For example, if company A creates an innovation but cannot protect the innovation through patents or sufficient secrecy, the idea might "leak" to company B, which, in turn, can benefit from it. Dr. Kesidou demonstrates that the wider and stronger the social networks between companies, the higher the likelihood of knowledge spillovers, which ultimately benefit the country in which the companies are located. These spillovers accelerate the benefits gained from the new technology, which has an aggregative effect that increases the country's capability to profit from adoption of the new technology.

Local knowledge spillover is one of the reasons high-tech companies gravitate to the same geographical area. Here in the United States, Silicon Valley in the West, or the 128 corridor in the Northeast have been traditional technology magnets. These tightly knit regions not only benefit the local economy, at least partially due to local knowledge spillovers, but they also drive the GDP of the country.

Local knowledge spillovers are a powerful indicator that social networking serves to efficiently disseminate and propagate tacit knowledge, which accelerates the use and adoption of new technologies. Dr. Kesidou's findings offer compelling evidence that a country that fosters collaboration and social networking between industries and organizations (including universities), and with international companies, will accelerate the pace of technology adoption. As a by-product of increased technology adoption, greater business advantages are generated, resulting in GDP growth.

There appears to be a strong correlation between the social networking capacities of a country and its capability to realize efficiencies and opportunities derived from new technologies. Countries such as China and Mexico, which have made exceptional efforts to adopt new technologies, are nevertheless still lagging in their GDP, perhaps in part for this reason (Figure 11.2).

The tremendous acceleration of communication technologies in the Social Age has been indispensable to the growth of economies around the world. This acceleration has also created new phenomena that are the result of nearly instantaneous dissemination of information. As we explore one of these phenomena in the next section, in a way we're returning to concepts first suggested in Chapter 9, "Social Brain and the Ideation Process," about the workings of the human brain. As we said, when the brainpower of many people is joined to foster innovation, the results can be amazing. But group thinking, or perhaps we should say, "group enthusiasm," can also cause headaches—or opportunity—for your innovation efforts, depending on the way you manage it.

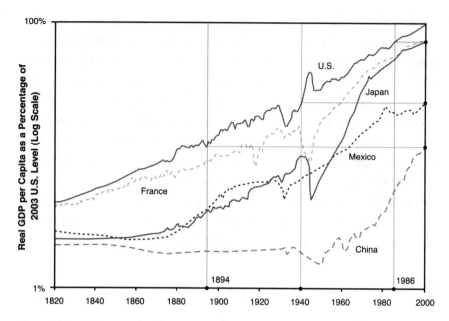

Figure 11.2 GDP per capita, illustrating GDP lags across the years.[8]

Recognizing and Exploiting the Hype Cycle

If you've seen news reports of lines of people stretching around the block waiting to buy the latest gadget, you have an idea what this section is about. Although we're each individuals, with individual thought processes, our various communities—work, home, neighborhood, online social networks, the broader culture—heavily influence us and our perceptions.

Traditional media and our social networks combine into a "crowd perception" that surrounds us and constantly influences our subconscious. In fact, our values and judgments might not be as original as we'd like to think. This crowd perception also drives unrealistic expectations about new innovations. These overly enthusiastic expectations are often referred to as the "hype" associated with a new technology. It is crucial for a business to recognize the reality and influence of hype if it is to be successful in its innovation efforts.

The most recent example of hype is probably the dot-com bubble and the subhypes that sprang up around a host of Internet companies, many of which quickly became worth billions of dollars (on paper) and yet had not generated a single dollar of profit. With a mighty crash the hype ended and reality set in, as the dot-com boom turned to bust.

Although stunning in its scope, the dot-com boom and bust represented the normal "perception cycle" of communities who adjust their expectations after going through a thoughtful evaluation process. The hype cycle model was developed by Gartner in 1995 to help its customers distinguish between true value and mere hype. In 2008, the concept was published by Jackie Fenn and Mark Raskino in their landmark book *Mastering the Hype Cycle: How to Adopt the Right Innovation at the Right Time.*[9]

Fenn and Raskino demonstrate that the introduction of a hot, innovative product to market triggers high expectations. Early adopters tend to overestimate its value and consequently create considerable hype around the innovation. A period of disillusionment follows, but eventually a rebound occurs. This step is the "slope of enlightenment" period, and is based on more realistic expectations; here customers begin to properly judge the true value of the innovation (Figure 11.3).

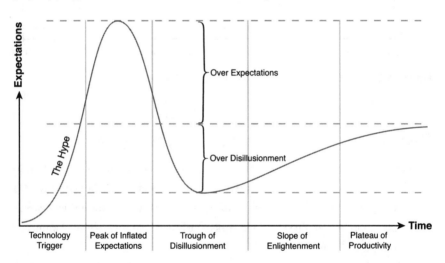

Figure 11.3 The hype cycle.

The Personal Digital Assistant (PDA) in the late '90s is a recent example of the hype cycle. Multiple failed attempts with early operating systems and cumbersome, nonstandardized interfaces quickly turned excitement about the PDA to a period of disillusionment. The PDA's astronomical expectations and hype actually brought down many companies during the 2001 recession. The PDA technology eventually evolved into today's smart phones. Now, there are nearly four billion cell phones subscribers worldwide, claiming a staggering 61 percent market penetration as of 2008.[10]

Helping people get organized was the original intent of the PDA, but millions of smart phones have demonstrated that low-cost communication and community collaboration are primary drivers of new technology in this area. The faltering start of the PDA merely laid the foundation for a better solution—the smart phone, whose primary value is to connect with others in a more natural and convenient way.

The classic hype cycle curve in Figure 11.3 reveals the overly enthusiastic expectations at the beginning of the cycle triggered by the innovation. The disillusionment period follows, before enlightenment, when the true value of the innovation is realized. Expectations finally plateau, and the hype cycle curve flattens out as the technology matures.

The Adoption Cycle

People and companies—which are actually just groups of people—are heavily influenced by the hype around a new technology and often jump in, hopeful of gaining an edge on the market. As we consider the hype cycle, however, it's helpful to keep in mind that behind the volatile and sometimes dramatic hype cycle is the somewhat less volatile adoption cycle. In Chapter 10, "Social Innovation," we reviewed the adoption cycle up close through the Technology Adoption Program (TAP). The adoption cycle identifies essentially three different personality types, each of which takes a slightly different view and approach to new technologies. These three types can be broadly categorized as early adopters, mass market adopters, and laggard adopters.

Early adopters, although being relatively fewer in number, tend to be a bit more daring, while at the same time making their thoughts and feelings known (sometimes loudly) about new technology. They're willing to collaborate with innovators to improve new technologies. They publish their enthusiasm and their criticisms on their blogs, often greatly influencing others.

As a product evolves and improves to satisfy the needs of a wider market, adoption increases. After some time the pressures of the market and standardization lead to the commoditization of the innovation, and mass adoption takes place. Technology laggards finally begin adopting the new technology as a substitute for earlier, less-efficient products. This natural process of technology adoption traces a normal bell curve shape[11] (Figure 11.4).

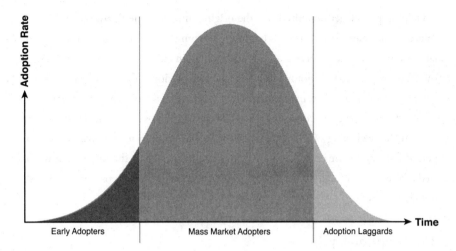

Figure 11.4 The technology adoption curve follows a normal distribution.

Managing the Hype Cycle

Business strategists need to understand that there is overlap between the hype cycle and the adoption cycle. By failing to properly manage expectations about a new technology, the hype cycle can get out of control, creating astronomically unrealistic expectations about the new technology, and potentially deepening the disillusionment channel that inevitably follows. This phenomenon is more easily understood when we combine the dramatic extremes of the hype cycle with the natural adoption curve.

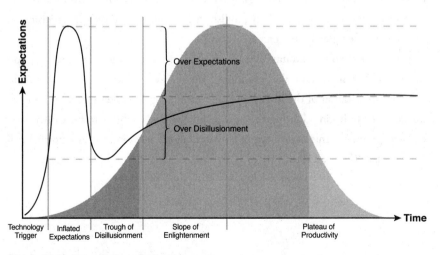

Figure 11.5 Hype cycle and adoption curve.

Most of the hype for a new technology is driven by early adopters, as illustrated on the left side of Figure 11.5. They act as sort of the main booster rocket, getting the innovation off the launch pad. Because they are often perceived as experts in their field, early adopters attract a lot of attention, and their opinions—in blog postings, magazine articles, or other media—carry relatively greater weight. If not properly managed, however, early adopters can create inflated expectations about the technology, leading to an uncomfortable period of disillusionment and possible dissatisfaction.

This is a good reason to establish a well-managed innovation program. By segregating early adopters from mass market adopters, you can essentially calibrate expectations during the critical early stages of new product introduction. As you introduce the product into the broader audience of mass market adopters, the capabilities and limitations of the product are fully known, and the disturbing disillusionment period is left behind.

Hype Can Be Expensive

This analysis of the hype cycle is important for another reason. If your company is considering a new technology for internal use, it pays to understand where that technology is in the hype cycle. Perhaps you've identified a technology that will be perfect to solve one of your business challenges, or that you believe will be well received by your customers. It's a hot technology. The trade magazines have been running the inventor's picture on their front covers, and you heard that the company across town is installing version 1.0 for its engineering teams.

CEOs and CIOs are, by definition, professional risk managers. They know there's a time to jump in and a time to take a step back. Understanding the hype cycle can help. In general, the best time to adopt a new technology is not during the first leg of the hype cycle. Instead, that's usually the time to take a step back and watch for the beginning of the period of disillusionment. During the disillusionment period, the market tends to over-penalize companies for any shortcomings of the product or the new technology. This provides the opportunity to adopt the new technology at a lower cost and with more realistic expectations.

The Cost of Transformation

You know you need to transform your business, and it appears a new technology might be the way to do it. But is it really? Successful implementation of a new idea to transform your business requires careful consideration and analysis.

Be sure to evaluate the return on investment (ROI) and Pre-Tax Income (PTI) not only of the technology under consideration, but also of possible alternatives. To maximize your ROI and PTI on new ideas or products, take into consideration the timing and maturity of the market to receive you innovation. Great ideas ahead of their time don't produce good ROI.

To maximize the chances for the success of a transformation or innovation project, plan for an assessment period to simulate multiple business scenarios. Simulating various business scenarios on a spreadsheet is far less expensive—and stressful—than watching your Profit and Loss statement suffer because of ill-conceived, real-world experiments. Give yourself enough time for the transformation, and protect your innovation project during the fragile development process and early adoption cycle. Don't let innovations get killed before they have a chance to prove themselves to the market. Ensure that your innovation process evaluates new ideas in a way that takes into consideration future market conditions, and ways they could lower cost of operations.

Ultimately, the analysis of a new technology should demonstrate that the cost efficiencies gained will outweigh the overall cost of transformation (Figure 11.6).

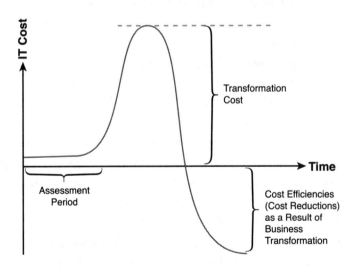

Figure 11.6 Cost-benefit curve—Investments in IT transformation enable reduction over time in overall IT cost.

Becoming President with Social Networking

The Social Factor is about this tremendous revolution we are a part of—a revolution of low-cost communication and unprecedented social connections. This revolution is possible only because of the powerful and amazing Social Age tools at our disposal.

For the users of social networking tools, they now wonder how they were ever able to live without them. We've offered many examples of the advantages and opportunities available with social networking. But if you're still not convinced, consider the case of a relatively unknown U.S. senator from the state of Illinois, who only a few years ago was laboring in the south side of Chicago as a community organizer.

SocialAge
Factoid

Do you know what this text message says?

> P911 TAFN CUL8R_

If not, you're probably from a pre-Social Age generation!

Parents in room, that's all for now, see you later!

From his days in Chicago, this young senator understood something very powerful. He understood that when people got organized at a local level, about issues of local interest, they are eager to work together. And he understood something else as well—he understood that we are living in the Social Age. He took what he knew about getting people organized at the local level, and combined it with what he knew about social networking, and he created a presidential campaign unlike any ever seen before.

Previous presidential campaigns (most notably that of Howard Dean in 2004) provided early and powerful evidence that the political game had changed. If someone hoped to compete for the highest office in the land, a comprehensive Internet strategy was not just an option, it was a necessity. And it was Howard Dean's IT team at Boston-based Blue State Digital that created the framework of the socially networked locomotive that became the Obama campaign. Using Dean's Internet campaign machinery as its foundation, Blue State Digital forged a completely new strategy that made use of every possible social networking tool to reach the electorate.

When I interviewed Blue State chief technology officer Jascha Franklin-Hodge for this book, he provided incredible insights into the Obama campaign. He told me about the way Obama used social networking to help empower his supporters. He said that Obama realized democracy worked best when you have high participation from people, and social tools are the best vehicle to accomplish that.

"Early on," Franklin-Hodge said, "the emphasis in the campaign was on traditional fund-raising, using the Obama campaign Web site. But after Super Tuesday—when more than half the delegates were committed—it became apparent that Obama had a strong emotional appeal that carried him to a virtual tie with Hillary Clinton in those crucial primaries. For much of 2007, conventional wisdom held that Clinton would easily win the nomination. For ten years Clinton had been building the most powerful political machine anyone had ever seen. But here was Obama, really connecting with the average voter. We knew we had to tap into the excitement of those voters to help drive the campaign."

Franklin-Hodge paused briefly, and said with a laugh, "And we only had eleven months to do it."

Franklin-Hodge went on to explain the way Blue State used social networking to harness "local power" in the national presidential campaign to maintain momentum and build excitement right up to the general election. Rather than using social tools merely to fund-raise, Blue State quickly realized Obama was winning the money battle, so the focus shifted.

Instead of an emphasis on fund-raising, Blue State began to build the social networking tools needed to empower individual supporters. For example, Obama volunteers used the resources on the Obama Web site to establish local organizations. These local organizations might have been as few as three or four people, or literally hundreds of people. The Web site allowed supporters to enter their ZIP code, and lists of local Obama organizations in that area (and upcoming local campaign events) were offered. If there wasn't a local organization, the Web site provided the tools to establish one. (By the date of the general election, there were more than 35,000 Obama organizations across the country.) Local events such as a county fair could be used as the ad hoc gathering spot for local supporters. The word could go out through the local social network to stop by the Obama table at the fair. Parties were also organized by local organizations in which the excitement and momentum could be sustained.

On the Obama Web site there were podcasts of speeches and streaming video to view or download. And most powerfully, there was a nearly seamless connection not just to the individual supporter who signed up on the Web site, but also to everyone in his or her e-mail address book. That's right—the Obama campaign offered the option to open your address book to help you reach additional supporters.

"You could provide access to your iPhone address book," Franklin-Hodge said, "and you could download an application that analyzed your address book by area code. As the campaign progressed, races were tight in certain states—the battleground states, such as Ohio and Pennsylvania. This application essentially searched your address book and presented you with contacts in your address book who lived in battleground states and then asked you to call them to persuade them to vote for Obama."

In addition to giving you a list of your friends and colleagues in battleground states to call, the application also suggested a few bullet points to highlight while having the conversation.

"We realized that you can only tell people to give money or do something so many times," Franklin-Hodge said. "They need to make their own decisions about the best way to campaign. We provided the tools they needed and then got out of their way. Most people, for example, weren't interested in putting an Obama widget on their Facebook page. But when they posted an activity they did on behalf of the campaign, that activity appeared as a news item on the Facebook account of their friends. This low-touch model offered powerful synergies for the campaign."

"On the one hand," Franklin-Hodge said, "we were establishing something of a directed anarchy by giving supporters the tools and getting out of their way. On the other hand, we were able to close the data loop very effectively and efficiently. We provided mobile applications the supporters could use to gather data about potential voters as they campaigned. That data could easily be uploaded to the campaign database by a supporter, essentially giving us a street-by-street reading on support for the candidate."

"Traditionally," said Franklin-Hodge, "that job was done by a campaign worker staying up until 3:00 a.m., entering all that information by hand into a database. We streamlined and automated the whole process through social tools."

Not only did the campaign use fresh data to get an accurate snapshot of support as the campaign progressed, they also used that same data to "micro-target" areas where support for the candidate was soft.

The incredible fund-raising efforts of the Obama campaign are well documented, at one point totally more $100 million a month.[12] This success was a function not just of a great Web site, but also of the millions of social connections that were made through each of Obama's supporters. The campaign demonstrated that a small financial investment in social networking tools provided a national impact and even a worldwide awareness of this young senator from Illinois. Social networking created an exponential multiplier effect that left Obama's opponents scratching their heads and his critics baffled.

As a relative unknown, he organized the south side of Chicago and gave the people hope. Using social networking he organized his supporters in the 2008 presidential campaign and gave the nation hope. As Obama fulfills his duties as president, he can serve as something of an inspiration to the rest of us, especially to those who still have their doubts about the power of social networking.

Because after all, if it helps get you elected president of the United States, is there anything social networking can't do?

Summary

- There is a direct relationship between technology adoption and GDP growth. The more new technologies are adopted and exploited by a country, the more the country's GDP grows.

- The service component of the U.S. GDP has increased considerably to become more than 43 percent of the total.

- Social networks, especially across businesses, appear to have a direct relationship to the pace at which a country develops.

- The hype cycle, especially when combined with the adoption cycle, provides valuable insight into the excitement about new technologies and the way you can avoid falling into the hype trap.

- Adoption of social software tends to change peoples' attitudes and helps break silos. Leverage social tools to corral your organization into a common purpose, as the Obama campaign did.

12
Mobile Society

Connect anywhere, any time with any device—that has long been the promise of technology for the busy professional, and the Social Age generation is perhaps the first that will see that promise fulfilled. High-performance cell phones, smart phones, and PDAs now offer the connectivity and computing power needed for ubiquitous data access.

In this chapter, we explore the way mobile devices have changed user expectations and the ways mobility is becoming a critical enterprise service. We touch briefly on trends in mobile computing devices, including the evolving role of 4G (fourth generation) networks and the way Social Age interaction will take advantage of the extraordinary power of these mobile networks. In the second half of the chapter, we discuss the role of 3D virtual worlds in the Social Age and the potential impact these interactive worlds will have on your business.

Mobility as a Critical Enterprise Service

Social applications such as MySpace are nice to have, but are they appropriate—or relevant—for the mobile enterprise user? Is it reasonable to expect social tools to join e-mail, calendar, and address books as part of the mobile computing core for business productivity and efficiency? The answer to both these questions increasingly seems to be "Yes."

Business people everywhere are beginning to appreciate the tremendous power of having more than just name, address, and phone number at their fingertips as they're about to walk into an important customer meeting. You can always use more information about a customer as a way to accelerate or enhance the relationship. But with today's mobile applications, you can also quickly access product information, or even connect with a product expert who can provide the answers you need at the critical moment in the meeting.

SocialAge
Factoid

Still have a wired telephone? Sorry, you might be part of a pre-Social Age generation.

Around the world, to support this trend, mobile devices are becoming increasingly "social." In the United States, BlackBerry and Windows Mobile-based devices remain the most popular smart phone choices, while in Europe, Symbian platforms on Nokia and Sony Ericsson devices dominate. Applications such as *MySpace for BlackBerry* are a natural step in the overall evolution of the Blackberry as an enterprise-centric platform, joining the foundational "push e-mail" technology responsible for the Blackberry's initial wide acceptance.

Mobility and User Expectations

Our connected culture is evolving rapidly. Children and young adults see a world in which mobility is not the exception, but the rule. For them, the connected office is much less important than making a social connection with a friend on their smart phone. Several factors are in play here to make all this happen, including many applications that were born on the Internet but which are quickly maturing in the increasingly mobile world. Three of these applications are *MySpace, LinkedIn,* and *Facebook.*

MySpace

MySpace users have the ability to contribute profile information, create blogs, maintain groups, upload photos, embed music and video, and become part of a network of friends or associates. In June 2006, MySpace was the most successful social networking site in the United States,[1] and as of April 2008, it was surpassed only by Facebook in terms of total unique monthly visitors worldwide.[2]

In November 2008, MySpace went mobile. For the first time, *MySpace for Black-Berry Smart Phones* extended the MySpace desktop user experience to the mobile phone. Within the first month of release, *MySpace for Blackberry* users downloaded more than 1 million copies of the application. More than 15 million messages were sent, and user "mood" and "status" were updated over 2 million times.

With the introduction of the Blackberry application, MySpace appears poised to capitalize on the emerging workforce already familiar with MySpace. This demographic was introduced to MySpace in high school, college, and in their early working life. Although not currently focused on the corporate landscape, MySpace remains a popular friend-oriented contact gathering and management tool.

LinkedIn

As we touched on in Chapter 7, "Social Media and Culture," although LinkedIn is more "Contact Networking" than strict

"Social Networking," it is poised to address the critical need of merging these two worlds and playing an important role in the way Customer Relationship Management (CRM) is done in the Social Age. LinkedIn Mobile (m.linkedin.com) gives users the ability to create a profile that includes current and past employment, education, primary connections to others, links to Web sites, and a public profile that can easily be added to e-mail closings or web pages.

Recent enhancements to LinkedIn have included the ability to subscribe to a more extensive tool set for finding people and resources more effectively and a LinkedIn Answers feature, similar in nature to Google or Yahoo services. LinkedIn Answers differentiates itself from other services in its capability to provide answers that contain information related to specific business needs or industry sectors. For the mobile, socially networked professional, these tools can offer a powerful tactical advantage during customer interactions.

Facebook

Also born on the Internet, Facebook has created mobile applications for several device platforms. The BlackBerry application is in many ways similar to the MySpace mobile

application. Although aligned with the "friend" metaphor, the Facebook application lends itself more closely to corporate use than MySpace. At the same time, an alphabetized list with pictures and names provides Facebook with a look and feel more closely resembling the contact-oriented LinkedIn interface.

Corporate Directory Hits the Small Screen

A number of years ago, IBM anticipated the increased dependence on mobile computing and began building a variety of mobile-ready applications, including the IBM Bluepages employee directory. Bluepages is a mission-critical application, so successful extension to mobile devices was considered vital to the organization.

Given the diversity and the global nature of the IBM employee population, using a web application approach (rather than a dedicated mobile application) proved much more flexible. The web-application approach readily accommodated a vast array of smart phones that were already in common use within the global corporate community, including Samsung, Windows Mobile, Nokia, Sony Ericsson, Blackberry, and iPhones.

In parallel with the application development process, key decisions were made about the rollout of the application. User documentation, videos, and other supporting communications were developed to support the deployment. These forms of communication proved invaluable when seeking validation and stakeholder support for the overall effort.

What's Next for Social Age Mobile?

IBM estimates that by the year 2015, the world will have more than five billion people connected to the Internet, most of them by wireless connection. The billion users we see coming along over the next few years will be in emerging markets, where broadband growth will be driven by demand for access to the Internet for the first time. These emerging markets will deploy ubiquitous mobile broadband across vast regions, providing many of the same wireless services now enjoyed in major metropolitan areas around the world today.

As we discussed in Chapter 1, "Dawn of the Social Age," the speed of the communications revolution has amazed all but the most prescient experts. You might remember the excitement of doubling the speed of your Internet connection...to

56K…via dial-up modem! Now multimegabyte download speeds are common for even the least expensive wired connections.

Broadband connectivity in the home and office quickly led to an expectation that service at these speeds would be available everywhere, any time, on every device, wired or wireless. As with every step in the evolution of communications, the challenge for mobile developers has been to push as much information as possible through the infrastructure, as quickly as possible, and deliver it to the end user at a competitive cost. Mobile users increasingly demand the computing power—and resulting productivity gains—on their mobile computer that they have long enjoyed on their wired computers. The concept of the triple play (data-voice-video) and quadruple play (data-voice-video-broadcast) networks becomes more applicable to consumer and business users as these networks become more capable of automatically recognizing the device used. An application can then deliver the desired content and information in an appropriate format.

Functions, features, and the ubiquitous nature of today's social networking applications will continue to evolve. With the integration of GPS, cell tower localizations, and Wi-Fi positioning systems, a new opportunity is emerging for geosocial networking. These same services have empowered a number of applications that enable users to find out "who's here," or find and connect with a particular product or service that is available locally.

Although most social networking sites promote and enable virtual relationships, emerging location-sensitive, geosocial networking sites will likely promote more in-person collaborations. Brightkite.com is a good example of a location-based social networking tool that enables you to remain in touch with your friends through an iPhone application. Brightkite automatically keeps track of your friends' locations and suggests places of interest to get together, such as a local restaurant or club. These same applications might even serve to extend opportunities back to brick-and-mortar retail outlets and services opportunities. If you're driving by your favorite home improvement store, for example, you might find an advertisement from the store on your GPS-enabled handheld, notifying you of a sale that day. By agreeing to have this service on your handheld, you save money. But at the same time, the store has immediate feedback about the effectiveness of its push-advertising over the mobile medium.

All these capabilities and opportunities will continue to evolve as 4G wireless matures and becomes the standard for mobile—and fixed—communication.

4G Wireless

The WiMAX Forum is an industry-led, not-for-profit organization with more than 500 member companies formed to certify and promote the compatibility and interoperability of broadband wireless products. There are currently more than 300 WiMAX deployments and trials underway by operators in 118 countries worldwide.[3]

In addition to higher transmission speeds, WiMAX solutions will make use of advanced multi-antenna signal processing techniques, allowing for true mobile computing for the first time. 4G wireless holds the promise of bringing together under a single umbrella a variety of previously separate telecommunications media, as illustrated in Figure 12.1.

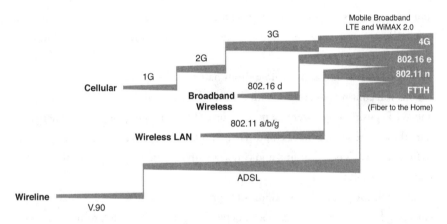

Figure 12.1 Mobile Broadband Evolution to 4G.[4]

Mobile WiMAX[5] (802.16e) is focused on the concept of personal mobile broadband and is complementary to WLAN and 3G cellular. Mobile WiMAX was developed as an open IP network architecture technology platform that outperforms 3G and has less demanding intellectual-property licensing terms. With a WiMAX account the subscriber can use the same broadband account for Internet access at home, in the office, or for mobile roaming.

Evolving User Expectations

Beyond just voice and short messaging services (SMS), consumers and business users expect increasingly easy access to bandwidth-ntensive, value-added services and applications. These services include

- Enhanced communications such as VoIP (Voice over IP)

- E-mail and Instant Message service that is secure and auditable

- Music downloads

- Games

- Interactive TV and radio

- Video on Demand (VOD)

- Web browsing

- News and real-time financial information

- Podcasting

- Mobile office and mobile workforce solutions such as VPN, Intranet access, corporate e-mail, scheduling and rich multimedia Unified Communications (UC) applications

- Social computing and GPS-powered, location-based services

Wireless Personal Broadband and 4G

A worldwide boom in Wireless Personal Broadband (WPB) is now under way, following the successful launch of 3G (3rd Generation) mobile broadband services such as High-speed Downlink Packet Access (HSDPA) and Evolution-data Optimized (EVDO), and by 4G technologies such as Mobile WiMAX.

Mobile voice traffic is especially noteworthy in developing markets with large populations such as China, India, and Africa. Parts of the world where people have never used a fixed phone or computer before are also experiencing explosive growth in mobile telecommunications. On a global basis, however, mobile data, rather than mobile voice, is in ever-greater demand. According to *Informa Telecoms & Media*, mobile data traffic will overtake mobile voice traffic globally in 2011 and will account for an amazing two-thirds of total mobile network traffic by 2012.[6] Future mobile broadband converged devices will include WiMAX, a key part of the 4G wireless standards. Mobile WiMAX operators will provide hot spot coverage across an entire city—and not just for stationary users. Fully mobile users, even in a moving vehicle, will access all the same content and applications.

Convergence of WPB will occur as fixed, mobile, and media join to reduce costs and enable new integrated services (see Figure 12.2). Industry consolidation is likely to continue, with fixed and mobile telecom companies merging with the media industry (broadcasting) to deliver new services, applications, and content across IP-based mobile platforms. This consolidated approach will be more appealing for the end user and be less expensive and easier to use.

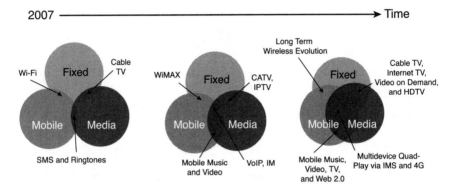

Figure 12.2 Convergence of fixed wire connectivity, wireless solutions, mobile solutions, and new media will enable new integrated services.

Triple- and quadruple-play networks become more applicable to consumer and business users as these networks become better able to recognize which device is currently used. The desired content and information can then be formatted and delivered most efficiently. Mobile broadband devices today can already sense whether Cellular or Wi-Fi access offers a better means for connectivity to the network and respond accordingly. Future converged mobile devices will include WiMAX, which will support multimedia applications and web-based content that was previously available only on a fixed broadband connection. These applications can now include nomadic office services, access to personalized entertainment, and network-based storage applications. As these applications become increasingly common, the distribution of traffic will continue to evolve, as shown in Figure 12.3.

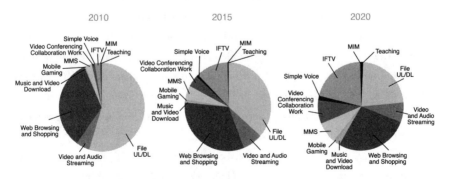

Figure 12.3 Predicted traffic distribution by Wireless Personal Broadband (WPB) Applications from 2010 to 2020.[7]

Earlier we looked at the migration of applications such as LinkedIn, Facebook, and MySpace from the desktop context to a fully mobile context. Bandwidth restrictions have long limited which fixed applications can effectively operate on mobile devices. Those restrictions are being rapidly addressed, and with the growing acceptance of 4G, a host of other Social Age applications are now lined up to make the jump to your handheld device.

Perhaps among the most bandwidth-hungry applications in the desktop world are graphics-intensive 3D game platforms such as *World of Warcraft* and virtual worlds like *Second Life*. Graphics, however, are only half of the equation. In addition to a sharp graphical display, these applications require high-speed connectivity to ensure a realistic, real-time participant experience. Technologies such as 4G—and beyond— will increasingly make even these applications available to mobile users.

Social Networking in 3D

As the virtual world Second Life (www.secondlife.com) has demonstrated, immersive, interactive 3D environments (three-dimensional virtual worlds) motivate, stimulate, and inspire users in ways never before seen. The potential impacts and opportunities of 3D virtual world environments are just beginning to be understood. But we will focus primarily on the implications of virtual worlds on social networking and its impact on the enterprise.

Creative modern inventors have always built electronic devices to facilitate game and play. The earliest computer games pitted human against computer, just as they do today. A.S. Douglas programmed a tic-tac-toe computer game in 1952 for his Ph.D. dissertation about human-computer interaction.[8] But leveraging computers, networks, and displays does not necessarily result in isolated interaction with machines. Computers have also long been used to create a competitive environment in which one person can engage with another in a gaming interface. In 1958, Brookhaven National Laboratory's William Higinbotham got things rolling when he programmed an oscilloscope for two users to play virtual tennis. These early beginnings had already identified the major features of games and virtual worlds: the graphical display, the real time simulation of physical laws, and the interaction of multiple users.

Fast-forward to 2009, where by age 21, the average person will have spent 10,000 hours playing video games.[9] Many of these games are still human against computer, but a host of other games now facilitate person-to-person competition, and increasingly, person-to-many-person competitions across the Internet. The "Massively Multi-player Online Role-Playing Game" (MMORPG) *World of Warcraft* has millions of players worldwide.

A number of years ago we also began to see the next stage in the evolution of online gaming and social interaction: 3D virtual worlds. The authors of "3D Social Virtual Worlds—Research Issues and Challenges" contend that Virtual Worlds "are beginning to shape the knowledge-based and globalized societies and economies of tomorrow."[10]

Social India—The Mobile Revolution

Behind many of the amazing advances in India is the mobile phone, whose popularity has absolutely exploded. Introduced only 15 years ago, 280 million mobile devices are now in use nationwide. This makes the mobile device one of the most disruptive technologies to impact India, literally revolutionizing the way Indians communicate and stay in touch. In the past five years, the growth has been more than 500 percent. Call charges have dropped almost 90 percent in recent years, and mobile phones are now a ubiquitous accessory for nearly every urban citizen. Mobile operators are now extending their reach into rural India, and the number of subscribers is expected to multiply threefold to 750 million in as little as three years.

Social networking in India is now an integral part of the culture, thanks to low-cost mobile devices. The rapid adoption of the technology can be attributed to low usage cost, ease of use, and India's tradition that attaches great importance to relationships among family and friends. Combine these factors with the many social networking tools now available, and it's easy to see why mobile is a key driver of India's societal transformation.

Social Networking in Rural India

Internet penetration in most of rural India is still limited. Broadband is expensive to build in rural areas, but the cost of mobile is much more reasonable. Wireless service providers continue to invest heavily in upgrading the technology and expanding their reach and coverage. This has made the mobile phone the primary mode of communication and networking in rural India.

Robust multilingual social networking platforms are being built for access through voice and SMS and are designed to support local communities and mobilize social change.[11] Wireless service providers are also moving fast to provide specialized services to rural India to effect a social change and also to cash in on the huge market at the bottom of the pyramid. Idea Telecom, one of India's largest wireless providers, has launched an innovative campaign to provide education via the mobile phone network.

Social Age Cricket

If cricket created excitement in India before the Social Age, that excitement has now turned into frenzy. Updates on cricket matches, including live broadcasts, were previously limited to television and radio. Now, minute-by-minute updates are available by SMS, on Web sites, and on web channels such as YouTube. Matches, teams, and individual performances are subjected to extensive analyses on thousands of blogs.

Cricket has spawned socially networked groups and communities that rival those devoted to Bollywood. Thousands of communities worship their favorite cricketing heroes. An Orkut community devoted to famed batsman Sachin Tendulkar has more than 400,000 members.

Cricinfo.com is one of the oldest and most popular Indian Web sites dedicated to cricket. RSS feeds of content, photo galleries, blogs, advertisements, opinion polls, newsletters, online games, and quizzes are all available on cricinfo.com. Cricinfo Mobile (cricinfomobile.com/india/) takes the game out to mobile phones and offers live scores, commentary, news, search options, statistics, player profiles, and match reports.

Characteristics of Virtual Worlds

Virtual worlds create three-dimensional space as a graphical representation on the computer display and allow navigation through that space. The space is filled with objects that have spatial relation to each other. Virtual worlds can often be shaped according to taste, with custom landscapes, plants and trees, building structures, furniture, machines, and a virtually unlimited range of objects. These objects can be completely imaginary or they can have a real-world counterpart.

In a virtual world, "simulation" introduces a sense of dynamic time and action. Simulation often also re-creates basic laws of nature. Virtual world gravity causes objects to fall, for example, as we expect them to do on earth; or the progression of morning dawn, bright noontime sun, and an orange-red sunset glow in the virtual world mirrors our own real-world quotidian cycle. But simulation can also be used to create machines; for example, in the form of vehicles to provide transportation.

Just as simulation inserts the concept of time into a virtual world, simulation also introduces the characteristic of "state" and state persistence. As we would expect in the real world, governed as it is by the laws of physics, the wall of a house is expected to remain standing until someone destroys the house. An object that falls to the ground to a stable position is expected to remain there unless it receives another impulse. A parked car should stay parked until someone moves it. For that purpose, virtual worlds update and preserve the state of all objects in a logical, aggregated data set known as "the world state."

Socially-Networked...Avatars

But all that's just context. In the Social Age, our focus is on *people*, how they interact in virtual worlds, and the ways they behave. TV shows and movies share one characteristic—our interaction with them is passive and unidirectional. Virtual worlds are, by contrast, an interactive environment. Because of this 3D, interactive environment, we can know and be known on a much deeper level than we can be with just the text-based medium of the community-oriented wiki environment.

In the virtual world, you're represented by a graphical image known as an avatar.[12] The avatar is guided by keyboard, mouse, or other input devices by the real-world participant. The avatar allows the participant to observe and interact with the virtual world and make his or her presence known. For example, as a participant enters a scene in the virtual world, a door opens and the avatar walks through. Other participants know that someone has come into the world, and they can watch as the avatar engages in activities, or as the avatar approaches other avatars for social interaction.

Noticing another participant's avatar is the first step to interaction. As in the real world, you can start a conversation with someone you've never met before as you walk by him. Interacting and conversing in a virtual world is facilitated through text chat and voice conversation. Avatar gestures can be used to offer nonverbal communication. Simple animations of the body to clap the hands, for example, show support and excitement. Movement of the avatar away from a conversation can show disinterest in a nonverbal way.

Many users invest considerable time and effort to customize and design their avatar. Just as in the real world, the outward appearance and the first impression is the basis for judgment in the "blink of an eye."[13] Some virtual worlds allow a wide range of avatar representations and detailed modifications. Human forms in all sizes, shape variations, and colorations can be combined with all kinds of hair styles, clothing, and accessories. Many users choose nonhuman avatars that take the form of fantasy characters, comic book heroes, furries,[14] or more abstract forms such as machines and vehicles.

Avatars allow for freedom of expression and provide the opportunity to break out of the limitations of the real world. A BBC documentary[15] tracked the lives of two couples who met and fell in love as avatars on *Second Life*. When they met in the real world, one of the couples (who looked not at all like their avatars), apparently were still sufficiently attracted to one another to marry (in real life, but using a *Second Life* virtual ceremony) and have a child (yes, a real one) together. A study in *Second Life* concluded that, "on average, people report making their avatars similar to themselves, but somewhat more attractive."[16] For business settings, however, it is usually preferable for an avatar to look at least similar to his or her real-life counterpart and maintain that appearance over time as a way to establish and foster trust relationships by visual recognition.

IBM recently held a global internal kickoff meeting in a private virtual world, with participants joining from locations around the world. A select group of employees sat on a virtual stage and answered questions from a senior vice president about their current projects, in front of the audience of avatar participants. Avatars intentionally looked similar to the real-world participants so that employees in other locations, countries, and continents could get to know each other without the usual travel, hotel bills, and conference room rentals.

One participant commented on the realism of the avatars: "I have [personally] met [the senior vice president], and [his] avatar really looked like him. I haven't met the other panelists, but I think I would recognize them now if I saw them." Although most of the avatar clothing reflected the daily appearance of the participants at work, the *salwar kameez* of the participants from India and the traditional dress from Japan allowed for expression of the rich cultural backgrounds.

Socializing with Other Avatars

As previously mentioned, the virtual world state of objects persists until the objects are acted on and state changes propagate to all observers in real time. That means that all virtual world participants see an avatar waving his hand at the same time.

Avatars make it much easier to have a shared experience in the real world, even something as simple as watching the same TV show. One study found that people liked to know—in real time—which TV shows their social group was watching.[17]

The benefits of learning in a group setting have shown to include motivation through collaboration, innovation, and shared purpose.[18] In a virtual world, shared experiences are possible in countless situations. Even passive presence at a speech in a virtual world can create the sense of "having been there together."[19]

The shared experience is taken even further when the real-time shared state is combined with the ability of users to create new objects and content in the 3D world. A user can create new objects by copying and modifying existing objects or by creating completely new geometrical objects. Several avatars can build a house; one can change the color of the wall while another is putting on the roof and a third is moving in the furniture. Because all these activities are performed—and observed by participants—in real time, they can be coordinated and discussed through voice conversation or text chat.

As we previously said, for social interaction to take place in a virtual world, the following characteristics are required: 1) represent the environment in three dimensions, 2) simulate the real world and update the persistent state of the objects; and, 3) represent the participants through avatars, and allow them to interact and communicate in real time.

Types of Virtual Worlds

In his analysis of the history of social interaction, Ray Oldenburg described the "Third Places"[20] where people congregate. In many cases, Oldenburg found, people don't go to German beer gardens with a specific goal or with the intention to consume entertainment. Although the beer is certainly a good excuse, it appears there is a more generalized appeal to this setting. Meeting and spending time with friends, enjoying the outdoor setting, doing some people watching, and conversing with others is just as important. Such unplanned interactions sometimes lead to great inventions or are the start of business dealings. Virtual worlds have the potential to provide the same kind of creativity and business success.

One participant at a recent corporate kickoff commented on the ability of the virtual world to create a sense of sharing, not only of the space and content and information, but also a sense of sharing the same experience, moment, and presence. "There's something about that sense of co-presence," she said. "There was some sense of them being together somehow, that ability to bring everyone together from India, Tokyo, and China. Rather than having four distinct screens, where everyone is separated with different phone hookups, this felt more cohesive."

People have flooded into virtual worlds, created avatars, acquired islands, built houses, and designed landscapes. Some of these worlds have hundreds of thousands of users logged on at the same time and individuals often spend several hours a day "in world." Interactions between users are started with little effort, offering a unique security that allows adults to approach each other as children do at a playground—with boundless curiosity, innocent trust, and an ever-present sense of wonder. Virtual worlds bridge countries, cultures, social status, and many other barriers that serve to limit unfettered interaction in the real word. A person's profile, interest, and favorite places are easily viewable in the virtual world, making it easy to find like-minded people.

But what value is there in a virtual world for business and professional users? Three use cases in marketing, product lifecycle management, and learning provide valuable evidence of the effectiveness of virtual worlds in a business setting.

Marketing and Advertising

Marketing professionals are always on the lookout for the next hype, the next subculture, the next medium to carry their message. Brands in the real world have a presence in online games and virtual worlds, and surveys have shown that consumers' attitude toward brands and companies is influenced as a result.[21]

These results should come as no surprise, considering the obvious match between the characteristics of virtual worlds and the objective of advertisers to reach the largest number of people with content personalized to their interests. At the same time, advertisers can more easily gauge the response of the audience in a virtual world to a particular advertisement or promotion. Companies seek to present their products and brands in the best possible light, with the highest resolution, and with the most realistic rendering and natural colors. Although virtual worlds still lag glossy print media and high-definition movies and television in these areas, they compensate by breaking free of the limitations of traditional, passive media.

A car shopper can experience the product in a three-dimensional perspective, for example, by looking at a new Mercedes Benz[22] in all imaginable camera angles. Through interactive simulation the car buyer—in avatar form, of course—can "drive" the car on a race track. After the car shopper successfully finishes the course, his avatar can keep the race suit as a souvenir. As the avatar moves around the virtual world, he is now known for his driving prowess and for his interest in a particular car brand. At the same time, the advertiser gains a dynamic presence in the virtual world through the avatar, much like the "Morris columns" seen throughout Europe that serve as advertising platforms. For example, in Figure 12.4 you can see a virtual "Morris column" advertising this book.

Much higher levels of involvement are available to advertisers in a virtual world than in traditional lean-back media. In a virtual, 3D world, the consumer is compelled to engage, lean forward, and experience the product, leading to greater desirability for the brand and the product.

Additional interest in a product can happen in 3D space when social elements come into play. For a family interested in a kitchen upgrade, for example, a 3D kitchen shop enables them to combine cabinets and to experiment with design variations. By working with a detailed virtual model of the actual kitchen space, they ensure that the selected parts actually fit. The family can "walk around" and

Figure 12.4 Virtual worlds can be an effective advertising channel for activities and goods that exist in the physical world. This virtual world "Morris column" advertises *The Social Factor.*

get various perspectives, and even invite extended family and friends to join them to offer opinions and suggestions before they place the order.

Product Design and Life Cycle Management

As three-dimensional objects, furniture, cars, fashion and clothing, toys, and consumer products are ideal for representation in a virtual world. Computer-aided design and manufacturing (CAD/CAM) has been in use for several decades, and is one of the earliest uses of IT in small and medium businesses.

Until recently, however, CAD/CAM applications and programs were optimized for a single user interacting with the tool. The design was shared by forwarding the data set after completion of each design phase. This approach ignored the creative and problem-solving process on which much of product design is based. In traditional CAD, a draft is sometimes printed out on paper and discussed by a team of people that marks up the paper with possible changes. Or the team gathers around a single workstation, possibly crowding together to have a good view of the monitor. Participants point out features or elements they want to change or discuss and sometimes even swap back and forth the input controls to update the draft.

This traditional approach is slowly giving way to a new perspective on product life cycle based on socially networked virtual worlds and the four primary elements of product life cycle: development, production, distribution, and after-sales management.

Product development is affected by current trends toward crowd sourcing, where extensive feedback is solicited and highly valued. Geographically dispersed populations participate in early functional evaluation, focus groups and clinics, and R&D cooperation between manufacturers and suppliers. Consumers are motivated to participate in product design for a variety of reasons. Perhaps they have a personal interest in a product, or they enjoy interacting with like-minded people to create an exciting new product. Self-esteem, including possible feedback through commendation and respect, motivates others, whereas some participants might just enjoy taking on and succeeding at a challenge.

Even if consumers are not included in the initial design, the early feedback they provide in functional evaluations and product clinics is invaluable. The earlier such a dialog can be established for customer feedback and insights, the more closely risk can be managed. Facilitating feedback with a representative and large group on early prototypes is either costly, for example in the case of a coffee maker, or outright impractical when the product is a car. With virtual pilots, a company can easily get feedback on models presented in a virtual space.[23] In 2008, IBM created a pilot for a 3D game called *PowerUp* to engage high school students with this new collaboration medium (Figure 12.5). The students were introduced to several engineering tools with which they designed solutions for energy problems encountered during the game. The result of the students playing the game was an overwhelming interest in the fields of engineering and science. Students and parents alike loved *PowerUp*, demonstrating the power of this 3D technology not only to effectively market the study of engineering and science, but also to bridge the generation gap!

Figure 12.5 Virtual world created for IBM's *PowerUp* game to engage high school students in the fields of engineering and science.

Many companies use virtual environments to facilitate product configuration and gain an edge into a more personalized marketing approach. The automotive and furniture industries have a particular advantage in this area, but clothing and fashion also benefit. Web pages now offer choices of components, designs, shapes, and colors and then present the result in 3D with navigation for rotating and zooming.

Finally, in after-sales management the use of virtual worlds for interaction with the customer is somewhat limited. Service and maintenance, however, often require extensive training. This is the perfect context for the use of collaborative 3D spaces. To train a mechanic on a new car model, for example, traditionally requires a substantial commitment in time and money. But exceptional service has a direct connection with customer satisfaction, so compromise in this area can be detrimental to the business.

In a virtual world, a new car model can be disassembled, parts replaced, and repairs easily demonstrated. These processes can be practiced in the virtual world until the learner feels comfortable with the process, and the trainer's avatar can offer tips and suggestions to make the job go more quickly. Also, training can take place before the first product is even shipped, without the high capital expense for "training models." The risk of damaging real products during trial-and-error training is also avoided. The trainer's avatar can demonstrate procedures, and there is no practical limit to the number of participants. The interactive nature of a virtual world allows easy interaction between trainer and learners. Virtual products can be manipulated faster than real-world products.

Failure conditions or problems that would be difficult or impossible to re-create in the real world can also easily be simulated in the virtual world. Such environments can also be used for problem determination or for getting expert help. When a mechanic encounters an issue, for example, he can reach out to a product expert from the manufacturer who joins him in a virtual world around the virtual product to point out methods and options.

Technology Outlook

The basic technology of virtual worlds has been around for some decades. Today's large scale implementations of social virtual spaces, however, still lag the immersive experience that the leading PC and console games offer through superior graphics, resolution, user interface, and sound. Challenges remain for virtual space engineers to solve, such as the real-time distribution of user-created content and the large-scale, shared space that differentiate virtual worlds from online games.

Bollywood in the Social Age

Four billion. That's the number of people worldwide each year who watch movies produced in Bollywood, the Mumbai-based, Indian equivalent of Hollywood. Bollywood movies are known for their music and melodrama and are an eclectic mix of song, dance, comedy, and action.

Web sites with rich Bollywood content have mushroomed in the last several years. Movie clips, reviews, interviews, downloads of audio and visual content, screensavers, and wallpapers are all available. But now blogs, forums, contests, and polls draw even more attention to Bollywood productions. The fate of a movie now rests as much with the public as it previously did with professional reviewers. Within hours of release, blogging reviewers and forum participants have either doomed the latest production or given it the kind of buzz that the producer could only dream of when he started the film project.

The December 2008 release of the hugely popular movie *Ghajini* was promoted with a variety of social and mobile media. Samsung released a *Ghajini*-edition *Ghajini*-mobile phone. A local FM station invited SMS messages and phone calls for a chance to win the signature Ghajini haircut—given by the actor himself. Findghajini.com quickly became a viral application, offering an online game with clues that led to the direct phone number of the movie's star.

Virtual space and worlds will become increasingly valuable to business users when relevant content (business procedures, documents) and interaction is possible. Existing applications, data, and documents must be connected to virtual worlds, and the flow between the 2D Web, mobile devices, and virtual worlds must become seamless.

As we explored briefly in Chapter 10, "Social Innovation," interesting advances are being made in the area of human-computer interfaces, including devices such as Emotiv Inc.'s EPOC headset. A couple of generations of kids have been trained to use the A, W, S, and D keys on their keyboard to move a character on the screen forward, backward, and sideways, but such a primitive approach does not make good use of our dexterity and tactile capabilities.

Haptic[24] technology, on the other hand, which "interfaces to the user via the sense of touch by applying forces, vibrations, or motions to the user," is an exciting field of ongoing research, and prototypes offer a promising glimpse into the future. Similarly, the true impact of a Cave Automatic Virtual Environment (CAVE) where projectors display a virtual world on three to six walls of a room must be experienced in person to be appreciated. Such an installation is remarkably realistic and immersive.

One tester commented about his experience in the CAVE: "When I put on the glasses and looked around the room," he said, "I involuntarily ducked down to avoid hitting my head on the large jet engine that was suspended in the virtual space." Wired gloves that are worn in a CAVE capture arm, hand, and finger movements and offer a more natural interaction with the objects in the space. "There was no need for training, education, or even a word of explanation," the tester said. "Rotating and interacting with the jet engine happened naturally through the data glove."

A Closing Thought

Like many technologies in an earlier day, whose long-term viability was hotly debated, but which are now ubiquitous, virtual worlds are met with a range of opinions about their future. The excitement and hype surrounding virtual worlds is real, but there are also legitimate criticisms and sometimes outright rejection based primarily on technical capabilities and limitations.

As the characteristics and use cases of virtual worlds have shown, however, the biggest motivation to participate in a virtual world is the insatiable drive people have for being with other people. We need social interaction and shared presence. We recognize that business and work are built on collaborative processes, and a 3D virtual world offers a connectedness unknown in earlier technologies. Geographically dispersed families, peer groups, and work teams all come together in a virtual world. A shrinking world gets even smaller when countries, time zones, and cultures are bridged in a virtual world. Virtual spaces that allow people to interact in real time and share an experience can become alternative places for some of our work and our life.

As we've previously discussed in detail, organizations realize that success depends on collaboration. 3D virtual spaces that allow people to interact in real time and to share an experience—no matter the actual geographic distance—are an ideal context for this purpose. And with the increasing speed of our mobile devices, these interactions will increasingly take place any time, anywhere, on any device.

Summary

- Mobility applications are of critical importance to businesses to ensure that employees on the road stay connected with each other and the rest of the enterprise.

- Expectations have changed to the point that connectivity is taken for granted.

- Digital convergence is bringing together traditional wire line services, wireless, and new media. This creates new ways to communicate and collaborate in a connected world.

- 3D is still in its infancy but is evolving quickly in ways that provide an increasingly immersive experience.

- 3D is a new way to collaborate with others and advertise your products and services.

Endnotes

Introduction

1. http://en.wikipedia.org/wiki/Millennials, retrieved February 24, 2009.

2. Thomas Friedman, "Meet the Zippies," The *New York Times* (op-ed), February 22, 2004.

Chapter 1

1. Patented May 1, 1849, patent number 6,420: National Museum of American History, from the U.S. Patent Office, http://www.150.si.edu/150trav/remember/r819.htm, retrieved February 24, 2009.

2. Central Pacific Railroad Photographic History Museum: http://www.cprr.org/Museum/Pacific_Railroad_Acts.html, retrieved February 24, 2009.

3. http://www.enchantedlearning.com/usa/states/area.shtml.

4. Henry Ford, *Today and Tomorrow, Anniversary Edition* (Garden City, NY: Doubleday, Page & Co., 1926); (Reprint edition, Cambridge, MA: Productivity Press, 1988), 234.

5. Wikipedia, "George Westinghouse," http://en.wikipedia.org/wiki/George_Westinghouse, retrieved February 24, 2009.

6. *IBD (Investor's Business Daily)*, "His Radios Dazzled Listeners," January 26, 2009.

7. Sungook Hong, *Wireless: From Marconi's Black-Box to the Audion (Transformations: Studies in the History of Science and Technology)* MIT Press, 2001, (Cambridge, MA).

8. Ibid.

9. Government Archives, "Crafting the Day of Infamy Speech," http://www.archives.gov/publications/prologue/2001/winter/crafting-day-of-infamy-speech.html, retrieved February 27, 2009.

10. http://images.google.com/imgres?imgurl=http:/farm3.static.flickr.com/2183/2036985734_ c262bceff9.jpg%3Fv%3D0&imgrefurl=http://flickr.com/photos/39735679%40N00/2036985734&usg=__W0tZ7_FQcPdWIfcH-W2IEx6_Zio0=&h=369&w=500&sz=94&hl=en&start=106&um=1&tbnid=O4J_yQINZBQjQM:&tbnh=96&tbnw=130&prev=/images%3Fq%3Dfranklin%2Broosevelt%2Bphotos%2Bdated%26ndsp%3D18%26hl%3Den%26sa%3DN%26start%3D90%26um%3D1.

11. "Television History—The First 75 Years," http://www.tvhistory.tv/Annual_TV_Households_50-78.JPG and Encyclopedia of TV, http://www.museum.tv/archives/etv/index.html.

12. Sam Palmisano, Speech to the Council on Foreign Relations, http://www.cfr.org/publication/17696, retrieved February 6, 2009.

13. Henry Ford, *My Life and Work,* (Garden City, NY: Doubleday, Page & Co., 1922), 72.

14. D. Comin and B. Hohijn, "Cross-Country Technological Adoption: Making the Theories Face the Facts." *Journal of Monetary Economics*, January 2004, pp. 39-83, and U.S. Department of Commerce, U.S. Census.

15. "Toshiba Dumps HD DVD," *SkyNews*, http://news.sky.com/skynews/Home/Technology/Blu-Ray-Sony-Wins-DVD-War-As-Toshiba-Dumps-HD-DVD/Article/20080231305804?lpos=Technology_Article_Related_Content_ Region_5&lid=ARTICLE_1305804_Blu-Ray_Sony_Wins_DVD_War_As_Toshiba_Dumps_HD_DVD, retrieved February 19, 2008.

16. U.S. Patent Number 7,082,306, granted to the author: "Apparatus and method for merging wireless telephone service with existing wired telephone equipment in a facility, allowing instantaneous connection with credit card companies, banks and other payers from a cell phone at the point of sale."

17. Jared Bernstein "Good Reception: Using Cell Phones to Predict Behavior." *EContent* 28(10): 8, http://www.econtentmag.com/Articles/News/News-Feature/Good-Reception-Using-Cell-Phones-to-Predict-Behavior-14183.htm, retrieved October 29, 2008.

18. Wikipedia, "Folksonomy," http://en.wikipedia.org/wiki/Folksonomy, retrieved February 27, 2009.

19. http://myspace.com, http://facebook.com, http://friendster.com, http://orkut.com, http://home.live.com/, http://cyworld.com, http://hi5.com.

20. http://24htennis.com, http://taltopia.com, http://travellerspoint.com, http://www.librarything.com, http://www.goodreads.com, http://myartspace.com, https://www.cakefinancial.com.

21. http://blackplanet.com, http://migente.com, http://geni.com.

22. http://linkedin.com, http://plaxo.com.

23. John F. Gantz, Christopher Chute, Alex Manfrediz, Stephen Minton, David Reinsel, Wolfgang Schlichting, and Anna Toncheva, "The Diverse and Exploding Digital Universe, An Updated Forecast of Worldwide Information Growth Through 2011," IDC, March 2008, http://www.emc.com/collateral/analyst-reports/diverse-exploding-digital-universe.pdf, page 2.

24. Ibid.

25. Frederick P. Brooks, Jr., *The Mythical Man-Month (Essays on Software Engineering)* (Boston: Addison-Wesley Longman, Inc., 1995), 292.

26. YouTube.com, *Shift Happens,* http://www.youtube.com/watch?v=ljbI-363A2Q, retrieved February 24, 2009.

27. Ibid.

28. Elizabeth Haas Edersheim and Peter Ferdinand Drucker, *The Definitive Drucker: The Final Word from the Father of Modern Management* (New York: McGraw-Hill Professional, 2007), 97.

Chapter 2

1. IBM Corporation, *Expanding the Innovation Horizon: The IBM Global CEO Study 2006*, http://www-935.ibm.com/services/us/gbs/bus/html/bcs_ceostudy2006.html?re=ceo, p. 22.

2. Malcolm Gladwell, *Blink, The Power of Thinking Without Thinking* (New York: Little, Brown and Company, 2005), 36.

3. Interviewed January 9, 2009, by IBM employee Michael Roche.

4. Wikipedia, "Service-oriented Architecture," http://en.wikipedia.org/wiki/Service-oriented_architecture, retrieved February 27, 2009.

5. Valdis Krebs, "Social Capital: the Key to Success for the 21st Century Organization," *IHRIM Journal* 12(5), http://orgnet.com/IHJour_XII_No5_p38_42.pdf, p. 38, retrieved February 27, 2009.

6. Ibid.

7. Oxford Internet Institute, University of Oxford, http://www.oxford-internet-institute.net/research/project.cfm?id=45, retrieved February 27, 2009.

8. Malcolm Gladwell, in *The Tipping Point, How Little Things Can Make a Big Difference* (New York: Little, Brown and Company, 2000), 38 and 41, defines Connectors as people who, "link us up with the world…people with a truly extraordinary knack of making friends and acquaintances."

9. Malcolm Gladwell, *The Tipping Point, How Little Things Can Make a Big Difference* (New York: Little, Brown and Company, 2000).

10. M. Granovetter, "The Strength of Weak Ties," *American Journal of Sociology* 78(6): 1360-1380.

11. M. Granovetter, "The Strength of Weak Ties: A Network Theory Revisited," http://www.si.umich.edu/~rfrost/courses/SI110/readings/In_Out_and_Beyond/Granovetter.pdf, retrieved February 27, 2009.

Chapter 3

1. Melanie Lindner, "What Are People Actually Doing on the Web?" *Forbes.com*, August 20, 2008, http://www.forbes.com/2008/08/20/google-yahoo-microsoft-ent-tech-cx_ml_0820wheregoweb.html, retrieved October 24, 2008.

2. Quarter ending December 31, 2008.

3. Malcolm Gladwell, *The Tipping Point: How Little Things Can Make a Big Difference*, op. cit.

Chapter 4

1. Ed Brill, telephone interview by IBM employee Laurisa Rodriguez.

2. http://www.edbrill.com/ebrill/edbrill.nsf, accessed February 27, 2009.

3. Malcolm Gladwell, in *The Tipping Point, How Little Things Can Make a Big Difference* (New York: Little, Brown and Company, 2000), 34, 62, 64-71, quoting Linda Price, marketing professor at the University of Nebraska: "A Maven is a person who has information on a lot of different products or prices or places…they like to be helpers in the marketplace."

4. Wikipedia, "Institutional memory," http://en.wikipedia.org/wiki/Institutional_memory, retrieved March 4, 2009.

5. Ioannidis JPA, "Why Most Published Research Findings Are False" (2005), http://medicine.plosjournals.org/perlserv/?request=get-document&doi=10.1371/journal.pmed.0020124&ct=1, retrieved February 27, 2009.

6. Luis Suarez Rodriguez, interviewed by the author on December 10, 2008.

7. http://docs.google.com.

8. Reed Cartwright (ed.) Bora Zivkivic (series ed.) *The Open Laboratory: The Best Science Writing on Blogs 2007* (Lulu.com 2008).

9. http://lulu.com/en/about/index.php.

10. http://flickr.com.

11. http://jacketflap.com.

12. Luis Benitez, interviewed by the author, December 12, 2008.

13. Wikipedia, "RSS," http://en.wikipedia.org/wiki/RSS_(file_format), retrieved February 27, 2009.

14. *Wired* magazine editor Chris Anderson popularized the term "long-tail" in an article he wrote for *Wired* in October 2004. Chris treated this subject to an extended analysis in a book of the same name. http://www.wired.com/wired/archive/12.10/tail.html.

15. http://wordpress.com, http://blogger.com, http://typepad.com.

16. http://twitter.com, http://flickr.com.

17. http://codingrobots.com/blogjet/.

18. http://illuminex.com/ecto/.

19. http://windowslivewriter.spaces.live.com/.

20. http://livejournal.com/, http://typepad.com.

21. http://www.qumana.com/.

22. http://www.scribefire.com/.

23. http://blogger.com, http://livejournal.com, http://www-01.ibm.com/software/lotus/products/connections/.

24. http://wordpress.org, http://drupal.org/.

25. Wikipedia, "Software as a Service," http://en.wikipedia.org/wiki/Software_as_a_Service, retrieved March 2, 2009.

26. Malcolm Gladwell, in *The Tipping Point, How Little Things Can Make a Big Difference* (New York: Little, Brown and Company 2000), 38 and 41, defines Connectors as people who, "link us up with the world…people with a truly extraordinary knack of making friends and acquaintances."

27. Malcolm Gladwell, in *The Tipping Point: How Little Things Can Make a Big Difference* (New York: Little, Brown and Company 2000), 34, 62, 64-71, quoting Linda Price, marketing professor at the University of Nebraska: "A Maven is a person who has information on a lot of different products or prices or places…they like to be helpers in the marketplace."

Chapter 5

1. Wikipedia, "Folksonomy," http://en.wikipedia.org/wiki/Folksonomy, retrieved February 6, 2009.

2. Wikipedia, "List of social networking websites," http://en.wikipedia.org/wiki/List_of_social_networking_websites, retrieved March 5, 2009.

3. T. J. Allen, *Managing the Flow of Technology*. Cambridge, MA: (MIT Press, 1977). See also a discussion of the "Allen Curve" on Wikipedia: http://en.wikipedia.org/wiki/Allen_curve.

4. Marc Strohlein, "Enterprise Search Gets Lost," *BusinessWeek*, May 15, 2006, http://www.businessweek.com/technology/content/may2006/tc20060515_393086.htm?chan=technology_ceo+guide+to+technology_executive+guide+to+search.

5. http://delicious.com/.

6. Dogear was an enterprise social bookmarking service created by Jonathan Fienberg of IBM Research; it has been incorporated into the Lotus Connection product Suite.

7. David R. Millen, Jonathan Feinberg, and Bernard Kerr, "Dogear: Social bookmarking in the Enterprise," pp. 111-120; Rebecca E. Grinter, Tom Rodden, Paul M. Aoki, Edward Cutrell, Robin Jeffries, and Gary M. Olson (ed.), Proceedings of the 2006 Conference on Human Factors in Computing Systems (CHI 2006), ACM Press, Montréal, Canada, April 2006, 1-59593-372-7.

8. Stephen Farrell, Tessa Lau, Stefan Nusser, Eric Wilcox, and Michael Muller, "Socially augmenting employee profiles with people-tagging," pp. 91-100, Proceedings of the 20th annual ACM symposium on User interface software and technology (ACM 2007) ACM New York (ISBN:978-1-59593-679-2).

9. See Harvard Business School professor Andrew McAfee's blog post on Serena Software's use of Facebook as an intranet: http://blog.hbs.edu/faculty/amcafee/index.php/faculty_amcafee_v3/facebook_on_the_intranet_no_facebook_as_the_intranet/.

10. http://www.topcoder.com.

11. IBM Research.

Chapter 6

1. Wikipedia, "Cloud Computing," http://en.wikipedia.org/wiki/Cloud_computing, retrieved March 2, 2009.

2. Irving Wladawsky-Berger, telephone interview with the author, November 25, 2008.

3. http://www.Google.com, http://www.Yahoo.com, http://www.apple.com/mobileme/, http://YouTube.com, http://Skype.com, http://aws.amazon.com/ec2/, http://public.Soonr.com, http://Mosso.com.

4. *Creating Energy-Efficient Data Centers,* U.S. Department of Energy, Office of Energy Efficiency and Renewable Energy, Industrial Technologies Program, Paul Scheihing, May 18, 2007.

5. Ibid.

6. Creating Energy-Efficient Data Centers, U.S. Department of Energy, May 18, 2007.

7. http://vmware.com/.

8. http://www.xen.org/.

9. http://www.gnu.org/.

10. "IT Doesn't Matter," http://www.nicholasgcarr.com/articles/matter.html, originally published in the *Harvard Business Review*, May 2003.

11. Wikipedia, "Geek," http://en.wikipedia.org/wiki/Geek, retrieved February 6, 2009.

12. "In web development, a mashup is a Web application that combines data or functionality from two or more sources into a single integrated application." Wikipedia, "Mashup," http://en.wikipedia.org/wiki/Mashup_(web_application_hybrid), retrieved May 5, 2009.

13. Creating Energy-Efficient Data Centers, U.S. Department of Energy, Office of Energy Efficiency and Renewable Energy, Industrial Technologies Program, Paul Scheihing, May 18, 2007.

Chapter 7

1. http://covestor.com.

2. Peter Lunn, *Basic Instincts—Human Nature and the New Economics* (New York: Marshall Cavendish, 2008).

3. http://edbrill.com/ebrill/edbrill.nsf/dx/new-zealand-herald-it-sellers-talk-up-social-links.

4. Interview of IBM employee Andy Piper by IBM employee Laurisa Rodriguez, on December 30, 2008.

5. Wikipedia, "Facebook," http://en.wikipedia.org/wiki/Facebook.

6. Malcolm Gladwell, *Tipping Point, How Little Things Can Make a Big Difference*, (New York: Little, Brown and Company, 2000).

7. http://www.youtube.com/watch?v=EwTZ2xpQwpA.

8. http://www.youtube.com/user/fordvideo1?blend=1, retrieved February 6, 2009.

9. Wikipedia, "Tay Zonday," http://en.wikipedia.org/wiki/Tay_Zonday, retrieved February 6, 2009.

10. IBM Marketing Research.

11. Interview of IBM employee Adam Christensen by IBM employee Laurisa Rodriguez, on December 23, 2008.

12. Keith Brooks interview by IBM employee Laurisa Rodriguez, on December 18, 2008.

13. http://mibancoblog.popular.com/.

Chapter 8

1. Wikipedia, "Standing on the shoulders of giants," http://en.wikipedia.org/wiki/Standing_on_the_shoulders_of_giants, retrieved February 6, 2009.

2. Elias Torres, telephone interview by the author, February 3, 2009.

3. Giuseppe DeCandia, Deniz Hastorun, Madan Jampani, Gunavardhan Kakulapati, Avinash Lakshman, Alex Pilchin, Swaminathan Sivasubramanian, Peter Vosshall, and Werner Vogels, "Dynamo: Amazon's Highly Available Key-value Store," *SOSP*, October 14–17, 2007, Amazon.com, Stevenson, WA.

4. http://project-voldemort.com/.

5. http://bwnt.businessweek.com/interactive_reports/global_brand_2008/.

6. Jeffrey Dean and Sanjay Ghemawat, "MapReduce: Simplified Data Processing on Large Clusters," Google, Inc., 2004.

7. Wikipedia, "Hadoop," http://en.wikipedia.org/wiki/Hadoop, retrieved March 1, 2009.

8. Interviewed on August 14, 2006, by IBM employee Brian Goodman.

9. Ibid.

10. Ibid.

11. Ibid.

12. http://www-01.ibm.com/software/webservers/httpservers/, http://drupal.org/, http://www.sun.com/software/products/mysql/.

13. http://www-01.ibm.com/software/websphere/.

14. http://acquia.com/.

15. Frederick P. Brooks, Jr. *The Mythical Man-Month, Anniversary Edition* (Reading, MA: Addison-Wesley Longman, Inc., 1995).

Chapter 9

1. "Expanding the Innovation Horizon: Global CEO Study 2006," IBM Corp., http://www-935.ibm.com/services/au/bcs_ceostudy2006.html.

2. Scienceblogs.com, "Exorcising animal spirits," Category: History of neuroscience, Posted on: July 10, 2007, by Mo; http://scienceblogs.com/ neurophilosophy/2007/07/exorcizing_animal_spirits.php.

3. Mary Bellis, "Magnetic Resonance Imaging MRI—Raymond Damadian— MRI Scanner," Paul Lauterbur, Peter Mansfield, About.com; http:// inventors.about.com/od/mstartinventions/a/MRI.htm.

4. Tan Le interviewed by the author, March 18, 2009.

5. *Genographic Project*, National Geographic Society, www.nationalgeographic. com/genographic.

6. http://www.engineeringchallenges.org/.

7. Adrianne Fox, "The Brain at Work," *HR Magazine*, March 2008.

8. Thomas R. Insel and Russell D. Fernald, "How the Brain Processes Social Information: Searching for the Social Brain," *Annual Review of Neuroscience* 27: 697–722.

9. Adrianne Fox, op. cit.

10. http://en.wikipedia.org/wiki/Endorphins.

11. James Surowiecki, *Wisdom of Crowds: Why the Many Are Smarter Than the Few and How Collective Wisdom Shapes Business, Economies, Societies and Nations*, 2004, ISBN 978-0385503860.

12. http://www.innocentive.com/.

Chapter 10

1. IBM CIO Insight Survey on Emerging Technology, April 2008.

2. Clay Shirky, New York University professor, was the first to refer to "situational applications" in his publication "Networks, Economics, and Culture," March 30, 2004.

3. 2008 IBM Global Human Capital Study, http://www-935.ibm.com/services/us/gbs/bus/html/2008ghcs.html?sa_campaign=message/laft2/all/hcstud.

4. Sacha Chua, Enterprise 2.0 Evangelist, IBM Global Business Services, Canada.

Chapter 11

1. The Financial Forecast Center™—U.S. Gross Domestic Product GDP Forecast, forecast retrieved March 17, 2009.

2. Gross Domestic Product—Monetary value that includes private and public consumption, government, investments, and imports and exports. GDP = Consumer spending + Government Spending + Country business spending on capital + export – imports.

3. World Economic and Financial Surveys 2008—World Economic Outlook Database World Economic and Financial Surveys 2008—World Economic Outlook Database.

4. *Bureau of Economic Analysis (BEA)—National Economic Accounts. Table 1.1.5 Gross Domestic Products, February 27, 2009.* The Financial Forecast Center™—U.S. Gross Domestic Product GDP Forecast, retrieved March 17, 2009.

5. D. Comin, B. Hobijn, and E. Rovito, "World Technology Usage Lags," version 2, April 2007, JEL-codes: O33, O47, O57. D. Comin and B. Hohijn, "Cross-Country Technological Adoption: Making the Theories Face the Facts." *Journal of Monetary Economics*, January 2004, pp. 39-83.

6. D. Comin and B. Hohijn, "Cross-Country Technological Adoption: Making the Theories Face the Facts." *Journal of Monetary Economics*, January 2004, pp. 39–83.

7. Business School, Nottingham University, England.

8. D. Comin, B. Hobijn, and E. Rovito, "World Technology Usage Lags," version 2, April 2007, JEL-codes: O33, O47, O57.

9. Jackie Fen and Mark Raskino, *Mastering the Hype Cycle—How to Choose the Right Innovation at the Right Time* (Boston: Harvard Business Press, 2008) (ISBN 978-1-4221-2110-8).

10. Measuring the Information Society: The ICT Development Index. International Telecommunication Union, 2009, pp. 108. (ISBN 9261128319). http://www.int/ITU-D/ict/publications/idi/2009/material/IDI2009_w5.pdf.

11. Geoffrey A. Moore, *Crossing the Chasm—Marketing and Selling Disruptive Products to Mainstream Customers* (New York: Harper Business, 1997) (ISBN 0-06662-002-3).

12. MSNBC, "Obama raises $150 million in September," http://www.msnbc.msn.com/id/27262116/, retrieved April 3, 2009.

Chapter 12

1. http://mashable.com/2006/07/11/myspace-americas-number-one/.

2. Techtree News Staff (2008-08-13). "Facebook: Largest, Fastest Growing Social Network." *Techtree.com.* ITNation.

3. WiMAX Global Market, WiMAX Forum, August 2008.

4. Mobile Broadband Evolution to 4G, Intel® Corporation.

5. WiMax: *Worldwide Inter-Operability for Microwave Access.*

6. Mobile Networks Forecasts: Future Mobile Traffic, Base Station & Revenue, Informa Telecoms & Media, June 2008.

7. Figure Predicted Traffic Distribution by WPB Applications from 2010 to 2020, Telecompetition Group, September 2007.

8. See http://www.pong-story.com/1952.htm.

9. See http://net.educause.edu/ir/library/pdf/NLI0425.pdf.

10. Adel Hendaoui, Moez Limayem, and Craig W. Thompson. IEEE INTERNET COMPUTING. Published by the IEEE Computer Society, 1089-7801/08.

11. Mobichange.com.

12. From the Sanskrit word " अवतार " that means "descent" and origi-
    nally refers to incarnations of Hindu deities. "Avatar," Wikipedia, http://
    en.wikipedia.org/wiki/Avatar, retrieved July 10, 2009.

13. "When you meet someone for the first time, …your mind takes about two
    seconds to jump to a series of conclusions." http://www.gladwell.com/blink/
    index.html.

14. See http://en.wikipedia.org/wiki/Furry_fandom.

15. Wonderland, Virtual Adultery and Cyberspace Love, aired January 2008,
    http://www.bbc.co.uk/programmes/b008vrht.

16. Paul R. Messinger, School of Business, University of Alberta; Xin Ge,
    School of Business, University of Northern British Columbia; Eleni Stroulia,
    Department of Computing Science, University of Alberta; Kelly Lyons,
    Faculty of Information Studies, University of Toronto; Kristen Smirnov and
    Michael Bone, School of Business, University of Alberta; "On the Relation-
    ship between My Avatar and Myself," https://journals.tdl.org/jvwr/article/
    view/352/263.

17. Ambient Social TV: Drawing People into a Shared Experience, http://web.
    mit.edu/bentley/www/papers/chi1227-harboe.pdf.

18. Social Network Methods and Measures for Examining E-learning, http://
    www.wun.ac.uk/elearning/seminars/seminars/seminar_two/papers/
    haythornthwaite.pdf.

19. http://www-03.ibm.com/press/us/en/photo/20820.wss.

20. Ray Oldenburg, *The Great Good Place: Cafes, Coffee Shops, Community
    Centers, Beauty Parlors, General Stores, Bars, Hangouts, and How They Get You
    Through the Day* (New York: Marlowe, 1997).

21. See "Real Life Brands in Second Life," 1st Quarter 2007, by Market Truths
    Limited.

22. See http://www.youtube.com/watch?v=Myqwxc0YKwo&mode=related&
    search=.

23. See "Fiat 500 Wants You," http://www.fiat500.com/.

24. "The word haptic, from the Greek ἁπτικός (haptikos), means pertaining to the sense of touch and comes from the Greek verb ἅπτεσθαι (haptesthai) meaning to 'contact' or 'touch.'" ("Haptic technology," Wikipedia, http://en.wikipedia.org/wiki/Haptic_technology, retrieved March 30, 2009).

Index

Serena Software, 81

service, cloud computing as a, 86

service economy, 181-182

services, 181

services layer, cloud computing, 91

services businesses, 182

sharing files, 42

sharing information, value of social
networking, 110-111

sharing knowledge, power, 28-29

Shift Happens, 14-15

short messaging services (SMS), 200

skills development, social networking
and organizations, 26

slope of enlightenment, hype, 186

smarter employees, value of social
networking, 111

SMS (short messaging services), 200

SOA (Services Oriented
Architecture), 24

Social Age

CIO (Chief Information Officer),
97-98

communication, 6

events leading up to, 1

exabytes, 14-15

expectations, 23-25

overview, 98

social networking and, 7-8

Semantic Web, 8

technology, evolution of, 5

versus Information Age, 95

Social Age clouds. *See* clouds

Social Age employees, 21

Social Age organizations, 20-21

Rheinmetall, 22-23

social networking, 25

innovation, 26

recruitment and on-boarding,
25-26

skills development, 26

succession planning, 26

teaming and collaboration, 25

social bookmarking, 78-79

Social Brain, 145. *See also* minds
ideation process and

social fragments, tag clouds, 67

social graphs, 80

social ideation, 153

best practices, 159-160

business benefits of, 153-154

InnoCentive, 154

process of, 155-156

ThinkPlace, 154-155

social ideation events, Jams, 156-157

anatomy of, 157-158

benefits of, 158

social innovation

innovation communities, 162-163

investing in, 172-173

socializing

with avatars, 207-208

social networking, 59-60

social media

defined, 101

financial services Web sites,
116-117

U

Y

Z

The Social Factor

Innovate, Ignite, and Win Through
Mass Collaboration and Social Networking

Maria Azua

FREE Online Edition

D0325443

Your purchase of **The Social Factor** includes access to a free online edition for 45 days through the Safari Books Online subscription service. Nearly every IBM Press book is available online through Safari Books Online, along with more than 5,000 other technical books and videos from publishers such as Addison-Wesley Professional, Cisco Press, Exam Cram, O'Reilly, Prentice Hall, Que, and Sams.

SAFARI BOOKS ONLINE allows you to search for a specific answer, cut and paste code, download chapters, and stay current with emerging technologies.

Activate your FREE Online Edition at www.informit.com/safarifree

> **STEP 1:** Enter the coupon code: WMRCKFH.

> **STEP 2:** New Safari users, complete the brief registration form.
> Safari subscribers, just log in.

If you have difficulty registering on Safari or accessing the online edition, please e-mail customer-service@safaribooksonline.com

Addison Wesley   Adobe Press   ALPHA   Cisco Press   FT Press   IBM Press   lynda.com   Microsoft Press   New Riders

O'REILLY   Peachpit Press   PRENTICE HALL   QUE   Redbooks   SAMS   SAS   Sun   Wrox   WILEY